God, Growth
& Great Adventure

"This book is more then a wilderness guide, it's a community building tool. Steve Sears has created a remarkable resource for individuals and small groups to experience God in a unique and powerful way!"

—Brandon Beard,
Life Groups Pastor,
Real Life Church, Valencia, CA

"I love hearing people share how an individual or book has helped them to better understand our God. Steve Sears is one of those individuals and this is one of those books…His experience, enthusiasm and communicative skills will inspire you to get out of your comfort zone and face the challenges awaiting you in the great outdoors."

—Ken Eichler,
Director of Family Life and Counseling Ministries,
Adventure Christian Church, Roseville, CA

"Someone once said that when people get together in a common place with a common purpose something completely uncommon happens: hearts are connected and relationships are deepened. What better place for this to happen then on a trail, next to a waterfall, or while watching the sun set over the Pacific Ocean? This practical and inspirational resource is perfect for…people who want to grow deeper in their relationship with God and one another."

—Scot Irwin,
Adult Life Pastor,
Discovery Christian Church, Simi Valley, CA

"Steve Sears is a godly man [with] a wealth of knowledge [concerning] the outdoors. He has given the Christian community in Southern California a…book, which I know will spur [them] on to great retreats with God. I wholeheartedly recommend this book for any Christian who wants to have a closer relationship with God."

—Caleb Kaltenbach,
Life Groups Pastor,
Shepherd of the Hills Church, Porter Ranch, CA

God, Growth
& Great Adventure

Fifteen Life Changing Wilderness Retreats
In The Southern California Area

Steve Sears

Forward by Mark McKinney

Photo credits: Bureau of Land Management
National Park Service
Palm Springs Aerial Tramway

Pleasant Word (a division of WinePress Publishing, PO Box 428, Enumclaw, WA 98022) functions only as book publisher. As such, the ultimate design, content, editorial accuracy, and views expressed or implied in this work are those of the author.

Unless otherwise noted, all Scriptures are taken from the Holy Bible, New International Version, Copyright © 1973, 1978, 1984 by the International Bible Society. Used by permission of Zondervan Publishing House. The "NIV" and "New International Version" trademarks are registered in the United States Patent and Trademark Office by International Bible Society.

Scripture references marked KJV are taken from the King James Version of the Bible.

Scripture references marked NASB are taken from the New American Standard Bible, © 1960, 1963, 1968, 1971, 1972, 1973, 1975, 1977 by The Lockman Foundation. Used by permission.

ISBN 13: 978-1-4141-0839-1
ISBN 10: 1-4141-0839-7
Library of Congress Catalog Card Number: 2006907551

"You turned my wailing into dancing;
you removed my sackcloth and clothed me with joy,
that my heart may sing to you and not be silent.
O Lord my God, I will give you thanks forever."
—Psalm 30:11-12 (NIV)

This book is dedicated to my Jesus,
for whom my heart beats.

Table of Contents

PART TWO: INTO THE WILDERNESS

PART THREE: THE SPIRITUAL COMPONENT

PART FOUR: THE RESOURCES

Foreword

Not too long ago, as I was preparing to go pick up my very adorable adopted son from Taiwan, I called up my *Surfing Sensei* (an older friend & mentor who has taught me about both surfing and life) and said, "Hey man, we've got to get wet before I leave. Can we fit it in?" We both knew that, given my pending father-hood, it would probably be awhile before I could get out again, and so before long we had worked out our schedules and were headed for the beach at County Line.

Once there, in between sets of waves, I took in my surroundings; I looked down at the clear, blue water, and up at white, puffy clouds. Off to my left there was a seal playing in the kelp, while behind me the hillsides were covered with beautiful green, yellow, and white plants.

Sitting out there on my board that morning it really hit me; God did all of this for us to enjoy. He had orchestrated the schedules for Sensei and I, had brought the seal near to play, had made the hills alive and beautiful, and had even arranged the pace of the incoming sets of waves so that we had time to take it all in. I could just feel Him while I was out there. I knew that He was alive and well, and I could sense his pleasure in knowing that we were enjoying His creation. I went home that day with a greater understanding of God's character and his love for me, as well as a greater connection with Sensei because we had shared this time together.

My good friend Steve has combined his passion for God with his passion for the outdoors to create this sweet book. I'm confident that it will lead you into experiences like the one that I had that day on the water.

God bless you as you seek him out there,
Mark McKinney

My good friend Mark, his wife Michelle, and their new son, Jaxon, lives in Simi Valley, CA, where he serves as the executive pastor of Discovery Christian Church. Mark is quick to laugh and quick to love; I hope that you have the chance to meet him some day.

Acknowledgments

As Richard Foster said, books are best written in community. The community that wrote this one, and who I want to recognize and thank here, includes my wife and best friend, Lesley, who has loved me, encouraged me, and kept me moving forward on this journey. Thank you for all that you are, sweetheart: I love you!

My mom, Suzan, for the love and selflessness that she so faithfully modeled throughout my life. You made Jesus real and attractive, Mom, and I know that it was your many prayers that carried me to Him. I'll be grateful to you for all eternity.

My dad, Jerry, who instilled in me a great love for the outdoors and the adventure found there. I love you dad.

Pastor Mark McKinney, a great friend, a great source of encouragement, and a great example of what it means to be real, and loving, and in the struggle to do right by God. Thanks for the contribution that you've made to this book, and to my life.

Sharon Benson and Jonathan Hart who crafted my jumbled, miss-spelled, and grammatically incorrect words into the coherent ones which you now read; Brianna Maxwell who put so many hours into creating the cover and the sweet maps that will help keep you oriented; Dustin Kellstedt who filled in the photographic gaps & went on a wild goose chase to double-check several of my facts; and Doyle and Marsha Hoth (and their 3 biological, 16 adopted and, they believe, nearly 1000 fostered children) who, in addition to instructing me in the use of their computer to prepare the photographs in this book, also allowed me a behind the scenes look at a whole new level of love. All of you are a huge blessing! Thanks so much for your friendship, and all that you've done to advance this book.

I also want to thank the many people who offered up activities for *The Spiritual Component* section of this book, including professor Chris Dyck, of Columbia Bible College, and his students—Whitney Atkinson, Jerome Gabriel, Joleen Kruselnicki, Melissa Schinkel and Troy Stelmach—who created several exercises in their curriculum development class, Kari Sievert and the other folks at Young Life Wilderness Ranch who allowed me to use a number of the activities found in their *Backcountry Manual*, and the many, many others who responded to my appeal by emailing me their ideas. I'm grateful to all of you.

I want to thank my awesome friends Jennifer Lingafeldt (Dell), Mike Edwards, Jeff Guldalian and Sam Lee, co-founders of 'The Adventure Ministry', the success of which was the seed for this book, Pastor Ken Eichler of Adventure Christian Church who unknowingly, and from a great distance, continues to influence who I am and who I am becoming, and Larry, Brian, and the staff at Dioko Coffee House (Joplin, MO), who provided me with friendship, a great creative environment, and enough caffeine and sugar to go the distance.

Finally, as I proofed the galley for this book, I listened obsessively to a CD by my friend Matt Bayless titled, *Come Down*. Sample it at myspace.com/mattbayless.

Wilderness: The Possibilities

"Early the next morning Jesus went out into the wilderness…"

—Luke 4:42a NLT

The grassland of the Carisso Plains National Monument is one of my absolute favorite places. This vast plain, the home of

Pronghorn Antelope and Tule Elk, is bordered by huge sandstone outcroppings that shelter nesting Prairie Falcons and ancient Chumash Indian paintings. The highlight of winter at this place is the migrating waterfowl, of spring, the stunning wildflower displays, and at night, the piercing cry of the Screech Owl and the lonesome song of the Coyote. It is absolutely beautiful!

Southern California is wildly diverse and holds many other fantastic jewels; the lowest, hottest point in the western hemisphere and the highest point in the lower 48 states are both here, as are magnificent offshore islands, high mountain glaciers, caves, hot springs, sand dunes, cinder cones, waterfalls, wild rivers, salt flats, narrow slot canyons, beautiful forests & meadows, three distinct deserts, many mountain ranges, and hundreds of miles of coastline.

Southern California is a place where one may ponder the migration of whales and butterflies, a life giving desert oasis, and the millions of stars visible on an inky black night. A place where antelope & wild mustangs may still be found, where wintering Sandhill Cranes huddle up in a fascinating mineral lake, and where that great survivor, the California Condor, is carried aloft on a sweeping nine-foot wingspan.

Wild places such as these are the perfect setting in which to connect with our Creator. In the silence, the solitude, and the grandeur we can stand in awe of his majesty, refocus our hearts on his beauty, and reflect on his love & grace. It is there we can listen for his voice, develop a sense for who we are as his children, and renew our commitment to pursue him. As my friend Mark wrote in the Forward to this book, God intends for us to discover his loving presence in such fantastic places and experiences.

In the wilderness we can also genuinely connect with one another. The slower rhythm of these places—and the extraordinary adventures and experiences that we share there—naturally lead us into deeper friendships. It is there, without the distractions of life at home, that we share meaningful conversation, join together to overcome hardships and achieve common goals, pray for and encourage one another, learn to care for and serve one another, and are forced to admit our weaknesses and receive help.

Finally, the wilderness is a place where we may discover more of our own selves through the freedom, as nature photographer Guy Tal describes it, "… to go and get lost in a place like no other…to find solitude, to challenge and test [ourselves] against the elements…to be inspired, to be scared and vulnerable and threatened, to watch the stars at night with no sign of humanity… and to wake up to a blissful silence in a world that is pristine and beautiful." (*Scenic Wild Newsletter,* December 2005. www.scenicwild.com)

God, Growth, & Great Adventure was written to equip the Christian wilderness traveler—alone or in a group, and with almost any level of previous experience—to plan and carry out just such physical & spiritual adventures in any or all of fifteen fantastic wilderness locations in the Southern California area. It is organized into four parts:

Part One: Preparing For Your Journey covers trip planning, safety & ethics, and a few basic outdoor skills that will enhance your adventures tremendously.

Part Two: Into The Wilderness covers the trips themselves; fifteen wild, adventure-filled destinations guaranteed to blow your mind.

Part Three: The Spiritual Component contains dozens of great outdoor-based spiritual & relational activities that can be woven into your trip to help you and your group grow closer to God and each other.

Part Four: The Resources is loaded with great supplemental information to help you purchase and pack the right gear, find the right maps, research your destinations, strengthen your wilderness skills, and more.

The first step is planning your trip. Let's get started…

Part One

Preparing For Your Journey

"You will go out in joy and be led forth in peace;
the mountains and hills will burst into song before you,
and all the trees of the field will clap their hands"
—Isaiah 55:12 (NIV)

Planning Your Trip

"God's beauty cannot be revealed through one form, but is so vast and infinite that it can fill an entire world with wonder."
—Gary Thomas, *Sacred Pathways*

Okay. So you've made the decision to go on a life changing adventure in the wilderness. This first section will walk you through six of the major elements necessary to plan your trip:

1. Deciding where to go.
2. Gathering information about your destination.
3. Preparing your people: getting everybody onboard, geared up and in shape.
4. The logistics: equipment, supplies, transportation, etc.
5. The last minute tasks: checking your gear, the extended weather forecast, etc.
6. The efficient use of your travel time.

DECIDING WHERE TO GO

With so many awesome destinations to choose from, the most difficult aspect of your trip planning may be deciding where to go. Simplify this decision by answering the following three questions: (1) What time of year will you go? (2) How long you will go for? (3) What are the interests and abilities of your group?

The time of year is an important consideration; the diversity of Southern California allows for fantastic year-round adventure, but not everywhere at once. In the summertime, temperatures are pleasant in the mountains, but can exceed 120-degrees in the low desert. Winter is a beautiful time to visit Death Valley and Anza-Borrego, but deep snow and road closures are possible in the White, Sierra Nevada, & San Gabriel Mountains. Along the coast conditions are usually fairly temperate, though winter can be quite chilly and wet.

While you or your particular group may lean more towards the hard core, desiring to camp in the snow or trek in the hottest spot in the western hemisphere, it is to the *average* group that I suggest the following:

- Save the desert trips—Death Valley, Red Rock Canyon, Mojave Preserve, Joshua Tree, and Anza-Borrego—for the months of October through May.
- Visit the mountains and the ocean—White Mountains, Mount Whitney, San Jacinto, San Gabriel, Catalina Island, Leo Carrillo Beach and the Channel Islands—from May through October.
- Havasupai is best in spring & fall.
- The awesome wildflowers of the Carrizo Plain are a springtime event.
- The Kern River Valley is great anytime of year; the exceptionally warm summers can be alleviated by a swim in the lake or a float on the river.

Wherever you end up, be sure to consider the phase of the moon when planning your trip. Full moons are my favorite; there is nothing in the world like wandering through canyons, across deserts, or above treeline by bright moonlight. It is enthralling and something your group will never forget. A new moon, on the other hand, means inky black nights, which are perfect for gazing at the stars and listening to the night sounds.

The second item that you'll need to consider is your available time. Do you have a day, a weekend, or a week? Closer destinations, with shorter driving times, are better for day and weekend trips. For example, the San Jacinto Mountains would be a great one or two day trip out of Los Angeles. They are only a couple of hours away, and all of the sights are within a short distance of each other. Death Valley on the other hand, at more than 250 miles from Los Angeles, and with sites that are spread out over great distances, would be better as a three (or more) day trip.

The third element that you'll want to consider, when choosing an adventure destination, is the desire and ability of your group. Are your people younger or older? Are they very physically fit or couch potatoes? Are they bringing children? Do they want to car camp, backpack, or spend their nights at a motel? Do they want to do a bit of light hiking around the Visitors Center, or do they want to raft some class IV whitewater and then bag the gnarliest peak in the area?

Because the excursions in this book have components that range from short strolls around roadside attractions to very challenging summit hikes with several thousand feet of elevation gain—and because most of them are also located within a reasonable distance of a motel—it's possible to plan a trip that satisfies the needs of everybody. Determining the interests and the level of fitness and ability among your people, ahead of time, will help you decide where to go, and what to do when you get there.

One more thing: You'll also want to keep your pastor informed of your plan—ahead of time—if your trip is in any way church-related.

Don't do what I did. One Sunday morning the leadership of my church, including the church's attorney, found that I had planned a skydiving adventure by reading, in the bulletin, an invitation for the congregation to join in the fun.

Save your pastor some gray hairs…keep him informed!

GATHERING INFORMATION

After deciding where to go, you'll want to gather information about that destination. Begin this process by using the information provided within this book to contact the land management agencies (Bureau of Land Management, National Park Service, etc.) that administer the lands you're headed to. Let them know what your plans are, ask for any advice and/or tips they may have (including recommended maps & guidebooks), apply for any necessary permits, and then request that all of the information that they have available—maps, brochures, newsletters, flyers, etc.—be sent to your home, church or office.

Next, visit your local outdoors store (R.E.I., Adventure-16, Sports Chalet, etc.—their contact information is in '*The Resources*' section of this book) and ask about the maps and books suggested by the land managers. If they have others that look good, grab those too. While there, survey the staff to see if any are familiar with the area; they are very often great sources of up-to-date and/or little known information.

Swing by your American Automobile Association (AAA) office, advise them of your plans, and have the agent dig up all of the resources that he or she can find. Don't forget to tell them about the sites you want to see on the drive up and back.

Your local library and bookstore are excellent resources for area guidebooks, history books, and maps—look for them under the headings of "Travel" and/or "Local Interest." Check Amazon.com or barnesandnoble.com as well to see if these titles can be purchased for less as 'used' items.

Of course the Internet is a crucial component of your research, too. For help in this area, check *The Resources* section of this book for trip planning sources such as recommended websites, books and maps.

Digging deep during this time will help to uncover the fascinating history, natural wonders, plants and animals that will enhance both your adventure and your time together.

PREPARING YOUR PEOPLE

More than likely, your group will have been involved in the planning process up to this point. If not, this is the time to bring them on board by calling a meeting, spreading your maps out and sharing your vision of an adventure-filled wilderness trip, and of a deeper and more intimate connection with God and each other.

At some point during this process you'll also want to:

- Share the fascinating things that you've learned through your research.
- Outline the food, gear and transportation needs. A good way to do this is to provide handouts and checklists so that everybody is equally clear on what they'll need to bring. (See '*The Resources*' section of this book for lists of recommended gear.)
- Outline and assign participant responsibilities and roles; some to purchase groceries, others to cook, clean, drive, lead worship, etc. Establishing these responsibilities before you head out will help to assure that the trip goes smoothly.
- Survey your group in regards to their talents and gifts. For example, do any of the members have outdoor experience or medical training? Are there any musicians, artists, photographers, or poets among them? How about amateur biologists, botanists, or astronomers? Think of ways that you can utilize the talents and skills of each of your participants for the betterment of the group's experience. Everybody can contribute; really, even 'scrap-bookers' can document your time together and produce a great keepsake for the group.
- Create a questionnaire form for each participant to fill out—prior to leaving on the trip—asking such questions as
    1. Name
    2. Address

3. Phone number
4. Age
5. Prior hiking experience & fitness level
6. Any known allergies
7. Medical conditions
8. Prescribed medications
9. Special dietary needs
10. Emergency contact & insurance information.

This information can really be an asset when you are making decisions affecting trip planning, and may be crucial in the event of an emergency. Photocopy these completed forms, keeping one copy with your group as it travels and the other with a responsible party at home.

- You may also want to consider having the participants sign a medical release and a liability waiver.

As mentioned earlier, you'll want to determine ahead of time—both for safety's sake and to help maintain a low frustration quotient among your people—the level of fitness that your group members will be required to function at on the trip. For example, do you have it in mind to climb 14,246-foot high White Mountain? If so, you'll need to clearly state this to your group and then plan a few high elevation training hikes together to get in shape for it. Lesser challenges will require less training; a couple of half-day hikes in the local mountains should prepare your people for the hike out to the Kelso Sand Dunes, or across the salt flats of Death Valley. Whatever the level of challenge, you don't want your group taking their first training hike on the day of the big climb.

Aside from the physical benefits, training together will also (1) give your group a head-start on developing intimacy and learning to function as a team, (2) help to determine each participants strengths and weaknesses, and (3) help to build a sense of anticipation and excitement for the upcoming trip.

I would use the first meeting to plan and calendar these training hikes, just to make sure they happen and then, as the departure date draws near, continue to meet together to pray, to hike, and to ensure that everything is on schedule and progressing well.

For ideas regarding nearby places to hike, contact your local outdoor store or swing by a major book chain and look for hiking guides under, "Local Interests".

LOGISTICS

In order for any adventure to be safe and satisfying one must have the proper clothing, equipment, food, maps, and transportation. What is 'proper' is determined by such factors as terrain, elevation, season, weather patterns, activities, the number of people in your party, whether you will be backpacking, car camping, or moteling it, and your desired degree of luxury while out there.

The one thing that you should have with you at all times are the basic survival items known collectively as, "The Ten Essentials".

These are the most basic and most critical items for the wilderness wanderer, and should <u>always</u> be in the pack (backpack) if on foot, or in the vehicle of <u>every</u> member of any party traveling outdoors:

1. A map of the area
2. A compass
3. A headlamp or flashlight w/extra bulbs & batteries
4. Sunglasses (in snow country)
5. Extra food & water
6. Extra clothing (layers)
7. Waterproof matches or lighter
8. A candle or fuel tablets
9. A pocketknife
10. A First-Aid kit
11. Toilet paper (11th essential)
12. Sunscreen (12th essential)
13. Emergency rain clothing or poncho (13th essential)
14. A sun hat (14th essential)
15. A whistle (15th essential)

In addition to these essentials, read through the gear and clothing lists found in '*The Resources*' section of this book, and choose the items best suited for your particular trip. If you still have questions, call the folks at your local outdoor store or the land managers of your chosen destination; they'll be more then happy to help you out.

LAST MINUTE TASKS

The wilderness is dynamic and things are liable to change at any time. Stay ahead of these changes by calling the land managers just prior to leaving on your trip and inquiring about trail, road, campground, and backcountry conditions or closures, as well as any other information that may affect your trip.

Below are a few other things that you should do and/or ask yourself just before setting out on your adventure:

- Re-check your gear, and the gear of the other members of your group. Is it all there? Do you have your maps, permits, and guidebooks?

- Is your vehicle(s) in good working order? How about the spare tire and the belts? Are the fluids and fuel topped off?
- Have you left copies of your itinerary and the participant's questionnaires with a *responsible* person(s)? Does that person(s) know when to expect you home and whom to call if you don't show up?
- Have you checked the extended weather forecast for your destination?
- If you are caravanning, have you exchanged cell phone numbers and agreed on meeting places in the event that you get separated?
- Have you prayed?

ON THE WAY

Be sure to utilize the considerable amount of time that you'll spend in your vehicles by really getting to know each other better; play ice-breaker games, have long talks, process your experiences, or wrestle with an exercise found in '*The Spiritual Component*' section of this book.

Once you have arrived at your destination be sure to swing by the local Visitors Center, museum, or park headquarters for a last minute check of road, weather & wilderness conditions, and to acclimate yourself to the area through the literature, maps, and interpretive displays found there.

Wilderness Travel and Safety

"New beauty meets us at every step in all our wanderings"
—John Muir

Though Southern California's backcountry is rarely hostile, wilderness is, by definition, a place of risks that we do not confront at home. Good preparation, common sense, and a solid knowledge of those potential risks are vital when it comes to safely adventuring in mountain, desert, and coastal areas…and all the more so when traveling with a group of people with varied abilities and experience.

In this section we'll touch on some of the major safety considerations for both vehicle & foot travel: managing your group in the wilderness (and what to do if they get separated), the importance of staying hydrated, how to help your body adjust to high elevations, avoiding heat and cold related health problems, a little about the plants and animals to watch out for and, finally, safety issues related to the exploration of the old mines and historic buildings that you'll come across in your wanderings.

Before jumping into the chapter, though, it's important to remember that while an understanding of these safety concepts will certainly make your trip safer and more fulfilling, they are not substitutes for the single most important rule, which is: *Know* your *abilities and limitations and operate within them*! Knowing when to back off and return another time, when conditions are better or when your abilities and experience have improved, is the single greatest quality that you can possess in the wilderness.

After reading through this chapter, check '*The Resources*' section for some advice on further strengthening your wilderness skills.

BEFORE YOU LEAVE HOME

Safety begins before you leave home. Did you pack all of your gear? Did you leave a copy of your itinerary and the questionnaires with a responsible party? Does that party know when to expect you and whom to call if you don't make it (i.e. the phone number(s) of the local ranger station, sheriff, etc.)?

Do you, or another group member, have medical knowledge and a proper first aid kit? Do you know where the closest hospitals, fire stations, and ranger stations will be and have you marked them on your maps? Are your people familiar with the maps and do they know where they will be?

Will you be hiking much? If so, has your group been training together for the past several weeks? Is everyone in decent shape? Can your group accomplish the goals that you have established, or should you reevaluate and set new goals?

VEHICLE TRAVEL

I have heard, and I believe, that more people find themselves in survival situations because of vehicle failure than for any other reason. One reason for this is that our vehicles give us a (often false) sense of confidence and security, which emboldens us to venture further away from civilization (and help) then we would otherwise go.

There are many ways to have vehicle problems in the boonies, such as bad roads, soft shoulders, traveling too fast for the conditions, and obstacles such as trees, ruts, washes, drop-offs, rocks, mud holes, etc. Vehicles themselves can overheat, radiators or tie-rods can be blown, tires can be shredded on sharp lava rocks, and gas tanks can be punctured.

With a few simple precautions, a little common sense, and a well-equipped vehicle, backcountry exploration can be a blast.

First of all, before heading out be sure that your fluids & gasoline are topped off and that your battery, belts and spare tire(s) are in good shape. If maintenance work is due (or nearly due) to be done on your vehicle, take care of it before leaving on your trip.

After making sure that your vehicle is mechanically reliable, the next most important consideration becomes stocking it with enough gear to get yourself out of a jam or, barring that, to comfortably spend a night or two outdoors. In addition to *the Ten Essentials* that we discussed earlier, backcountry travelers may want to carry the following articles of equipment in their vehicles:

- A basic tool kit with a full socket set, pliers, wrenches, screwdrivers, spark plug socket, wire cutters, vice grips, channel locks, Allen wrenches, hammer, knife, fuses, etc.
- A shovel, saw, fire extinguisher, & duct tape.
- A spare tire, jack, air pressure gauge, & tire inflator.
- A tow strap, jumper cables, flares, extra coolant, oil, fan belt, a current Auto Club membership card, and a shop manual for your vehicle.
- A first aid kit, flashlight & batteries, a charged cell phone, extra food, three gallons of water per person—plus five gallons of water per vehicle—blankets and/or sleeping bag.
- In the winter, snow chains and the ability to install them.

While all of the backcountry dirt roads described within this book are passable for two wheel drive vehicles, some do require higher clearances and even the finest dirt road can become washed out or an impassible quagmire in poor weather. Snowfall introduces new challenges & hazards, as do ruts, potholes, tire-shredding rocks, downed trees, and sandy washes & shoulders.

If you do plan to journey in the backcountry, try to travel in pairs. That is, a pair of vehicles. That way if one vehicle breaks down or becomes stuck, you'll always have a backup. If this isn't possible, leave an itinerary (including a description of your vehicle, specific route information, and when to expect you back) with a ranger or someone back at camp. If you fail to show up as planned the authorities will have a head start on searching for you—they'll know your exact route and what your vehicle looks like and won't have to waste the time it takes to search a wider area. (Note: If you do leave a note for the rangers, don't forget to stop back in when you return and let them know that you're ok.)

If you do somehow become lost or stranded, or if your vehicle breaks down, it is almost always better to stay with it; your emergency supplies are there and it is far easier to see a vehicle from a great distance then an individual on foot. If you must leave your vehicle, do so only if you are absolutely, positively sure of the route and distance to help—and of your ability to safely cover that distance—and then leave a note with your name, date, time, and direction of travel, and take your Ten Essentials with you.

If you choose to stay with your vehicle, open the doors and raise the hood & trunk to signal that help is needed, and then stretch a tarp or blanket out for shelter from the sun. If you are in the desert, remember that ground temperatures can be as much as 30-percent hotter then the air temperatures, so stay up off the ground to avoid overheating. A *nearby* hill may provide cell phone coverage; if it is *very* close leave a note on your vehicle, including date, time and your direction of travel, before climbing it.

If you left a detailed itinerary, and if you loaded your vehicle with the recommended survival gear, it should be a simple matter of waiting for the cavalry to show up—even if it takes a couple of days.

A couple of other thoughts regarding vehicle travel:

- Gas stations are often very few and far between on these adventures, so try to get into the habit of topping off at every opportunity.
- If in doubt about a tracks ability to sustain the weight of your vehicle, get out and walk it before driving onto it—a few minutes on foot may save you many hours of digging to extricate your vehicle.
- Stay on established roads and obey all local regulations; cutting roads is hard on the land, particularly in the desert where the scar from just one vehicle leaving the road just one time can take decades to heal.
- Checking on the road conditions with the local land manager, at every opportunity, is a good habit to get into as well.

For specific information about four-wheeling theory & technique, as well as some really great Southern California routes, I recommend the book: "Backcountry Adventures: Southern California" (Peter Massey & Jeanne Wilson)

Travel by Foot

Each of the adventures in this book has several hiking options—some easy, some extreme. The following tips will enhance your journey afoot, whether on trail or off.

Route Finding: Trail & Cross-Country Travel

Route finding—the art of working out a safe and efficient course through the wilderness—begins at home as you study the guidebooks, pour over the maps, search the internet, talk to people who have an intimate knowledge of the area which you'll be traveling through (land managers, other travelers, etc.), and answer the question, "Are we physically able, and properly equipped, to tackle the challenge that we are considering?"

Once you're out in the field, the key to route finding is to hike with your eyes as you move across the landscape, continuously evaluating:

- The terrain & potential hazards.
- Your location on the topographic maps (In case of emergency, each person in your group should always have a clear idea of where they are, where they are going, and how to get back).
- Your group's fitness level.
- The weather conditions.

Some elements that may cause you, the leader, to stretch your route finding skills or to modify the route, include landslides, burned areas, overgrown trails, rain swollen streams & rivers, private property or trail closures, severe weather (i.e. ridges exposed to lightning), and exhausted hikers.

Good route finding skills come with experience, and experience comes from doing; read books, take classes, join a local hiking club, and hike, hike, hike.

Group Management

Walking through the hills with a couple of your buddies can be a pretty casual affair; generally, you'll move along quickly, efficiently, and with great flexibility. Add a few people to that number, however, particularly people with varied fitness levels and backgrounds, and then it becomes prudent to put together a management plan.

The following is an example of such a management plan:

- Assign a *navigator*, perhaps one of the slower persons in the bunch, to lead by setting the pace and keeping the group on the correct trail, or route if heading cross-country. This person should consult with the leader regarding any navigational questions.

- Assign a *trail-sweep* to follow along at the rear of the group and make certain that no one falls behind. This person must be able to say, with absolute certainty, that, "I am the last one from our group, there is no one behind me." (If someone stops to use the bathroom, for example, the trail sweep should stop a short distance ahead and wait for that person to rejoin the group). The trail sweep will usually have the dual responsibility of encourager, since he or she will be at the rear with the slower hikers. The trail sweep must be patient and understanding and cognizant of the importance of his or her role; they encourage the struggling to accomplish the goal (hike) while assuring that no one becomes separated from the group. The sweeper should advise the leader if the pace is too fast.
- Assign an *encourager* to float among the group to chat with, and encourage, the other hikers, particularly any who might be struggling.
- The *leader's* job is to circulate through the group, as well, to monitor the fitness and morale levels within the group and to ensure that everyone is on track to accomplish the group's stated goals—it is vital that everyone accomplishes the goals and feels good about those accomplishments. The leader, who must be familiar with the trail (or map reading), has the ultimate decision making responsibility.

It won't be too hard to identify the fastest, fittest person; the one who is anxiously waiting to hurry down the trail. You might want to assign this person some responsibility too, such as encourager or trail sweep, to distract him or her from the fact that they are going much slower then they want to go (for a fast person, going slow can be just as demoralizing as going fast is for the slower person). Ideally, this person would be patient and compassionate, doing whatever is necessary—chatting, encouraging, and even carrying the others gear if necessary—to help keep moral up and see that everybody accomplishes the challenge in a positive way.

Pace, Rest Breaks and The Rest Step

There are several variables that will determine your group's optimum hiking speed, including their level of fitness, the terrain, the weight of their gear, and the elevation. You'll know that you or your group are walking too fast if:

- you cannot sustain your pace, comfortably, for long periods of time.
- you cannot carry on a conversation with your hiking mates.
- your rest breaks are less then one hour apart.

A hurried pace is often the result of anxiety about the distance remaining on the hike, or an internal sense that you may be holding up the rest of the gang or, and this is most often the case, trying to keep up with others who are much fitter.

Placing the slowest hiker in the front of the group, to set the pace for the whole, is probably the best way to be certain that everybody is traveling at a comfortable pace. However, if you do decide to do this, to put the slowest person in front, be sure to keep an eye on that individuals pace. If he or she is still working harder then everybody else, it could be a sign that they are feeling the pressure from those to the rear and are pushing themselves too hard. A physically exhausted person who feels that they are holding up the group will quickly become discouraged and that is the last thing we want. Remember, the real goals are a deeper connection with God and our teammates, and a real experience of Christ's love & grace. Every action should be to that end; the physical adventure (hike, climb, whatever) is secondary to the *true* goals.

All of the participants should be able to accomplish the goals and feel good about those accomplishments. It is the leaders job to keep the morale up and see that everybody completes the challenge.

As far as rest breaks go, establish these times (perhaps, a ten-minute break every hour) before heading out on your hike so that everybody is on the same page. Later, if necessary, you can modify your rest time to suit your particular group.

Remember, hikers who walk at a slower steady pace, and take short regular rest breaks, travel more miles more safely then the group that charges into the wilderness. So, take it easy and enjoy the fellowship and the fantastic scenery.

The *Rest Step* is a great technique to employ when hiking at high elevations, or on steep slopes, or with a heavy pack, or any other time that legs or lungs are struggling to climb uphill. The pace is slow, because for every step there is a pause, but it is designed to give your legs muscles an opportunity to rest between those steps.

Here's how it works: As you take a step, straighten and lock the knee of the rear leg, the load bearing one, while relaxing the muscles of the forward one. If you keep your knee locked, all of your weight will be supported on your skeletal system and not your muscles. Synchronizing your breathing to your steps (i.e. one breath per step) will give you a focus point as you climb, slowly but surely, to your goal.

Once you get a handle on this technique you'll find it to be a valuable addition to your mountain travel skills.

Staying Found

Here are some thoughts on staying found (i.e. not getting lost) in Southern California's backcountry:

- Be certain that you have a clear mental picture of the terrain and the routes that you'll be following by studying the area guidebooks and maps before leaving the house; familiarize yourself with the topography, landforms, landmarks & drainages (creeks, rivers, washes), roads, highways, and railways. Be sure to study more then just the route that you'll be traveling on, also familiarize yourself with the larger area.
- Even if someone else has planned and/or is leading the hike, it is still your responsibility to know where you are. Days before setting out, ask the leader for map and route information, and then study up on the intended destination. Aside from helping to stay found, you never know when the leader might have a problem, leaving you with the job of summoning help and /or leading the group out.
- As you travel through the backcountry (on foot or by car) make it a habit to regularly check your location against the map.
- My dad showed me the importance of simply looking back over my shoulder as I walked along. The trail looks completely different going the other way and may be unrecognizable to you should you get turned around (try this at the mall too, especially a couple of days before Christmas). Looking back periodically will help to keep your surroundings familiar and in perspective.

- As you travel through the mountains and desert, practice your group management plan and assign a trail sweep to make sure that no one falls behind. Divided groups are a major cause of lost hikers.
- Leave an itinerary detailing your hiking and traveling plans with a responsible party. Include your route information, your estimated time of return, and the phone numbers of who to call if you don't show up.
- Always carry your *Ten Essentials* with you.
- Remember, the most important thing that you can do to remain found is to *operate within your experience and abilities.*

If you do become separated from your group, or become unsure of your exact location, the first thing that you must do is *stop immediately* and think things through. Any search party will begin its search for you from the point that you were last seen; any distance that you continue to travel may place you further away from that point. Don't continue to travel until you have thoroughly thought things through.

At this point your biggest enemy is not the wilderness—it is you and your capacity for panic. Some people have been known, at the moment they realize they are alone and unsure of their location, to take off at a sprint in search of someplace they do recognize; a few, in their panic, have even left their packs behind. You must remain calm; anything that you do at this point that is not well thought out may only lead to more problems, including injury or further separation from your group or survival gear. You must stay calm; you are going to be fine. Your Ten Essentials will keep you alive and your group members, or itinerary if solo, will point searchers in the right direction.

After you have stopped, prayed and calmed down, reflect and make a plan before you take another step. Know where you are going, and why. Check your map and try to settle on where you might have gone wrong. Can you determine your location by area landmarks, or can you backtrack to a familiar point? No? Then are you within a *reasonable and safe* walking distance of a town or major highway? If not, and this is critical, you must remain in the area if you believe that somebody will be searching for you—search parties will begin to look for you from the place that you were last seen or along the route detailed in your itinerary.

If you decide to range out looking for familiar landmarks, only travel about one-quarter to one-third miles…max…and mark the route so that you can find your way back. One way to do this is to simply drag a stick or a trekking pole in the soil as you walk along. On the way back, use that same stick to draw arrows, or build them out of rocks or branches, pointing towards your direction of travel or where you have settled in to wait out the searchers.

As nightfall approaches, prepare for an evening outdoors by locating a spot that is out of the wind and *very close* to where you first discovered that you were 'lost' or separated. Build a fire if it's safe (no danger of starting a wildfire) to do so or, of course, if it is a matter of survival, and then make a place to bed down by building up a layer of insulation—pine needles, thin branches, leaves, grass, etc.—to keep your body off of the cold ground. If in the desert, and it's warm, use your rain poncho or emergency blanket to create a shady spot to wait out help.

If it's cold put on all of your clothing, and if you have a large enough pack put your feet into it as far as they will go. For more insulation, stuff your pack and the outer layer of your clothing with the same materials that you made your bed with.

Searchers should find you reasonably quick if you left an itinerary and/or your group has alerted them. Stay put and resist the urge to search for them, instead let them find you. Plan to signal an air or ground party by building a smoky fire, signaling with a mirror, or blowing your whistle (always carry a whistle—you can only shout for a very short time before going hoarse, but can blow a whistle indefinitely).

STAYING HYDRATED

Water's a Good Thing!

The human body is composed of water and needs to remain properly hydrated in order to:

- Metabolize energy & function efficiently (the loss of as little as 1% of your body's weight in water will lead to a serious decline in your physical performance).
- Regulate the body's core temperature.
- Eliminate metabolic waste.

The battle to remain hydrated is ongoing; we lose water through breathing, going to the bathroom, and perspiring. In fact, perspiring under strenuous physical labor can cause us to lose as much as 1 liter of water per hour—even more at higher, drier, elevations!

A continued loss of water, without replacement, will lead to dehydration, which begins with a sense of thirst and progresses to dizziness and/or nausea. Soon your head will ache, your mouth will become dry, you will find yourself urinating less frequently—and when you do it will become steadily darker in color—and your leg and/or abdominal muscles may cramp from the loss of water and electrolytes.

If you allow the dehydration to progress to a more critical level, your blood plasma volume will lower, causing your blood to thicken and your heart to strain to pump it throughout your body.

Eventually, if left unchecked, this condition will lead to collapse and death.

One of the secrets to staying hydrated during *strenuous* physical activity is to *prehydrate*, or tank up, before starting out. Later, on the trail, drinking small amounts often (perhaps a sip every fifteen-minutes or so), before you feel thirsty, will enhance your performance tremendously.

Another element to staying hydrated is conservation. There are several ways that you can help your body to retain water:

- Wear environment appropriate clothing, such as light colored clothing and a broad hat in the desert (the color white reflects about 90% of the suns radiant heat, while black absorbs about 90%). Long sleeves and pants also help to retard fluid loss through evaporation.
- Save the most strenuous activities for the cool hours of the day.
- Avoid caffeine and alcohol. These are diuretics that will cause you to urinate more, resulting in a greater loss of water. Also, sugar (and sugar drinks such as cola's) may actually impair your body's ability to absorb fluids. Stick with water & athletic replacement drinks.

Some other thoughts on water:

- A good rule of thumb, when preparing for your wilderness adventure, is to plan for at least 1 gallon of water per person, per day. You may have to adjust this figure upward if you will be in a particularly hot region, a particularly dry region, or if you will be participating in strenuous physical activities. Always carry, and drink, more water then you think that you will need.
- Fill up your water bottles or purchase more water at every opportunity (campgrounds, gas stations, etc.), and carry extra in your vehicles.
- Check locally before depending on a watercourse in the wilderness. The spring or stream "just over the next rise" may exist only on your map, or may be seasonal or affected by draught.
- Finally, except in emergencies, desert springs and small sources of water should be left to the area wildlife, which depend on them for survival.

Pure Water

Years ago we carried small metal cups, called 'Sierra Cups', which we used to dip into mountain streams for a drink of, what seemed to us, the best tasting water in the world.

Today these same streams have been overrun by a microorganism called Giardiasis (jee-ar-dye-a-sis), a nasty little parasite introduced by man's poor hygiene habits, which, if allowed to work its way into the hikers system will incapacitate him or her with diarrhea, bloating, and nausea.

Prevention is the key to avoiding Giardiasis. Most of the water you drink will probably be store bought or come from a tap, but if you do find yourself requiring water from the backcountry you must assume that all of California's streams are unsafe to drink from and follow one of the following procedures to treat it:

- The first method to make water safe is to strain it through a hand-pumped filter. Several very effective types of filters are available from your local outdoor store.
- A second way to filter your water is to bring it to a rolling boil for 1 minute at sea level (five minutes at 10,000ft).
- A third approach is to use iodine tablets (also available at your local outdoor store). Do so by placing one tablet (two if it is especially murky) in your water bottle and then allow it to sit for about fifteen minutes. Be sure to splash some of the treated water onto the threads of your water bottle to purify it too.

One more thing: Don't forget to use treated water to brush your teeth and wash your dishes.

GETTING ALONG AT ELEVATION

Many of the adventures in this book are to heights—from 8,000 to 14,000 feet—that require your body to adapt, or acclimatize, to the decrease in oxygen molecules. Properly acclimatized, your time at elevation will be much more enjoyable, the conversation and fellowship sweeter, and your experience greater.

Acclimatizing to Elevation

Acclimatization is the process that your body goes through to adapt to elevations that are higher than it is used to. Here's how it works: As you ascend to these greater heights, you enter an environment where the concentration of oxygen in the air remains the same, but the number of oxygen molecules per breath is reduced. This stimulates your system to take certain steps to help it to adapt to this new, oxygen-deprived condition. First, your breathing rate increases (both faster and deeper) to boost the oxygen content in your blood. Then your body begins to produce more red blood cells to carry that oxygen while at the same time increasing the pressure within your pulmonary arteries to force that blood into portions of your lungs that are normally not utilized. Different people acclimatize at different rates but, for most, this process takes from 1-3 days at a particular elevation.

The very best way to help your body properly acclimatize is to plan your trip to allow for a gradual ascent. For example, if you wanted to climb White Mountain (14,246ft) you might plan to spend the first night at Grandview Campground (8,200ft), day hike the Bristlecone Pine's (10,000-11,000ft), and then spend the second night either at Grandview Campground or at the White Mountain trailhead (11,200ft) before waking early to 'bag' White Mountain. This formula will allow your body time to acclimatize so you can climb strongly with fewer elevation-related health problems.

Aside from ascending gradually, there are a few other ways that you can assist your body in the acclimatization process:

- Stay hydrated—this cannot be emphasized enough!
- Move slowly and take frequent breaks.
- Snack often.
- Avoid tobacco, alcohol, and other depressants including barbiturates, tranquilizers and sleeping pills. These items will only decrease your respiratory drive and make matters worse.

While most people can climb to 8,000ft without effect, there are some who are more susceptible to elevation related problems than others and no amount of acclimatization will help. These folks may want to ask their doctors about available prescription drugs, such as Diamox, which may help them to go to elevation.

For more information regarding the effects of high elevation on the body, read "High Elevation Illness and Wellness" (Charles Houston M.D.)

Acute Mountain Sickness

Acute Mountain Sickness (AMS) is the condition that a person develops when their body is either not given the opportunity, or is unable, to acclimatize to the lower oxygen levels of higher elevations. For some people this condition can occur at the relatively low elevation of 8,000ft, but for most it is reached at heights closer to 10,000ft where more then 75% of all people will begin to display some sort of mild symptoms including headache, dizziness, fatigue, shortness of breath, a loss of appetite, nausea, and disturbed sleep. These symptoms, known as mild AMS, generally do not interfere with activities and will decrease within a couple of days as the body acclimatizes.

If a person with mild AMS races to greater heights without allowing their body to acclimatize, or if they are unable to acclimatize, their mild AMS may progress to moderate AMS. The symptoms of moderate AMS include a headache that cannot be relieved by medication, nausea & vomiting, increased weakness & fatigue, shortness of breath and a much-decreased level of coordination, known as ataxia. Though the individual may still be able to walk on his or her own, normal activity becomes very difficult and thinking becomes confused. It is critical that this person descends to a lower elevation right away; only descent (or advanced medications) can reverse this problem at this stage.

The condition of AMS is generally subject to the elevation, the rate of ascent, and an individual's susceptibility to it. If you begin to show symptoms of moderate AMS, don't go higher until symptoms decrease, and descend if they worsen. The best advice, in every case, is this: When in doubt, descend, descend, descend!

Hot, Cold, and Otherwise

The human body is designed to maintain a core temperature of 98.6-degrees. In cooler environments, below about 92-degrees, the body absorbs heat through sunlight, while at temperatures above 92-degrees the body absorbs it from the atmosphere. The body can also produce its own heat through such things as physical activity and eating.

When the temperature begins to rise above 98.6-degrees the body perspires, which then evaporates and causes cooling. Working optimally this system is very efficient to maintain the required temperature, but California's desert and mountain environments, which have the capacity for enormous temperature fluctuations within any given 24-hour period, can easily overload this system. In the desert, for example, a freezing dawn can give way to a 100-degree day, and mild mountain days can precede nights in the low-teens.

These temperature extremes have the potential to affect the human body through one of three negative conditions: *heat exhaustion*, *heat stroke,* and *hypothermia*. It is important to understand their prevention and treatment.

Heat Related Illnesses

Every year in July there is a foot race called the Badwater Ultra, which begins at the Badwater (Death Valley) parking area, where temperatures often exceed 125-degrees, and proceeds to Whitney Portal, about 135 miles and 15,000ft of elevation gain away.

There are two primary heat related illnesses that these runners are concerned about: *Heat Exhaustion* and *Heat Stroke*.

Heat exhaustion is a serious illness that occurs when the body gains heat at a faster rate than it can disperse it. Symptoms of heat exhaustion include dizziness, nausea, physical weakness, minimal (or no) urinating, headache, and vomiting. The victim of heat exhaustion should be seated out of the sun and given water or some sort of replacement drink (with electrolytes, if possible) to slowly sip until he or she feels better.

If the symptoms of heat exhaustion are not taken seriously, and dealt with, the victim's condition will progress to heat stroke. This is a considerably more serious condition that occurs when the body's temperature rises above 105-degrees, and leads to the victim's death if not treated immediately. The symptoms of this malady are the same as with heat exhaustion, but with the addition of pale, cool, damp skin (some victims progress to hot, dry skin), confusion, irrational behavior, and physical collapse. The victim must be cooled down immediately; put him or her in the shade, loosen tight clothing, swab with a water-soaked bandana, have him or her take small sips of water (if conscious), and get them to the hospital A.S.A.P.

Heat exhaustion can be easily avoided by:

- Simply saving your physical activities for the cool of the day—i.e. the early morning and late afternoon.
- Wearing appropriate, breathable, light colored clothing, a light colored broad-brimmed hat, and sunscreen.
- Not just carrying water with you, but drinking it too!
- Operating within your experience and abilities

One of the best books that I have ever read on the subject of survival in hot environments is, "Desert Hiking" (Dave Ganci). I highly recommend it!

Hypothermia

Hypothermia, the number one killer of the outdoor recreationalist, is a condition that is brought on by the rapid loss of body heat, which causes the victim's core temperature to drop to a level that impairs both brain and muscular function. *Hypothermia can happen anytime of year in cold or windy weather with a wet or tired victim.*

The first sign of hypothermia is uncontrollable shivering, followed by slurred speech, a sluggish gait, fumbling hands, memory lapse, apathy, drowsiness and, eventually, unconsciousness and death.

At the first sign of uncontrolled shivering you must make camp; the victim's life depends on getting their temperature back to normal as soon as possible. Get the victim out of the wind and their wet clothing and into a sleeping bag or a vehicle, if you have one, with the heater running. If he or she is conscious, get warm drinks and energy food into them. Skin to skin contact is another way to restore temperatures and should be used in extreme cases.

Note: If you are alone, you must take these steps as soon as you are aware that your shivering is serious; *your thinking will become progressively more confused and soon it will be too late for you to think through your survival requirements.*

The best prevention for hypothermia is to *know your limitations* and be well prepared with the appropriate clothing & gear. Dress properly—wool, polypropylene and other synthetic materials are the best insulators—and in layers. An example would be a first layer of polypropylene underwear (tops & bottoms) followed by a layer of wool or synthetic pants & sweater, and then a layer of windproof, waterproof, breathable pants and a jacket. Top this off with a wool ski cap and a pair of light, waterproof gloves. See *'The Resources'* section of this book for more about appropriate outdoor clothing.

Electrical Storms

Electric storms are common in the mountains and desert, especially in the summer. Lightning usually seeks the highest point in its strike area, so get into a deep forest, avoiding the highest tree, peaks, ridgelines, lakes, open areas, lone trees, or shallow caves. If you are caught in the open sit on something insulated, such as your foam-sleeping pad, and pull your feet up on it.

Oh, and avoid wrapping yourself in one of those metallic survival blankets.

UNFRIENDLY CREATURES AND VEGETATION

Southern California has only a few dangerous plants and animals that you need to be aware of on your travels:

Bears

If it comes to associate him with food, a bear will lose his fear of man and eventually become a nuisance to be trapped and destroyed. The single greatest thing that we can do to keep this from happening is to maintain a clean camp. Keep your food (food, to a bear, is anything scented—toothpaste, deodorant, etc.—or anything that he can visually identify as being edible) in bear-proof containers, and clean up your trash and food scraps. Many of California's campgrounds have bear-proof lockers for your use; if you are backpacking, inquire about renting or purchasing a bear-proof container before setting out.

While we're on the subject: Cars are not bear-proof containers! Every year many people learn, the hard way, that bears are super powerful, highly motivated, and more then a match for their Hyundai'. What usually happens is that the hiker leaves food (or chapstick, or toothpaste, or virtually any other scented or visually identifiable item) in his or her vehicle, goes for a hike, and returns to find that a local bear has destroyed their car to get at it. In Tuolumne Meadows (Yosemite) I once saw a Volkswagen bug after a black bear had peeled its roof back to get at an ice chest left on the front seat. I've seen others where the bear has broken a window, climbed into the car, and then torn through the back seat to get into the trunk. Most often, in addition to the damage, the vehicle's owner also receives a hefty ticket for leaving the food where the bear could get at it.

I have walked up on several of California's black bears through the years and can tell you that these magnificent animals are not at all prone to attack. There are, however, two scenarios that you should be aware of when this may not be true: The first is a sow with cubs—she should be given plenty of space—and the second is a bear that has managed to get your food; she now truly believes that it is her own, and you should too.

Mountain Lions

Mountain lions are found all over California, but are very shy and rarely seen. Most people, by far, go their whole lives without seeing a mountain lion in the wild, and you probably will too.

However, as a precaution, you should always keep children and pets very close to you in Mountain Lion country, and if you do catch sight of one of these magnificent animals, and it does not immediately melt away into the brush, do the following:

First, try to appear as large and as intimidating as you possibly can. Face the lion, lift your arms (or a jacket) over your head and yell at it. Do not crouch down and do not run; these actions will make you appear like prey and will trigger the attack instinct within the lion (Imagine your house cat's response to a ball rolling away from it). Back away, slowly, from the lion, while continuing to hold your arms up and speaking loudly. If there are others in your group, stay close and throw rocks towards the lion. A healthy lion will retreat.

Report the sighting of any lion, but particularly an aggressive one, to the local land manager or county sheriff as soon as possible.

Ticks

Ticks are found all over the country, especially in thick brushy areas. What they do is climb up to the very tips of grass and low bushes, attach themselves to you as you sweep past, and eventually make their way to your skin where they affix themselves for a meal.

The larger brown ticks are not a big worry; it's the smaller black ones, the deer ticks, which are the major concern. Deer Ticks can be as small as about twice the size of the period at the end of this sentence, and can carry Lyme disease, which often reveals itself through flu-like symptoms and a series of concentric rings around the bite. Caught early it can be treated with antibiotics; otherwise it can progress to arthritis and other problems.

Be sure to check yourself after every hike, recruiting a friend to help if necessary. If you find one that has fastened to you, remove it by grasping it with tweezers and gently pull it out.

Faithfully check for ticks after every hike in the brush and you won't have any problems.

Rattlesnakes

Rattlesnakes have a diamond shaped head, rattles on their tail, and can reach lengths of up to five feet or more. They are quite venomous and can be found at elevations up to about 11,000ft.

As with all reptiles, rattlesnakes have no internal means of controlling their body temperatures, and so are constantly either cooling themselves (under bushes, rocks, logs, burrows, etc.) or warming themselves (on rocks, trails, asphalt, etc.) to stay comfortable. Because of this, snakes often become nocturnal during the hottest part of the year and hibernate during the coldest. You are most likely to see rattlesnakes during the spring when they emerge from their dens to mate; the combat dance between males usually occurs during this time and is an awesome site to witness.

A rattlesnake will never pursue you but can, if threatened, strike out as much as 1/3 the length of its body. The best advice to avoid getting bit by a rattlesnake is to watch where you step, where you sit, and where you put your hands. Don't tease them and don't attempt to handle them, even if they appear to be dead; they have a nervous-system reflex that causes their jaws to work even in death.

If you are bitten, swelling at the site of the bite and a tingling & numbness around the mouth are symptoms that it was venomous, but not every bite will be.

Back in the day snakebite kits had razor blades and tourniquets, with instructions to tie the tourniquet off above the wound, and then make a cut at the bite and suck the poison out. It didn't take long to discover that the secondary wounds, caused by untrained people taking razorblades to the victims, were causing many more problems then the snakebites themselves. Contemporary wisdom dictates that you treat a snakebite victim by keeping them quiet and getting them to the hospital as soon as possible.

Poison Oak

Of all the safety issues and risks in the wilderness, this is by far—by far—the greatest concern to me. I have never been confronted by a Mountain Lion, or bitten by a Rattlesnake, or suffered from hypothermia, but I have over the years had more then my share of Poison Oak encounters. In fact, several years ago my doctor and I determined by my records that I had averaged a severe case of it every quarter for the prior four years! That was (at the time) sixteen major occurrences requiring a doctor visit—not to mention the countless minor ones! For the record, I have had many more episodes since then.

Poison Oak is the most wide spread shrub in California and can be found at elevations that range from sea level to about 5,000ft. Sometimes it looks like a bush (similar to a blackberry bush, but without the thorns) and other times like a vine. It has clusters of three leaves, often with red color on them, and may have tiny white flowers, which later become small berries. Poison Oak is usually found in damp, shadowy canyons, but can be anywhere within the coastal ranges.

The oils (Urushiol) in the leaves and stems of the Poison Oak plant cause allergic reactions in most people who come in contact with it, even secondarily by touching clothing or animals that have brushed against the plants. This allergy manifests itself in a nasty, seeping, itching, skin rash. I'm told that because the reaction is allergy based, with each exposure it becomes easier to contract and more difficult to relieve.

If you feel that even with all your efforts to avoid poison oak you may still have had some contact get back to camp, or home, A.S.A.P. and wash your clothes and body with a strong soap. If a rash develops, ask your pharmacist for an over-the-counter product. If it persists contact your doctor.

There are products on the market that, supposedly, act as a sort of barrier to the plants oils; you apply them to your skin before an exposure, and then wash off when you get home. I've never tried any of these products (I've learned the hard way to stay miles away from this stuff), but would love to hear a report from anybody who has. I can be contacted at www.Godgrowthandgreatadventure.com.

Not all people develop an allergy to poison oak. My dad, for example, can stomp through hillsides thick with it, literally breaking trail through it, and only end up with a rash the size of a nickel that lasts for a mere day or two. For the rest of us, though, the very best way to deal with Poison Oak is through prevention. An old adage states, *"Leaves of three, let it be."*—learn to identify poison oak, and then go out of your way to avoid it.

Author's note: Just before this book went to the publisher I did it again. That's right, I managed to get into some poison oak and, as usual, it spread rapidly. This time though, instead of going right to the doctor I swung by Wal-Mart and picked up an over-the-counter product called, ZANFEL (www.zanfel.com), which turned out to be extremely effective and fast acting. Let me know if it works for you, too.

MINES AND OTHER HISTORIC STRUCTURES

One of the coolest things about exploring the mountains and, especially, the deserts of Southern California is the certainty of eventually encountering old mines, outbuildings and other historic ruins, relics, and artifacts. These places—often littered with old tools, equipment, and other fascinating historical debris—are like windows to another time.

As cool as these places are, though, there are some potential hazards to consider when exploring them:

- These old structures can be littered with broken glass & sharp nails and are often rotted and in danger of collapsing.
- Rattlesnakes are often drawn to these places in search of the rodents that make their homes in the ceilings, walls, and among the debris; watch where you put your hands & feet while poking around.
- The most dangerous elements in mining areas are the mine shafts themselves, which often contain decayed support timbers, ladders, and hardware just waiting to

give out and either drop you into a void or bring a load of rock down on you. Blind shafts, some hundreds of feet deep, can be scattered throughout these complexes, too, and may be disguised with old, rotted timber, plants, and rocks that are not strong enough to hold your body weight. Southern California has tens of thousands of these open mine shafts, so stay alert!

- Some mines have oxygen deficits ('bad air') created when past mine fires, many of which lasted for years, depleted the available oxygen and left pockets of carbon monoxide. If the ventilation in that particular mine is poor, it may be many decades before the carbon monoxide is replaced with oxygen.
- Often explosives (blasting caps, dynamite, etc.) were left behind when the miners moved on. While I have found wooden lids stamped, "Danger" and "Explosives", I have never come across the contents. Nevertheless, there are certainly more out there. If you do come across any suspected explosives during your explorations, leave the area immediately—they will be highly unstable—and notify the appropriate authorities.
- Along with the abandoned historic mines are many, many active mining claims; please respect private property.
- The California Office of Mine Reclamation has a toll free number, 877-OLD-MINE, where the public may call to report abandoned mines.

Exploring old mines and ruins are a blast (uh, no pun intended), but as with everything else in the outdoors you will need to exercise common sense; watch where you walk and where you put your hands, and stay out of the shafts themselves. If you really have an itch to go underground, do it sensibly by hooking up with one of the caving clubs listed in '*The Resources*' section of this book. With these groups you'll participate in far greater, and far safer, adventures then you'll ever find in these old mines.

Wilderness Ethics

"The heavens declare the glory of God;
the skies proclaim the works of his hands"

—Psalm 19:1 (NIV)

It is just as important to tread softly in our wild places as it is to travel safely through them. This is especially true here in California, the nations most populous state, where the millions of people who annually escape to the mountains, deserts, and seashore leave behind beaten down meadows, garbage-strewn trails, and contaminated lakes & streams. California's wilderness is, quite literally, being 'loved' to death.

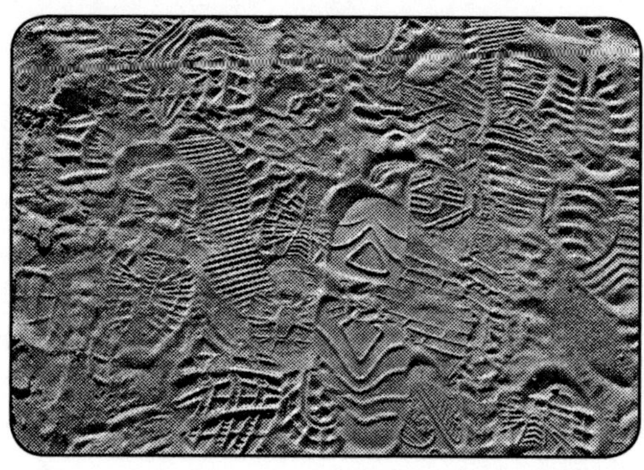

To counter this, several governmental agencies, including the Bureau of Land Management, the US Forest Service, the National Park Service, and the U.S. Fish & Wildlife Service got together with a number of private organizations and developed a program called, "Leave No Trace". This program has been used by tens of thousands to significantly reduce the impact that they've had on the environment.

There are at least two *great* reasons why we, as Christians, should also strive to follow these well thought-out guidelines:

The first reason is the matter of stewardship. The Lord, *our Lord*, created these wonderful places and we have a responsibility to care for them, and to preserve them for the generations to follow.

The second reason that we need to practice these low impact principles, I believe, is for our witness. Nothing generates respect in the eyes of the typical outdoors person as much as someone valuing the land. Our concern & respect for the environment will bring honor to our God.

Following are the basic principles of *Leave No Trace* wilderness travel & camping, many of which are designed for backpackers and primitive campers and may not seem to apply to you at all; to the degree that they do, however, please follow them.

TREADING SOFTLY: THE 'LEAVE NO TRACE' PRINCIPLES

Proper Planning

Your pre-trip planning is the time to gather important information about terrain, anticipated weather conditions, camping and/or fire restrictions, trail closures, road conditions, and the number of other visitors who may be in the area at the same time that your group is. The information that you glean during this period will help you to make important decisions about where to camp (i.e. away from restricted or fragile areas), when to go (i.e. other than times of high visitation and poor weather), what size and dynamic your group should be (i.e. some areas have group size restrictions), etc.

Group Size

As far as group sizes go, less is more. Here are a few of the arguments for keeping your group size to a minimum:

- Smaller groups have a lighter impact on the land.
- Local regulations may limit your group size.
- Smaller groups foster an intimacy that leads to deeper spiritual & emotional growth for the members. In smaller groups (1) there are greater opportunities to speak and be heard, (2) individuals are more likely to open up and share, and (3) there are more opportunities for personal care. It is also easier for smaller groups to daily debrief and process their experiences.
- It is much easier to make group decisions with fewer people. Your group can be more spontaneous and adaptable to changing circumstances.
- A smaller group is more likely to observe the wildlife and other natural wonders around them, translating into a much greater wilderness 'experience.'

So, if your group is larger then, say, 10 people you may want to consider splitting it and either assigning co-leaders to manage each group, or leading more then one trip to the same area.

Choosing a Camp Site

Several of the adventures in this book give you the option of establishing a primitive campsite, out under the stars, and away from crowded campgrounds. The main point to remember when establishing a primitive campsite is this: *Good campsites are found, not made.*

To minimize your impact, choose a site that has already been heavily used (first choice), or one that is very durable, such as exposed bedrock, snow, sand or gravel bars (second choice). If these elements are not present, and you are in the mountains, then try to choose a site under the pines where the carpet of dead needles will help absorb the impact of your presence. Easily trampled meadows and streamside vegetation are the most fragile environments and should not be camped in at all. To allow wildlife unfettered access to water, and to keep it free of pollution, your camp should also be at least 200-feet (70 adult steps) from any stream, spring, or lake, and to protect the wilderness experience for others, away from trails and screened from sight by vegetation or topography.

In the desert choose a campsite that is non-vegetated, out of flash flood prone washes, and at least 0.25 miles from any water source; your presence may keep shy wildlife from coming in for a life-saving drink.

'Improving' your campsite by digging rain trenches around the tent, hammering a nail into a tree to hang your mirror, or building a giant fire ring is unnecessary and unsightly and damaging to the landscape. Remember the adage above: A good campsite is found, *not made*.

Try to avoid trampling the vegetation and making trails around your campsite by establishing areas of high use (cooking areas, tents, etc.) on the most durable surfaces.

Store your food securely while you are in camp and then, when you leave, help to keep the wildlife wild by taking all of it with you, even the scraps. Never bury food or leave it behind—it will only be dug up.

Before leaving your site, be sure to completely restore it to its natural state; break down fire rings, return rocks to their former locations, and clean up every last scrap of trash and food. As always, honor the Lord by packing (carrying) out more trash than you brought with you.

Campfires & Cooking.

Whether you are talking & laughing with your friends, worshipping the Lord, or simply reflecting on life, there is nothing in the world like doing it fireside under a star-filled sky. Follow the principles below to make this activity a safe (and low-impact) one:

- First of all, it should be both legal and safe (no high winds, etc.) to build a fire where you are; some land managers establish a fire season, and others require that you obtain a fire permit, even for a stove. Check on any restrictions before heading out on your trip.
- Southern California is a desert, even along the coast, so it is vitally important that you bring your own wood & kindling with you whenever possible. The little bit of downed wood that you'll come across is necessary to help maintain a healthy ecosystem; mosses & lichens grow on the wood, wild creatures live in and under it, and as it decomposes it feeds nutrients back into the soil. With so many people, and relatively so little wood, without restrictions, self-imposed or otherwise, the land would quickly be stripped bare.
- In a campground use the existing fire ring. If camping primitively bring your own fire blanket or metal tub to contain your fire (some land managers will require you to do this) or, if you must, use a very small campfire ring,

keep your fire small and, when finished, take the ring apart and return the area to its natural state. Don't bury coals—they can smolder, insulated under the soil, for a very long time—instead thoroughly drown all campfires. Also, don't use your campfire as a trash incinerator; it rarely does an effective job.

- Modern cook stoves are so much more efficient, cleaner and, usually, faster then preparing a meal over an open fire. The fuel is lighter too. If you are in a primitive back-country camp, you may want to consider passing on the campfire altogether.

Be As Inconspicuous As Possible

Loud pets, boom box's, and voices ruin the wilderness experience for others who have escaped to the hills for peace and quiet. When you sing or play instruments in worship, do so in a manner that is considerate of your neighboring campers; establish a primitive campsite away from others if you think you want to worship like King David (See 2 Samuel 6).

Disposing Of Human Waste

Although many of the areas described within this book are located near bathrooms, you still may find yourself on a trail an uncomfortable distance from one. If this occurs, the question racing through your mind—as it did the minds of millions before you—will be, "How does one go to the bathroom in the wilderness?"

Here's the answer: Find a site at least 200 feet (70 adult paces) from any trail, campground or source of water and dig (using a stick, trowel, boot heel, whatever) a 'cathole' 6" to 8" deep. Do your business, and then backfill it with the original dirt and disguise the area with pine needles, small rocks, etc. It's that easy!

Burning toilet paper in dry areas, like Southern California, is usually a bad idea. First of all, the paper doesn't always totally burn and, secondly, more then one major wildfire has been started this way. Ideally, to keep animals from digging it up, you'll want to pack out all toilet paper, tissue, and feminine hygiene items (carry a plastic bag for this). Better yet, instead of toilet paper use grass, a rock, or a pinecone and bury it too.

Bathing

Even though a particular soap may be labeled as biodegradable, it still has an impact on the environment. Here's the procedure to minimize that impact as you bathe: If you are near a natural source of water, such as a creek, river or lake, take a dip and then haul water 200 feet (70 adult paces) from this source, lather up using the *least* amount of soap necessary to get the job done, and rinse with the water you carried with you. The idea is that you want to bathe far enough away that the soap cannot make its way back to the water source in a concentrated form.

Pack It Out

This goes without saying; *always pack (carry) out more trash then you brought with you, always leave your camp cleaner then when you found it*. If the nearest trash cans are filled, don't leave your trash bags on the ground next to the cans where animals can tear into them but, instead, throw them in the car and haul them to the next trash bin, or even home if necessary. Avoid the wind blown trash problem by keeping your camp tidy. Try not to use your campfire as a trash receptacle, and if some members of your party do, fish the unburned trash out the following day (making sure it's cool enough to do so) and pack it out. Include a few small trash bags, or plastic grocery-type bags, with your gear and, as you hike and explore, pick up the extra trash that you come across on the way. Watch even for small items, like gum wrappers and the plastic wrap around cigarette packages.

I know that I keep repeating myself, but it's true—this kind of stewardship is God honoring.

Trail Care

The best way to minimize your impact on the land, while hiking, is to have your group hike single file on trails (particularly in meadows where the temptation is to walk next to each other), and to spread out a bit when traveling cross-country.

One of the most wasteful expenditures of energy on a hike is the act of cutting trails, particularly switchbacks. Switchbacks are sections of the trail that zigzag up a slope to make the gradient less steep. While switch backing up a hill, the hiker may be required to walk dozens of circuitous yards to gain only a few feet of elevation. The temptation, then, is to cut off the meandering length of trail by climbing either straight up, or straight down. This seems like a good idea, at first, but in reality it is inefficient, exhausting, bad for your knees, and it greatly increases your risk of getting hurt, particularly if you are carrying a heavy pack. It is much more efficient, and much safer, for you to continue up the trail at a comfortable pace, then it is for your body to have to adjust to charging straight uphill or controlling a steep descent. Furthermore, cutting switchbacks breaks down the trail, hastens erosion, and is illegal in most places. Cutting switchbacks is just a bad idea!

While we can't be responsible for what everybody is doing out there, we can do our part—and our part matters! Learn more about the 'Leave No Trace' guidelines by visiting <u>www.lnt.com</u>.

CARING FOR ARCHAEOLOGICAL SITES & ARTIFACTS

Several of the adventures described within this book include side trips to such fascinating archaeological locations as ghost towns, historic buildings, and Native American village sites & rock art panels. Here are a few definitions and tidbits of information to help you better understand and protect these awesome places.

Ghost Towns & Historic Buildings

Southern California is filled with fantastic ghost towns that were once populated with folks drawn by the prospect of hitting it rich in gold, silver, or other precious resources. When these resources played out these same people often abandoned their homes and businesses in search of the next 'strike.'

Among the ghost towns in this book is the beautifully preserved Cerro Gordo high above Owens Valley, Ryholite in the Death Valley area, and Bonanza Gulch & Randsburg in the Red Rock Canyon area. The latter, Randsburg, is a really cool 'living' ghost town with year-round residents, antique stores, and an old-fashioned soda fountain.

Native American Rock Art

There are basically four types of rock art that you'll encounter on your adventures—*Petroglyphs, Pictographs, Cupules,* and *Intaglios*:

The first type, the *Petroglyph*, is an image incised (engraved) into the desert varnish, or dark coating, on rock surfaces. Petroglyphs are most commonly found in the desert areas of California and can be seen at such wonderful sites as the Volcanic Tableland near Bishop, Titus Canyon in Death Valley National Park, and Steam Wells near Red Rock State Park.

Pictographs are paintings made on the rock using, most commonly, red, white or black paint made from mineral earths mixed with a binder of some sort, such as animal fat or urine. Pictographs are widespread throughout the state; we'll see them in Little Blair Valley in Anza-Borrego Desert State Park and Painted Rock on the Carrizo Plain.

The third type of rock art is the *Cupule*, which is a small depression about 2 centimeters across carved into the rock. Usually created in a series, cupules can be found both vertically & horizontally and are believed to be associated with puberty rites. A good example of cupules can be seen in Little Blair Valley in Anza-Borrego Desert State Park.

The final, and perhaps most unusual type of rock art is the *Intaglio*. Also known as *geoglyphs*, intaglios are large figures (men, creatures, or shapes as much as 60-feet in length) created on the surface of the desert in one of two ways; either by moving dark rocks away to expose the lighter substrata beneath, or by outlining the figure with large rocks.

Intaglios are found primarily in the southeastern California desert; a good example of an intaglio can be seen in the Yuha Basin, just outside of Anza-Borrego Desert State Park.

Standing in front of a rock art panel, the question that comes to everybody's mind is, "What does it mean?" The short answer is: some rock art is an expression of the religious belief of the Native American artist who created it, some is related to puberty, fertility, or other types of rites or ceremonies and some, of course, is simply expressions of personality. You can learn more about the meaning of California's rock art by reading, *"Rock Art Sites of California and Southern Nevada"* (David Whitley).

While their original meaning is fascinating, my own passion is in the thrill that I get from their discovery. I love to dig up clues to their whereabouts, to pore over the maps, to plan a trip and then head out in search of an obscure panel painted or incised into the rock of some high mountain shelter, desert canyon, or hidden spring. I love to stand where the artist had, centuries or even millennia before, and try to imagine what his world was like; who he was, how he lived, what he believed, and what inspired him. It is a fantastic adventure, which I'm sure you'll appreciate too.

Native American Milling Stations

Milling stations are places that native peoples used to process their plant food (grains, acorns, seeds, etc.) into meal. There are three primary types of milling stations, all of which are found on flat boulders and/or bedrock.

The first type is called a *mortar*, or *mortero*. It is basically a round hole bored into the rock from one to several inches deep. Acorns, for example, would be placed into the hole and then pulverized with an oblong stone called a *Mano*.

The next type of milling station is a basin shaped depression, called a *metate*. Acorns placed into this depression would be ground with a rock in a pushing-pulling motion.

The third type of milling station is a smooth, flat shiny surface, usually on a boulder, called a *grinding slick*. This surface was used in the same fashion as the metate.

Midden Heaps

The refuse piles of Native American villages or camping areas that were inhabited for long periods of time, whether permanently or seasonally, are known as midden 'heaps.' Midden is a grayish-to-blackish soil—sometimes as much as 40-feet thick—made up of organic material, charcoal, bone, seashells, pottery shards, stone tools, and other debris.

Along the coast and on the Channel Islands, midden is comprised of large mounds of abalone (a staple) and other seashells discarded over centuries of time.

Look for midden heaps and milling stations near permanent sources of water.

Pottery Shards

Many of California's Native American peoples fired clay pots (sometimes called *ollas*), which they used to carry and/or store seeds, nuts, water, etc. The craft of pottery evolved over a period of centuries, making it possible for archaeologists to date a pot, or a fragment of a pot (and thus a site and a people), by its appearance and the technique by which it was created.

Though most of the complete ollas have been collected by archaeologists or thieves, or have been intentionally or unintentionally broken over the centuries, fragments (shards) do remain. Please appreciate these small treasures from a respectful distance.

Preserving Archaeological Sites

Here are a few guidelines that will help preserve the integrity of the archaeological sites that you are certain to discover in your wanderings:

- The position of artifacts (the clues) within these sites, and the relationship between the artifacts, usually provides more information to the archaeologist's then the artifacts themselves. Because of this, the removal of an artifact, or even just a context change (moving the artifact, even slightly) can often render a site worthless for study. This is why it is so important that any artifacts that you may come across remain undisturbed.

- If you do come across an artifact or suspected site, appreciate it from a distance, mark its location on your map, and advise the land manager as soon as possible.
- Camping and/or eating on or at an archaeological site will attract rodents, which then dig in the area and alter the site. Urinating on or about an archaeological site can change the chemical makeup of the soil, which will, in turn make it difficult for future archaeologists, with futuristic technology, to get accurate readings.
- Rubbing your hands or anything else against rock art (petroglyphs/pictographs) will accelerate the breakdown of the art. These treasures are finite; please help to increase their lifespan by appreciating them from a respectful distance.
- Please pack all of your trash out, and then some.
- Finally, the days of collecting arrowheads on the open desert are behind us; it is no longer legal to collect any historic or prehistoric archaeological artifacts or cultural material on public land (all of the lands in this book are public). Violators of the Antiquities Act of 1906 or the Archaeological Resources Protection Act of 1979 may receive penalties ranging from fines of $10,000 to ten years in federal prison.

Going Deeper (Again, no pun intended)

Check out '*The Resources*' section of this book for more archaeological resources, including clubs & organizations, and opportunities for involvement in actual digs.

CHAPTER FOUR

And Finally

Adventure / *n* 1: a risky undertaking 2: a remarkable and exciting experience

—The Merriam Webster Dictionary

Well, we've made it through the difficult stuff: We've talked about how to determine the best destination for your particular group, how to organize your people, and how to gather the information that you'll need to make your trip as rich an experience as possible.

We've discussed the various ways that, in your travels, you can get stuck on a back road, get separated from your group, and/or suffer from dehydration. We've said that it's not a good idea to allow yourself to get too chilly in the wilderness, to climb to high elevations too quickly, or to hike during the heat of the day, but that it is wise to continue to develop your outdoor skills through classes and such. We've learned that there are animals out there that can bite you and plants that can give you a rash, that mine shafts can be dangerous, that you should pack out your trash, and that it's not cool to pee on archaeological sites.

There is one final item to consider before you take off on your adventure. That's right, the liability disclaimer…

Traveling and adventuring in the wilderness can be the greatest experience of your life, but it does carry with it unavoidable risks that you must be aware of, respect and assume. These risks include deteriorated roads and trails, landslides, wildfires, erosion, adverse weather, hostile plants & animals, etc. Injuries are inevitable, too, including, but not limited to, cuts, scrapes, bruises, sprains, elevation sickness, poison oak, insect bites, broken bones, head injuries, heat exhaustion, dehydration, severe exposure to the elements, and drowning.

You must always be aware of your limitations. The activities described within this book vary in degrees of difficulty and the fact that a route, site or adventure appears in this book does not guarantee that it is now safe to pursue; routes change, conditions deteriorate and, often, lands are closed by managers or private owners. If, while pursuing an adventure you discover that you or a teammate are not properly conditioned, trained and/or equipped, or if conditions appear to be too dangerous, it is your responsibility to choose a different trip or adventure, or to return at another time when the dangerous conditions no longer exist.

As a reminder, this book is not intended as a replacement for formal training from a qualified instructor in an organized school or program. It is the responsibility of the reader to learn the proper techniques for safe participation in these wilderness activities, and to exercise prudence and good judgment at all times. The author and publisher can assume no liability for loss, injury or inconvenience sustained by any user of this guidebook as a result of information or advice found within it.

Whew…now you're finally ready to go. Be safe, have a blast, and don't forget to make time for the Lord…

Part Two

Into The Wilderness

"Climb the mountains and get their good tidings. Nature's peace will flow into you as sunshine flows into trees. The winds will blow their own freshness into you, and the storms their energy, while cares will drop away from you like the leaves of autumn."

—John Muir

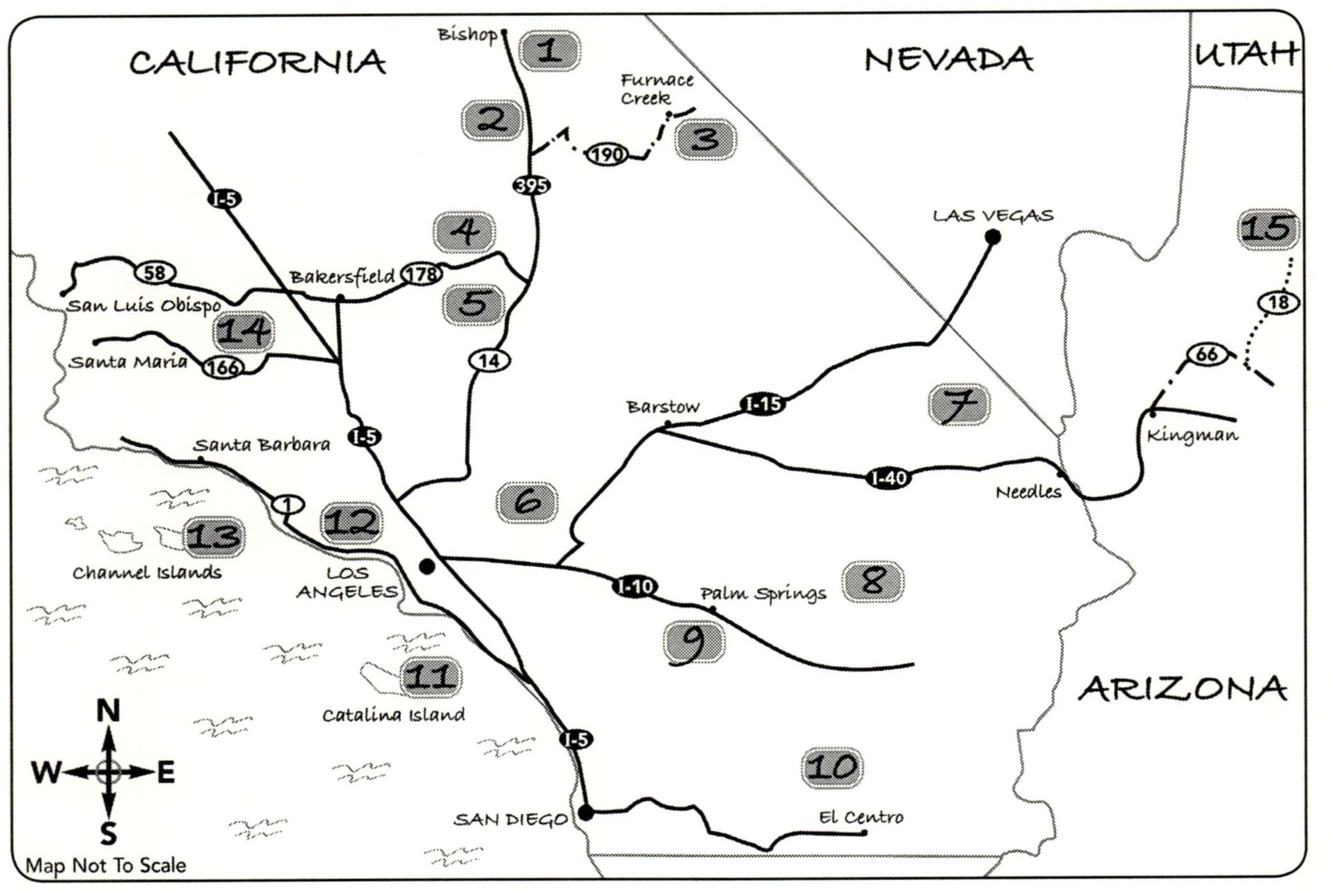

CALIFORNIA
NEVADA
UTAH
ARIZONA
Bishop
Furnace Creek
190
395
I-5
58
Bakersfield
178
San Luis Obispo
Santa Maria
166
14
Santa Barbara
I-5
1
Channel Islands
LOS ANGELES
Catalina Island
I-5
SAN DIEGO
Barstow
I-15
I-40
Needles
Kingman
66
18
LAS VEGAS
I-10
Palm Springs
El Centro
Map Not To Scale
N
W
E
S
1
2
3
4
5
6
7
8
9
10
11
12
13
14
15

The White Mountains & Northern Owens Valley Area

Walk among 4,500 year-old Bristlecone Pines; Take in 100-mile views of the Sierra Nevada Mountains, Death Valley, & beyond; 'Bag' a 14,000ft peak; Swim in a river; Explore Native American petroglyphs in a volcanic setting; Wander through hundreds of acres of amazing rock formations; Hike to an alpine waterfall; Sample sheepherders bread…and more!

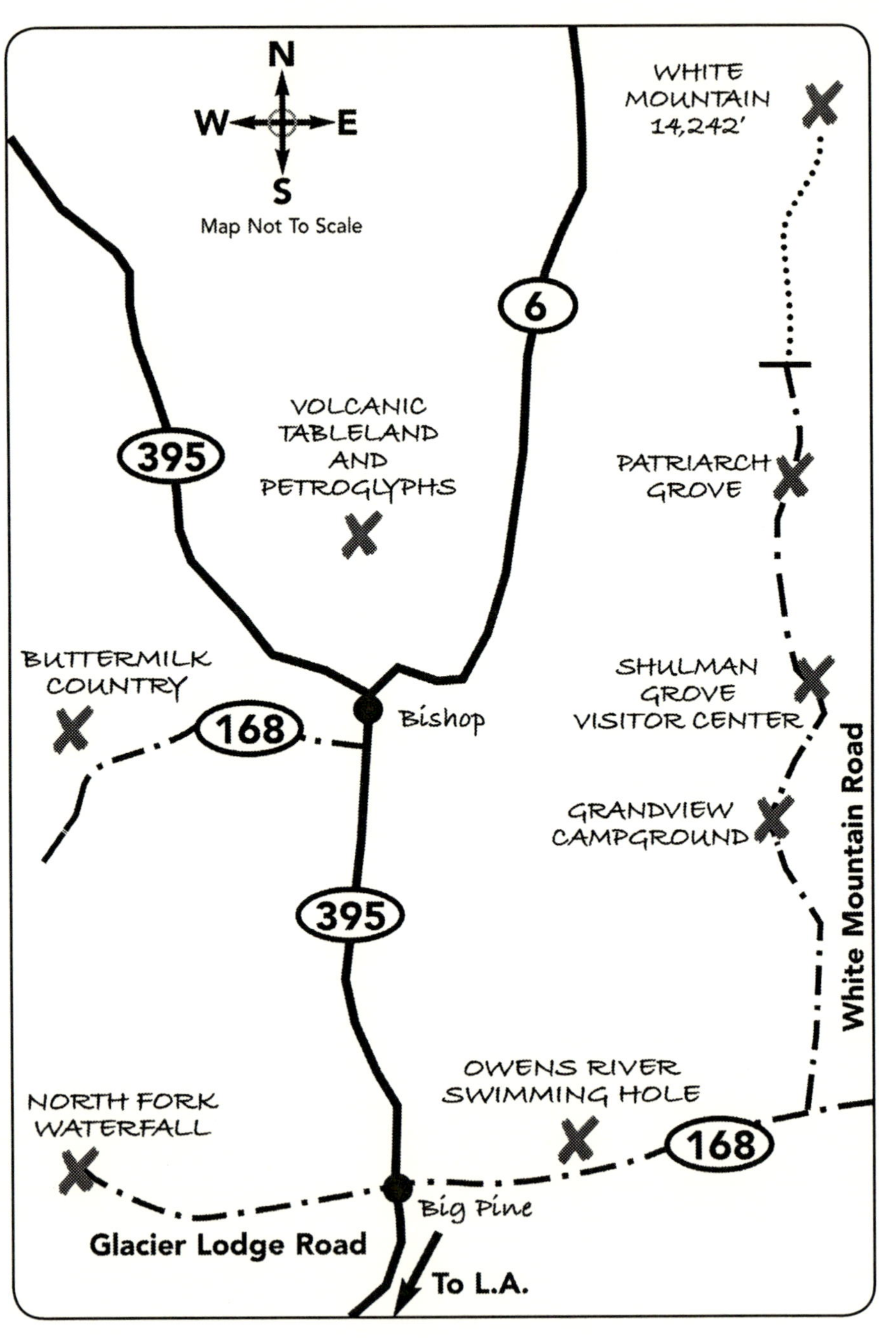

N
W E
S
Map Not To Scale
WHITE MOUNTAIN 14,242'
6
VOLCANIC TABLELAND AND PETROGLYPHS
395
PATRIARCH GROVE
SHULMAN GROVE VISITOR CENTER
BUTTERMILK COUNTRY
168
Bishop
GRANDVIEW CAMPGROUND
White Mountain Road
395
OWENS RIVER SWIMMING HOLE
NORTH FORK WATERFALL
168
Big Pine
Glacier Lodge Road
To L.A.

ABOUT THE WHITE MOUNTAINS & NORTHERN OWENS VALLEY AREA

In addition to being one of the highest ranges in the country, the wonderful White Mountains are also home to two groves of the oldest living trees on earth, as well as White Mountain itself, the third highest point in California.

High above the tree line, the upper reaches of White Mountain (14,216ft) are moon-like and ethereal, with 100-mile views that take in the High Sierra, as well as parts of Death Valley and Nevada. One of my favorite White Mountain experiences was of an evening spent at 14,000ft, looking across the Owens Valley, more then 9,000 feet below, at 13,000 & 14,000ft Sierra Nevada peaks, glaciers, and snowfields bathed in light from a full moon. It was magical.

The Owens Valley (the deepest valley in America) is a great place to adventure, too; there are ancient volcanic flows, Native American rock art, a river to swim in, beautiful rock formations to climb, and access to an endless amount of wonderful alpine scenery.

This is a fantastic place; you're going to love it.

Getting There

The directions for this trip begin just north of the town of Big Pine, at the junction of US 395 & CA 168, about 250-miles north of downtown Los Angeles. Get there, from Los Angeles, by taking Interstate 5 north to Hwy 14 north through the town of Mojave, where it eventually merges with, and becomes, Hwy 395; continue north on Hwy 395 for about 100-miles to the town of Big Pine.

From Big Pine, take CA 168 (Westgard Pass Road) east for about 13-miles and turn left (north) onto White Mountain Road (look for a sign directing you to the Bristlecone Pines). In a short distance you'll pass through the Cedar Flat entrance station which, when it's manned, is a good place to pick up maps and area information.

At about 5.4-miles from CA 168 you'll pass the Grand-view Campground (8,299ft), and then at 8.8-miles cross the boundary into the 28,000-acre area established as the Ancient Bristlecone Pine Forest. At about 10-miles you'll come to the Schulman Grove (10,000ft), the Visitors Center, and the end of the paved road. About 13-miles beyond this point, by good gravel road, is the Patriarch Grove (11,500ft), and then 4.6-miles further on a parking area and locked gate—the trailhead for the roughly 15-mile round-trip hike to the summit of White Mountain.

The total mileage from Big Pine to the end of the road beyond Patriarch Grove is somewhere around 40.5-miles.

Supplies, Lodging, Maps & Information

Gas, supplies and motels are available in Big Pine, Bishop and, to the south, Lone Pine, but they are not available at all between Big Pine and the end of the road beyond Patriarch Grove.

As far as camping goes, there are many, many great places to camp in the northern Owens Valley area, but I recommend that you stay at Grandview Campground (8,200ft). Located high in the White Mountains, in a beautiful pinion-juniper-sage setting, it's a great place to acclimate to the higher elevation while also enjoying phenomenal sunrises and sets.

Grandview Campground has tables and pit toilets, but is without drinking water; bring all that you'll need while keeping in mind that because high elevation air is drier than the air you breathe at home you'll need more than usual. Oh, and catch the sunrise or set by taking the unmarked trail at the western end of the campground to the vista near a pile of boulders.

If you would rather be further out in the sticks, primitive camping is legal anywhere in the Inyo National Forest, as long as you remain outside of the Ancient Bristlecone Pine Forest itself. Talk to the folks at the Schulman's Grove Visitors Center, or at the White Mountain Ranger Station down in Bishop, for more information about acceptable camping locations. Also, don't forget to request a free fire permit, required even if you only plan to cook with a stove.

For information regarding primitive camping, alternate campgrounds, road conditions, weather, or any necessary permits, contact: White Mountain Ranger Station, 798 North Main Street, Bishop, CA 93514, or by phone at 760.873.2500. For an alternative source of information regarding White Mountain weather, go to www.whitneyportalstore.com and click on the link at the bottom of the page.

To help you navigate, I suggest Delorme's Southern & Central California Atlas & Gazetteer, as well as the Northern California Atlas & Gazetteer. The Inyo National Forest Map is helpful too, and is available from your local outdoor store, any Owens Valley ranger station, the White Mountain Ranger Station in Bishop, and the Schulman Grove Visitors Center. The American Automobile Association's (AAA) "Eastern Sierra" map will be a great help in identifying the Eastern Sierra peaks that rise up dramatically across the Owens Valley.

On your way to the White Mountains/Owens Valley area, swing by the Interagency Visitor's Center, located at the junction of US 395 & CA 136, just south of the town of Lone Pine. Here you'll find books, maps, photographs, area information, and knowledgeable staff to answer your questions.

The best time of the year to make your trip into the White Mountains is from late spring through the fall. Summer at these elevations is wonderful—July and August is equivalent to springtime down in the valley—but remember that the weather above 8,000 feet is unpredictable, and there is always the chance of a thunderstorm, or even early season hail or snow. With fall comes a greater chance of snow, the first flakes of which lead to the closing of area roads until at least spring.

Whatever the time or season, expect wonderful views, an indescribable 'top-of-the-world' experience, an astonishing night sky, and a fresh understanding of God's awesome creativity and majesty.

The Ancient Bristlecone Pines

The Bristlecone Pine is thought to be the oldest living tree in the world. In fact, the most senior specimens of this species are more than 4,500-years old, which would have made them over 600 years old when Joseph, the Patriarch, was reunited with his family in Egypt (See Genesis 45)!

The two principal groves in the Ancient Bristlecone Pine Forest—the *Schulman* and the *Patriarch*—thrive at high, harsh elevations from about 10,000 to 11,000ft. Because of the difficulties of living in such high elevations—meager rainfall, long, cold winters, poor soil, harsh winds, etc.—most Bristlecone's grow slowly and are less than 25 feet high, gnarled, and polished smooth. This slow growth (less then an inch in diameter every century) allows the elements (water, sun, wind, sand, cold and heat) ample opportunity to mold them into beautiful, twisted shapes. See for yourself as you explore these beauties in the low-angle light of early morning and late afternoon, when their contorted forms are accented and made rich, warm, and alive.

Get to the Bristlecone's by following the above directions to the Schulman Grove—named after Dr. Edmund Schulman, the guy who first determined how old the Bristlecone Pines really are. It has a picnic area, restrooms, and a small, but dynamic, Visitors Center with great interpretive displays. One of two short loop trails, the Discovery Trail, takes off from here offering awesome views, and somewhere along its length, Methuselah the "Alpha Tree." This tree, unmarked to protect it against vandals, is believed to be over 4,700-years old! Aside from exploring the trees, the stroll on these trails will go a long way in helping your body acclimatize to the elevation.

Thirteen miles further north, beyond the Schulman Grove, is the Patriarch Grove. This grove, also with two short interpretive trails, is a fantastic spot to photograph the trees in warm, late afternoon light.

'Bagging' White Mountain

At 14,246ft, White Mountain is the highest desert peak in California, and the third highest point in the state, just behind Mt. Whitney (14,495ft) and Mt. Williamson (14,375ft).

Get to the trailhead for this fantastic 15-mile (round trip) hike up White Mountain, from the Patriarch Grove, by continuing on the main road a little more then 4-miles to the locked gate/parking area. The route to the summit begins just behind that gate and follows the old jeep trail the entire way.

While it is possible to drive up from sea level and bag this peak on the same day, I wouldn't recommend it. If you really want to enjoy the walk, share good conversation with your friends, and finish strong, you'll want to take the time to acclimatize. For example, you might spend the first night at Grandview Campground (8,200ft), then day hike the Bristlecone's (10,000-11,000ft), spend the second night at the White Mountain trailhead (11,200ft), and then wake early for a 'mountaineers start.' Following a regimen like this will allow your body to adjust to the elevation so you can climb strongly with fewer elevation-related health problems.

In the past, when time was scarce, I've left Los Angeles in the evening and driven directly to the trailhead, arriving late at night and catching a few hours of fitful sleep before the climb. This is not the preferred method, but even a few hours at a high elevation is better than going straight to 14,000ft from sea level.

If you decide to sleep at the trailhead—it's not a campground, just a very high gravel parking lot—bring a very warm sleeping bag, a wool hat, and extra water.

For this hike catch the jeep trail behind the locked gate and head upward, passing at about 2-miles the University of California's Bancroft Laboratory (12,470ft), dedicated to researching the effects of high elevation on the human body, before crossing a fantastic windswept plateau high above the tree line. This barren, otherworldly landscape is one of my favorite places; watch for deer and Bighorn Sheep from this point on.

At about 6.5-miles the route begins to switchback upward towards the summit before reaching the peak at about 7.5-miles and 3,000 feet of elevation gain from the trailhead. Relax in the sun or, if it's windy, against the stone summit hut. Sign the summit register, enjoy your lunch, and take a few photographs; the views are incredible and include the Sierra Nevada Mountains, the Owens Valley, and large portions of Nevada and Death Valley.

Be sure to bring plenty of water and warm clothing on this hike; even in the summer this route, entirely above tree line, is exposed to high and sometimes chilly winds. This can be especially true if you get a pre-dawn start, finish after sunset, or climb this mountain by full moon.

Oh, and because of the exposure, save the climb for another day if there's any possibility of an electrical storm.

A Dip In The River

About 1.6-miles east of US 395, the CA 168 crosses the Owens River and a great spot for swimming, tubing, fishing (license required), and baptisms, Lord willing. This is a great place to hit while traveling north or south on US 395.

Hike To A Waterfall On The North Fork Of Big Pine Canyon

One of my greatest memories is of the time that I snow-shoed into this canyon with a couple of very dear friends for a few days of camping and frolicking. We photographed ice-encrusted waterfalls, watched snow banners stream from the high peaks, listened for distant avalanches, glissaded on big mountains, fantasized about the hot meal we were going to eat when we got back to town, told each other semi-truth-ful stories, and laughed ourselves to sleep squashed into a less than adequate tent. It was a great time in a wonderful place.

The hike up this canyon to the waterfalls is a short 3-miles round trip, however with adequate maps and gear it can be extended to virtually any length you might want. For our purposes though, I'll describe only the hike to the falls.

From US 395 in the town of Big Pine, head west on Crocker Street (which eventually becomes Glacier Lodge Road) for about 10.5-miles, to the Big Pine Canyon Trailhead at the end of the road.

From the parking lot, at about 9,000ft, head west around the gate and over the footbridge below First Falls (a beautiful 200-foot whitewater cascade) and then, just beyond the bridge, bear right onto the narrow trail that switchbacks uphill alongside the falls.

After topping out above First Falls, cross the next bridge, and then take a hard left onto the dirt route paralleling the creek. Avoid the trail signed, "Upper Trail", but instead continue straight ahead towards the North Fork of Big Pine Canyon; Second Falls, larger and more remarkable then First Falls, is visible from the trail just about 1-mile ahead.

After enjoying the falls, exploring the area, and perhaps napping in the sun, retrace your steps to the parking area.

Volcanic Tableland Petroglyph Tour

On this fascinating journey to the Volcanic Tableland area you'll have the opportunity to explore the largest concentration of petroglyphs in this part of the state.

In an attempt to discourage vandals, the Bureau of Land Management (BLM) requires visitors to appear in person for directions to these fragile sites. Get to the BLM office, from Big Pine, by heading north on US 395 for about 15-miles, where it then becomes Main Street in the town of Bishop. The BLM office is located in the Cottonwood Plaza, 785 North Main Street, Suite E (760.872.4881). Pop in and tell the rangers that you would like directions to the Volcanic Tableland Petroglyph Tour.

While you're in town for the map be sure to visit Erick Schat's Bakery at 763 North Main Street; it's world famous for its Sheepherders Bread, and they bake a lot of other goodies too. Also, if you have time, visit Mountain Light Gallery at 106

South Main. Galen Rowell was an amazing mountaineer/landscape photographer, and his photographs of the White & Sierra Nevada Ranges will inspire you.

If you require more maps, books, or other information, stop in at the White Mountain Ranger Station, just down the road at 798 North Main Street.

As you gas up in Bishop, and then follow the BLM map to the first stop, the Fish Slough Site, keep in mind that the mountains which rise above you to the east are the White's, and that White Mountain itself is nearly 10,000 vertical feet above you.

The Fish Slough petroglyph site contains a few dozen petroglyphs and several grinding slicks—these flat-topped rocks with smoothly polished surfaces were used by the Owens Valley Paiutes to grind seeds, nuts, etc. The Paiutes, descendents of the people who created these petroglyphs, have a reservation in Bishop to this day.

The next stop is the Chidago Site. This site is larger than Fish Slough and is located among a pile of boulders, one of which is called, appropriately, "Newspaper Rock"; it is absolutely covered in petroglyphs.

Further on you'll come to the two concentrations of rock art that make up the Red Canyon Site. The first concentration is a small grouping around a parking area on the western side of the site. The second, the larger of the two, is just beyond the parking area, about 200 yards east of the first car park.

After you've explored Red Canyon, proceed to Chalfant—the largest and most spectacular of the sites—where more then 400 elements are spread out over 600 yards of cliff face. Look for a fenced-in area towards the northeast containing the most spectacular elements.

When you've finished return to Bishop via US 6, or backtrack the way you came.

Buttermilk Country Adventure

The Buttermilks, spread out over hundreds of acres at the base of the Sierra Nevada Mountains, are made up of several wonderful concentrations of boulders and rock formations known the world over for their challenging rock climbing routes. Take some time to explore these beauties, photograph them, identify the area peaks (using your AAA "Eastern Sierra" map), study, pray, journal, and worship our Lord, who made them. Also, if you're itching for some exercise, you can check with the White Mountain Ranger Station for tips on hiring a reputable guide/instructor to teach your group how to rock climb.

Get to Buttermilk Country, from Bishop, by taking Hwy 168 (West Line Street) west for about 3-miles, and then turning right on Buttermilk Road. After crossing a cattle guard continue on the maintained gravel road for another 3.5-miles, to the top of a rise. You are now in the heart of the spectacular Buttermilk's. There are several groupings of boulders around the area and several more a little further down the road.

Temperatures in Buttermilk Country can be very high in the summer. If it's too hot to hang out, you might want to avoid Buttermilk Road altogether and continue west on Hwy 168, climbing into the high country above the heat. There, in a short few miles, you'll find beautiful high mountain lakes, streams, and crags to explore. Check with the rangers in Bishop for more information regarding this high country.

Please note that Highway 168 above Buttermilk Road is closed in the winter.

More Local Adventures

Read through the next chapter, The Mt. Whitney Area, for additional adventures in the Owens Valley.

CHAPTER SIX

The Mount Whitney & Southern Owens Valley Area

Camp among wonderful, chaotic, rock formations or high in the pines; Discover an old mine & artifacts; Stand in awe of a classis Eastern Sierra sunrise, a 300ft cascade and an enormous pancake; Hike to an alpine lake and a high desert waterfall; Explore volcanic cinder cones & lava flows, a ghost town, charcoal kilns, and sand dunes; Soak in a hot spring; 'Bag' the highest mountain in the lower 48 States…and more!

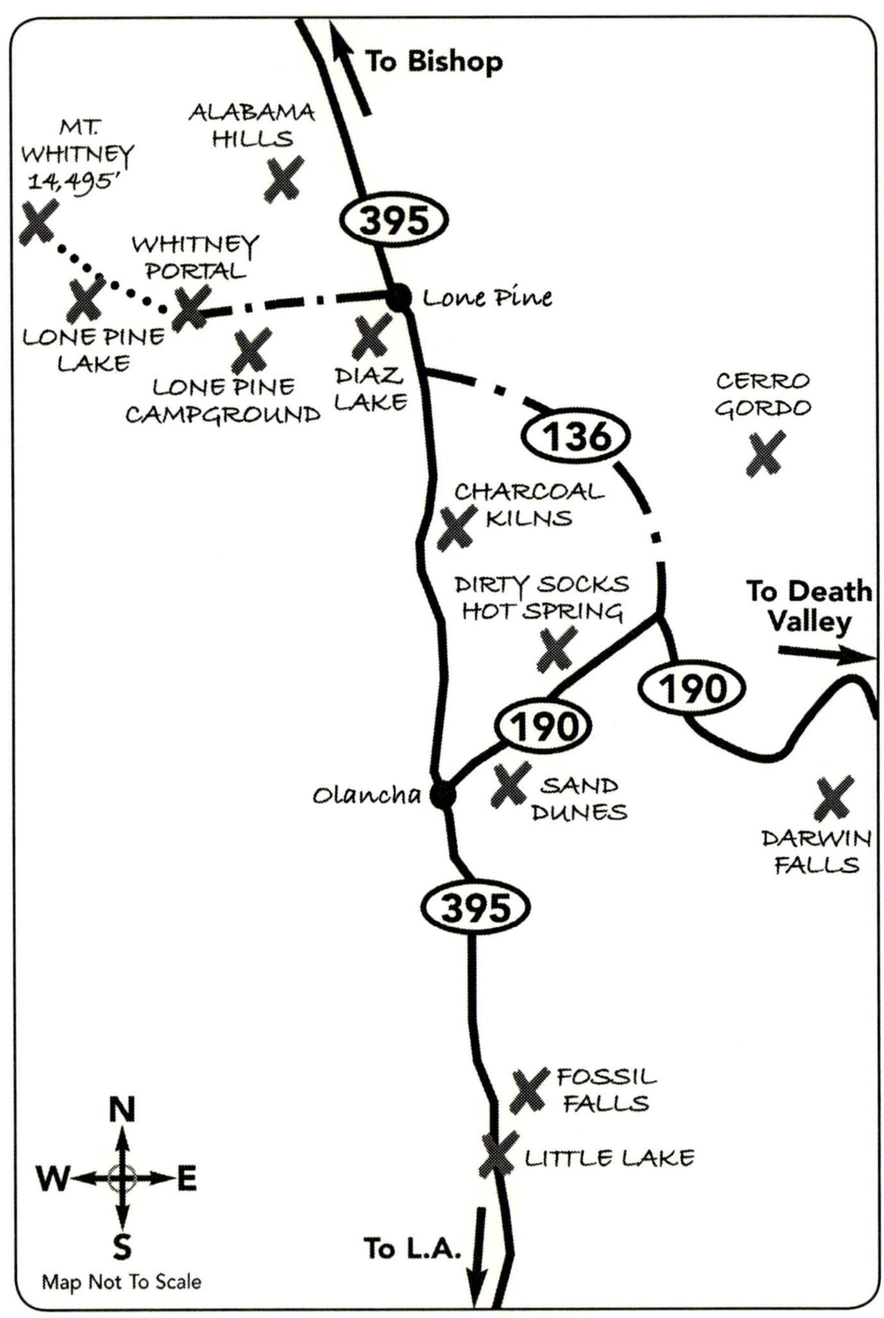

To Bishop
MT. WHITNEY 14,495'
ALABAMA HILLS
WHITNEY PORTAL
395
Lone Pine
LONE PINE LAKE
LONE PINE CAMPGROUND
DIAZ LAKE
136
CERRO GORDO
CHARCOAL KILNS
DIRTY SOCKS HOT SPRING
To Death Valley
190
190
Olancha
SAND DUNES
395
DARWIN FALLS
FOSSIL FALLS
LITTLE LAKE
N
W
E
S
To L.A.
Map Not To Scale

ABOUT THE MOUNT WHITNEY & SOUTHERN OWENS VALLEY AREA

The Owens Valley is the deepest in America, and one of the most ecologically diverse areas in the world. The landscape ranges from high desert to alpine and includes such fantastic features as sand dunes, thick forests, hot springs, cinder cones & lava flows, majestic granite amphitheaters, thousands of acres of fascinating rock formations, and a lake birthed in an earthquake. This same wide range of elevations—nearly 12,000 vertical feet from the valley floor to the summit of the highest peaks—makes it a great year-round retreat, with cooler summer temperatures high up in the pines and warmer winter temperatures in the valleys below.

The Sierra Nevada Mountains, which make up the western border of the Owens Valley, is also home to Mount Whitney, the highest point in the contiguous United States.

This is an awesome place filled with unlimited adventure and exploration opportunities…you're going to have a blast here!

Getting There

The directions to the various adventures in this chapter originate from the principal town in the area, Lone Pine, which is located on US 395, about 210-miles north of downtown Los Angeles. Get there, from Los Angeles, by taking Interstate 5 north to Hwy 14 north through the town of Mojave, where it eventually becomes Hwy 395. Continue north on Hwy 395 for about 60-miles to the town of Lone Pine.

Lodging, Supplies, Maps & Information

Gas, supplies, motels, and at least two campgrounds are available in and around the town of Lone Pine.

The first campground is at Diaz Lake, located about 3-miles south of Lone Pine on US 395. Diaz Lake was formed during the devastating earthquake of 1872 when the ground dropped between 16-20 feet, severing natural springs that quickly filled the depression with water. Open year round, it has 200 sites with water and flush toilets.

The other campground is Lone Pine Campground, located about 7-miles west of town on Whitney Portal Road. This campground has 38 sites and is open all year, although piped water is only available from May 15 to October 15.

A third camping option is the nearby Alabama Hills where it is free and undeveloped (no spaces, water, bathrooms, etc.); contact the BLM for specifics.

These campgrounds— Diaz Lake, Lone Pine, and the Alabama's—are suitable year round, though summers can be very hot. There are three more campgrounds, a little further west and higher up in the cool pines of the Whitney Portal area, which are great places to stay from late spring through the fall. We'll discuss these in greater detail below.

As far as maps go, you'll want DeLorme's Central & Southern California Atlas & Gazetteer, the American Automobile Club's "Inyo County" map, and Tom Harrison's fantastic topographic map titled, "The Mount Whitney Zone" (www.tomharrisonmaps.com).

Also, don't forget the Interagency Visitors Center located at the junction of US 395/CA 136, just south of Lone Pine. This is a great place to get oriented to the area and to obtain solid information, guidebooks, maps, etc. If you do visit the center, be sure to identify Mount Whitney before you leave.

The Alabama Hills

The Alabama Hills Recreation Area (4,500ft) embraces 30,000 acres of awesome rock formations, dramatic views, great hiking, wonderful photographic opportunities, breathtaking sunrises, and star-filled nights. This is a great place to explore, rock climb, journal, be silent, meditate on God, and sleep out under the stars.

From the town of Lone Pine, head west on Whitney Portal Road, crossing over the Los Angeles Aqueduct and into the Alabama Hills Recreation Area at about 0.6-miles.

At about 2.6-miles you'll come to an intersection with Movie Road, so named because of the hundreds of commercials & films that have been shot in the Alabama's since the 1920's. As you turn right here, onto Movie Road, be sure to catch the commemorative plaque at the intersection; it was dedicated by Roy Rogers, who starred in his first feature film here in 1938. Movie Road is nicely graded and meanders some ways through the Alabama's before intersecting with Moffet Ranch Road, and eventually emptying out onto US 395 a few miles north of Lone Pine.

The Alabama's are named after an area mine, which itself was named by southern sympathizers after a confederate battleship that was doing a number on Union shipping during the Civil War. A mining community to the northwest of the Alabama's, Kearsarge, was named after the Union ship that finally sank the Alabama. Look for the Alabama Mine and associated artifacts as you explore the northeast section of these hills.

As you cruise along Movie Road be sure to explore a few of the side roads that loop through the rocks, many of which end in cul-de-sacs that make perfect campsites. If you choose to camp out here, be sure to choose a site that has an unobstructed view of Mount Whitney; you won't want to miss the first rays of the rising sun striking the summit and minarets of this beautiful mountain. Once you've experienced one of these world-class sunrises, you'll see why the famous mountaineer and conservationist, John Muir, called the Sierra Nevada, 'The Range of Light'.

Winter is especially beautiful in the Alabama Hills; the snowcapped Sierra's provide an incredible backdrop, the air is wonderfully crisp, and there's a greater chance of having the area to yourself. Hiking and exploring the Alabama's by moonlight is a special treat too, and a great way to bond as a group.

For more information regarding the Alabama Hills, contact the BLM, 785 North Main Street, Suite E, Bishop, CA, 93514, or by phone at 760.872.4881.

Whitney Portal

From the junction of US 395 & Whitney Portal Road (the only streetlight in the town of Lone Pine), head west on Whitney Portal Road for about 12-miles, and a couple of sharp switchbacks, to its end.

Whitney Portal (8,361ft), high in the pines and surrounded on three sides by 1,000-foot high granite walls, packs a lot of interesting sights into a very small area. One of those sights is the world famous Whitney Portal Store.

Originally built in 1935, today the Whitney Store serves climbers & backpackers heading to the summit of Mount Whitney by providing basic gear, supplies, books, maps and Mount Whitney souvenirs, as well as up-to-date weather and trail information. Oh, and don't miss buying a pancake from the grill. That's right, "a" pancake, a single pancake. It's hubcap sized and comes served on two side-by-side paper plates. Ah, yes! The sun just seems to shine a little brighter when you're sharing one of these beauties with your sweetheart or closest bud.

The store is open from May to October, with varied hours. Check out their website, www.whitneyportalstore.com for more info about the store, the portal, the mountain, or area weather.

About 100-feet east of the store is the trailhead to Mount Whitney; the jump off point for, among other things, the most popular route to the summit, 11-miles and more then 6,000 vertical feet away.

Across the road from the store is a small fishing pond, which is stocked weekly from May to October. A license is required to fish here and, occasionally, you may have to share your space with a black bear.

Near the pond, and visible from the parking area, is a beautiful, 300-foot cascade. This is the lower falls; the upper one, just upstream, is perhaps 200 to 300 feet higher. In the spring, the roar of these snowmelt-driven falls reverberate from the granite walls. It is awesome!

Camping At Whitney Portal

The three campgrounds in the portal area are open from May to October. The first, the Whitney Portal Campground, is about 1.5-miles from the end of the road. It has 44 family-sized sites, with piped water and flush toilets.

The second campground, the Whitney Portal Group Site, is to the immediate west and can accommodate three groups of fifteen individuals.

To the west of the group campground, near the long-term parking area, is the Whitney Portal Trailhead Campground. This campground has ten walk-in sites that are for the use of hikers planning to begin their climb of Mount Whitney the following day. A stay at this campground is strictly limited to one night.

Campsites at these three campgrounds can be reserved by contacting Reserve America by phone at 800.444.7275, or online at: www.reserveusa.com.

Whitney Portal is a very active bear area, so be sure to store anything that you have that looks or smells like food in the bear-proof boxes provided in the campgrounds…even if it's broad daylight, and even if you only plan to be there a short while. If you are doubtful, take a look at the bear-related photographs on display in the Whitney Portal Store.

Lone Pine Lake Hike

The trail to Lone Pine Lake (9,420ft)—about 5.6-miles round trip in length and with about 1,060ft of elevation gain—begins at the kiosk 100 feet east of the Whitney Store, and follows the same route as the Mount Whitney trail.

The trail initially angles away from the mountain, then turns sharply back and switchbacks upward through a very exposed, and sometimes very hot, stretch of trail. At about 0.80-mile you'll cross into the John Muir Wilderness area; take some time here to enjoy the awesome views of the Owens Valley and the massive granite walls and spires that tower above you.

Continuing on, at somewhere just over 2.5-miles you'll encounter a fork in the trail that may or may not be marked; bear left here and descend slightly to this little alpine jewel. Spend the day reading, journaling, swimming, picnicking, sunbathing, or just soaking your feet and then, when you're finished, return to the Portal via the same route.

Bring your Ten Essentials and plenty of water, or a filter, and be aware that the weather at this elevation changes quickly; afternoon thunderstorms often crop up during the summer.

A permit is required to hike beyond Lone Pine Lake, into the area known as the Mount Whitney Zone. Permit information is described in detail below.

Climbing Mount Whitney (14,495ft)

Mount Whitney is a classic. It is the highest point in the contiguous 48 states, one of fifteen 14,000-foot peaks ('Fourteeners') in California and, for most of the year, a non-technical mountain attainable by virtually any prepared person. These factors, combined, have made Mount Whitney the most climbed mountain in the United States.

To protect both the fragile environment and the wilderness experience, a system limiting the number of hikers has been established requiring all who cross into the Mount Whitney Zone between May 1 and November 1, including those taking the main route from Whitney Portal to the summit, to have a permit in his or her possession.

Back when Mt. Whitney permits were issued on a first come, first served basis, aspiring climbers would simply drive up to Lone Pine the night before and sleep on the porch of the ranger station. In the morning, when the ranger arrived to open the office, he or she would issue the first permit to the person sleeping closest to the door. The next closest would get the next permit, and so on.

These days, because of the immense number of applications that the Forest Service receives, hikers are required to apply for a permit through the mail. A lottery system then determines who actually receives those permits.

Acquiring A Permit

Here's how to apply for a permit: First, go to <u>www.fs.fed.us/r5/inyo/recreation/wild/mtwhitney</u> to check for up-to-date information and download an application. Next, determine the number of people in your party and the dates that you can climb. Flexibility is the key here; having fewer people (4 or less) and several alternate dates will give you a better chance of getting your permit.

Fill out the application, making sure to totally fill in the alternate leaders section of the form. This will allow anyone named on the application to carry the permit, which can be helpful if it turns out that the leader is unable to make the trip for some reason.

If you plan to mail your permit, you'll need to write out a check in the amount of $15.00 per each person on your application (i.e. $60.00 for four persons). Make it out to *USDA Forest Service* and include it with the application (if you fax your permit, pay this amount by VISA or MasterCard only). If your permit is issued, you'll receive a confirmation letter and a receipt for these monies. If your attempt at getting a permit is unsuccessful you'll receive your check, or credit card number, back within two months of the date that you submitted it. Note: This fee is only for the permit and is separate from any other pre-trip fees that you may have incurred, such as campground reservation fees.

Finally, mail your completed application and fee to: Wilderness Permit Office, 873 North Main Street, Bishop, CA 93514, or fax it to: 760.873.2485

Permits are only received from February 1st-28th, with those received between the 1st and 14th processed first. All mailed applications must have a February postmark—early applications are not accepted.

If your group has some flexibility, there are other options available to you. For example, you can stop in at the Mount Whitney Ranger Station (on US 395, in the town of Lone Pine) first thing in the morning and see if there are any permits that haven't been picked up. Things happen between February, when permits are applied for, and the summer months when they are supposed to be picked up that prevent people from going on their hikes. When this happens, their permits are offered up on a first come, first served basis. There are no guarantees with this option, though, and it is a long drive, but the payoff would be well worth it if you have the time.

Also, there are other routes to the summit—*the Mountaineer's Route, the High Sierra Trail, the John Muir Trail, New Army Pass* and others—that have fewer people on them and no lottery application process. Contact the ranger station in Lone Pine for more information about these alternate routes and their permit procedures.

The Climb

The trail to Mount Whitney's summit—22-miles, round-trip, with about 6,000ft of elevation gain—begins at the kiosk, 100 feet east of the Whitney Store.

The trail initially angles away from the mountain, then turns sharply back and switchbacks upward through a very exposed, and sometimes very hot, stretch of trail. Cross the North Fork of Lone Pine Creek at about 0.65-miles (the *Mountaineer's Route* follows this creek upward from here) and then, at about 0.80-mile, cross into the John Muir Wilderness area. Take some time here to enjoy the awesome views of the Owens Valley and the massive granite walls and spires that tower above you.

At about 2.8-miles (9,420ft), you'll pass a spur leading down to Lone Pine Lake; continue on the right fork and shortly cross into the Mount Whitney Zone, the limit for those without a Mount Whitney permit.

Over the next 1-mile, or so, you'll cross through the beautiful meadow at Bighorn Sheep Park, and reach Outpost Camp at

10,360ft. There are some great tent sites here under the trees, a beautiful waterfall just to the east, and a solar powered toilet.

Continuing on you'll reach Mirror Lake (10,640ft) at 4.3-miles, Trailside Meadow (11,395ft) at 5.3-miles, and Consultation Lake at 5.8 miles.

At 6.3-miles you'll reach Trail Camp (12,039ft), the second of the two campgrounds on this route. This camp, much closer to the summit and in an awesome setting above treeline, is usually more crowded then Outpost Camp. It also has the last dependable water on the route, so be sure to tank up here—of course, treating or purifying it first.

Continuing on from Trail Camp, the route climbs at least 99 switchbacks over the next 2-miles before topping off at Trail Crest (13,777ft). Use caution on the switchbacks; if the route is clear this is a pleasant, if a bit monotonous, stretch of trail. If the route is icy or snowy (which is possible into July) it can be quite dangerous, requiring technical gear and the knowledge to use it.

At Trail Crest you'll cross into Sequoia National Park, and with it views of the Western Sierra, the headwaters of the Kern River and, below you, the Hitchcock Lakes. The John Muir Trail junction is another 0.5-mile *down* the trail (9-miles from Whitney Portal); hang a right here and continue climbing, now on the famous John Muir Trail.

The summit is still about 2-miles away—past Mt. Muir, Third Needle, Crooks Peak and Keeler Needle—but they are glorious miles, filled with mind-blowing views that extend for miles and miles before, at last, you snake through some large granite blocks, and past the stone hut, to the summit.

Congratulations…you are standing on the highest point in the lower 48 States! Enjoy the magnificent views, sign the register, savor your lunch, take photos, and connect with the other climbers around you—some of the coolest and wackiest people you'll ever meet will be with you on the summit of Whitney.

Remember, too, that if you plan to hike back to the trailhead at Whitney Portal today, then you are at this point only half done with your walk. Be sure to allow yourself more then enough time to get back down the mountain.

Some Thoughts On Climbing Mount Whitney

- To my mind, the four most important elements of a successful climb of Mount Whitney are: (1) training together as a team, (2) being properly equipped, (3) acclimatizing properly, and (4) climbing at a comfortable pace. Do these four things and you can't go wrong.
- Although achievable for nearly any prepared person, this climb is no pushover. Your training must be serious—hike aggressive trails together at higher elevations in the weeks leading up to your trip.
- Do your research; read (there are lots and lots of books on this hike), surf the web, and talk to others who have done it. Check out www.whitneyportalstore.com. Climbers from all over the world log on to this site to share information and have their questions answered.

- There are several options for climbing Whitney:
    1. Some people start out early and do the mountain—from the trailhead to the summit and back—in a single day. There are some benefits to doing it this way; it's easier to get a day-permit than an overnight one, you can carry a lighter pack, and it's a great physical challenge. The downside is the acclimatization process is thrown out the door, and you must be in excellent condition.
    2. A second option is to do the hike over a weekend. For example, you might drive up on Friday afternoon, stop at the ranger station before it closes to pick up your permit, and spend the first night at Whitney Portal. Waking up early Saturday morning, you'll hike up to Trail Camp and spend the second night. Sunday is summit day; set out early in the morning with light packs (just the basics—Ten Essentials, heavier jacket, lunch, camera, etc.), summit the mountain, and then return to Trail Camp, pack up your gear, and walk out to Whitney Portal for a celebration dinner and the drive home.
    3. A third option is to take several days and stay at Whitney Portal the first night, Outpost Camp the second night, Trail Camp on the third night, and then climb the summit the following morning. You could even stop at Outpost Camp on the fourth night before walking out. This plan would be the best bet for acclimatizing and for assisting the younger, older, or less fit to successfully summit the mountain.
- At the higher elevations of Whitney, ice and electrical storms are very real threats; before heading up, check with the rangers and the crew at the Whitney Store for the latest trail/weather conditions. Ice axes and crampons may be necessary in the spring and early summer;

know how to use them or save the hike for later in the season. Remember, the number-one greatest wilderness skill that you can ever posses is your aptitude for *knowing, and operating within, your abilities.* If at anytime on the walk you have doubts, turn back and save it for another day.

- This is a great full moon hike for a strong group. Contact the Lone Pine Ranger Station for more information about getting a full moon permit.
- Swing by the Whitney Store, before heading up the mountain, and purchase a labeled panoramic photo to help you identify the many, many wonderful peaks, valleys, and lakes visible from the summit.
- Don't forget to pick up an, "I Climbed the Big One" t-shirt at the Whitney Store before you head for home.

For more information regarding permits, recommended guidebooks (there are several very good ones out there), or the hike itself, contact: Mount Whitney Ranger District, PO Box 8, Lone Pine, CA 93545, or by phone at 760.876.6200.

Fossil Falls Natural Landmark & Cinder Cone

Get to Fossil Falls by heading south on US 395, from the town of Lone Pine, for approximately 45-miles. Turn left (east) onto the well marked, 'Cinder Cone Road' for about 0.6-miles, and then bear right (south) and drive another 0.6-miles to the Fossil Falls trailhead.

From the informational sign at the south end of the parking lot, follow the yellow and orange splotches of paint for about 0.25-mile across a very exposed lava field to the two falls, which are more then 40 feet high, and a couple of hundreds yards apart from each other. The falls are actually dry now, as the Owens River no longer flows this far south, but the amazingly sculpted and polished lava formations remain.

The whole Fossil Falls Natural Landmark area is volcanic; the mountains to the east are named the Coso Range, which means, "Range of Fire", and if you look closely you can see where the lava flowed from them. In fact, when you turned onto Cinder Cone Road from US 395, the hill to the north of the road was Red Hill, an actual cinder cone formed when molten material was ejected from a vent in the earth's crust. These days the cinder is being mined; drive around the cone counter-clock wise, to the northeast, to see where that's happening, and to explore interesting cinder dunes.

As you explore the area around the falls keep your eye out for flakes of obsidian, a dark, glass-like volcanic rock that ancient peoples quarried in the Coso's and used to manufacture tools (arrowheads, knives, scrapers, awls, etc). These flakes, left over from the creation of the tools, still litter the ground in great numbers.

Look, too, for circles of stones marked out on the ground, which held together the circular brush-and-Tule shelters the Paiutes once lived in. There is rock art (petroglyphs & pictographs) around the area also and, worn into the tops of nearby rocks, oblong basins called metates that were used to grind nuts, seeds, etc.

Have sunblock, a hat, and lots of water with you here, as shade is scarce and this lava field can be a very hot place on a summer day. Also, be sure to keep the kids close while exploring near the falls; the rim is quite high and can be very dangerous.

For more information regarding Fossil Falls Natural Landmark, contact the Bureau of Land Management Ridgecrest Resource Area, 300 South Richmond Road, Ridgecrest, California, 93555, or by phone at 760.384.5400.

The small, privately owned, spring-fed lake between the volcanic flow and Hwy 395 is called, appropriately, Little Lake. Next time you drive past Little Lake on US 395, notice the volcanic cliff that runs parallel to the freeway, on the other side of the lake. Locally, this lava flow is called, "The Snake." Can you see the snake's body? Its head is at the southern end, about where the lake is. Kinda cool, huh?

Owens Lake Charcoal Kilns

About 9.1-miles north of the junction of US 395/CA 190, near the town of Olancha, on the east side of US 395, you'll see a small, signed, spur road; the remains of the fascinating beehive-like charcoal kilns are 1-mile down this road.

At one time, on the other side of this dry lakebed, there were three charcoal-driven smelters that processed the silver produced by area mines. After these smelters—Swansea, Cerro Gordo & Darwin—had exhausted the local supply of trees, a new source of timber was located across the lake and high up in Cottonwood Canyon.

If you look northwest from the kilns, across US 395, you can see Cottonwood Canyon where the trees were logged. The logs were transported by way of a flume that ran down the mountain, and then fired into charcoal in these very kilns.

At the time these kilns were built, Owens Lake was 30 feet deep and had over one hundred square miles of surface area. At least two steamers, the Bessie Brady and the Mollie Stevens, ferried loads of charcoal and supplies across the water, returning with shipments of silver destined for Los Angeles.

Olancha Sand Dunes & Dirty Socks Hot Spring

From the junction of US 395/CA 190, in Olancha, travel east on CA 190 for just over 4-miles, and then look to the south (right) for some nice dunes. Sand loving flowers put on a beautiful display here in the spring, and what a place for solitude and prayer!

Just under 0.5-miles east of the sand dunes, on CA 190, on the opposite side of the road, is an unmarked turnoff that leads 300 yards out onto the playa. This road ends at a cemented hot spring called, "Dirty Socks", so named because it emits a slight sulphurous stench.

This is a great place to soak, despite the funky smell.

Cerro Gordo Ghost Town

Cerro Gordo is a sweet little privately owned ghost town that is all original and in great condition.

Get there, from the junction of US 395/CA 136, just south of Lone Pine, by heading east on CA 136 for about 12.6-miles to the small hamlet of Keeler, and the junction with Cerro Gordo Road. Head northeast on Cerro Gordo Road for about 7.5-miles—climbing past mining relics and artifacts—to the town site high on the flank of Cerro Gordo Peak.

Silver was first discovered in Cerro Gordo (Cerro Gordo means 'Fat Hill') in 1865, and by 1871 it had grown into a town of about 2,000. Most of the buildings in Cerro Gordo were built either during this period, around 1871, or during the next growth phase which occurred in 1916.

The Cerro Gordo Mine was the largest producer of silver, lead, and zinc in California's history. The ore was processed by the smelter in Swansea (on the shore of the now dry Owens Lake), which was itself powered by charcoal fired in the kilns you saw across the lakebed. Most of Cerro Gordo's silver was transported to Los Angeles, helping to put the small pueblo on the map.

After you've explored Cerro Gordo, retrace your route to Keeler and CA 136, while being sure to watch your brakes. This steep road is the same route that the teamsters used in the old days to haul ore down to the lakeshore. It's been said that, in those days, drivers would chain the wheels of their wagons to keep them from turning on this descent, and that many drivers quit their jobs upon reaching the bottom.

Note: The Cerro Gordo Road is a county maintained gravel road and is passable for the average vehicle with decent clearance; however, it is subject to washouts and can be blocked by snow. Check conditions locally before heading up.

To get more info, or to arrange a tour of Cerro Gordo, call 760.876.5030. The owners also rent out various buildings to help fund their preservation efforts; this may be the perfect place for your small group retreat. For more about Cerro

Gordo's fascinating history read, *Death Valley to Yosemite: Frontier Mining Camps & Ghost Towns* (L. Burr Belden & Mary DeDecker).

Hike to Darwin Falls

This is an easy 1.5-mile round-trip hike to a hidden desert oasis. From the junction of US 395/CA 136, just south of Lone Pine, head east on CA 136 for 18-miles, and then southeast on CA 190 for 30 more miles. The turnoff for Darwin Falls is on the right (south) almost exactly 1-mile before you reach the Panamint Springs Resort. Turning right onto the dirt road, continue on for 2.5-miles, and then bear right at the fork for 0.30-mile to the parking area.

From the parking area, head upstream on foot, following a tiny trickle of water that continues to grow as you make your way upstream. The trail is not well defined, but as long as you stay in the canyon bottom and follow the creek you can't go wrong.

Continuing upstream the vegetation increases with willow, cattail, and reeds all contending for positions near the water. Birds are here in abundance, too, with more then 80 species spotted each spring. In a very short time you'll come to the first in a series of falls, each one higher and more beautiful than the last. The colorful mosses and ferns, the willows, the musical sound of the waterfall—what an awesome place!

This is a nice stroll through a beautiful canyon, but it is a desert and can be very hot in the summer. For this reason, and for a better shot at solitude and wildlife observation, it is better done in the cool of the day.

Other Local Adventures

Read back over Trip #1, The White Mountains & Northern Owens Valley Area, for other Owens Valley adventures.

CHAPTER SEVEN

The Death Valley National Park Area

Stand on the lowest spot in the western hemisphere; Walk among incredible salt flats & formations, and other geological wonders; Scale huge sand dunes; Take in the views from awesome overlooks; Discover ghost towns, mining history, and Native American rock art sites; Soak in a hot spring; Hike to a 70 foot-high desert waterfall or along the rim of a huge volcanic crater; 'Bag' the highest summit in the park; Order an old fashioned malt at a 'living' ghost town; Traverse a canyon by moonlight…and more!

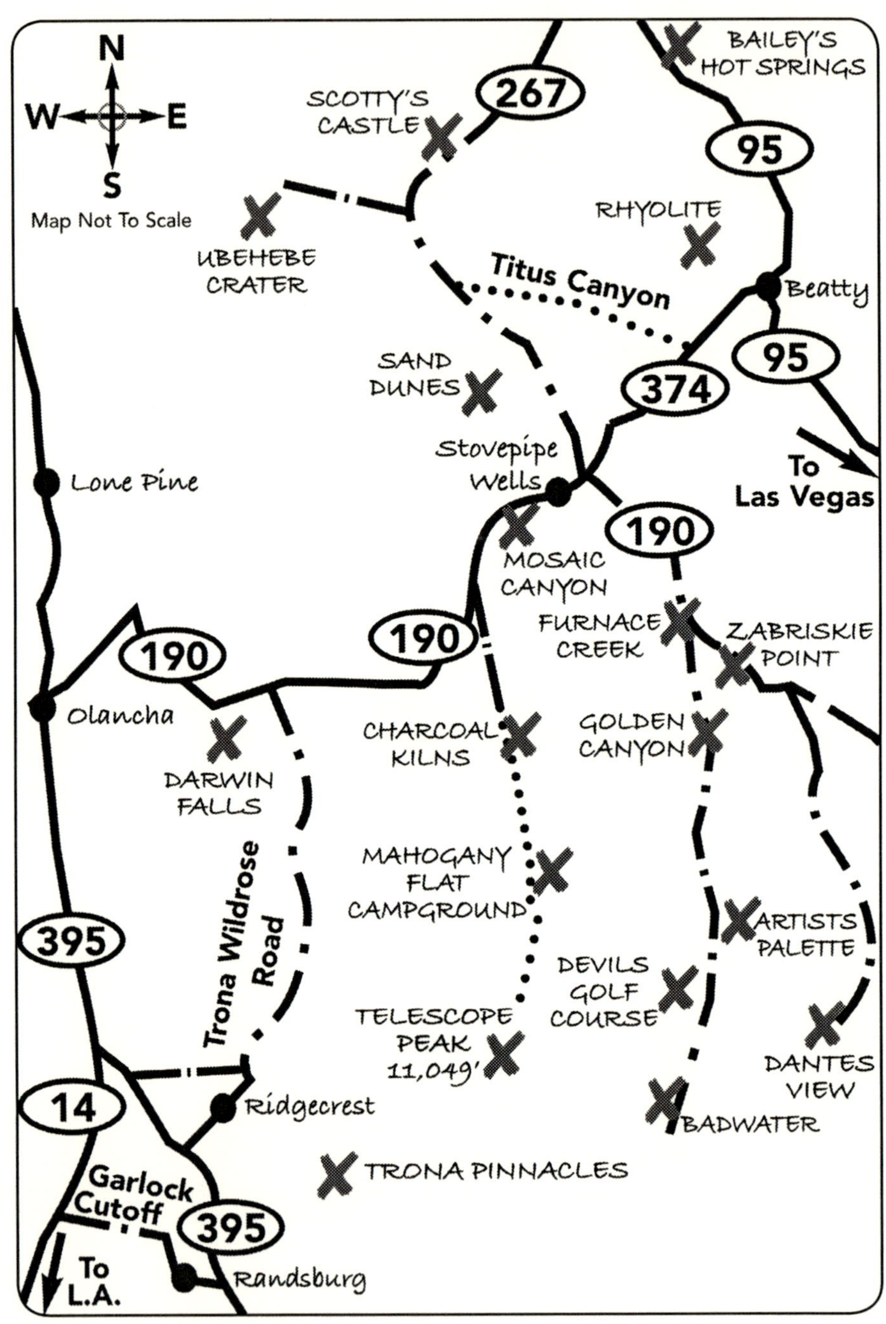

N
W E
S
Map Not To Scale
SCOTTY'S CASTLE
267
BAILEY'S HOT SPRINGS
95
UBEHEBE CRATER
RHYOLITE
Titus Canyon
Beatty
SAND DUNES
374
95
Stovepipe Wells
To Las Vegas
Lone Pine
190
MOSAIC CANYON
FURNACE CREEK
190
ZABRISKIE POINT
190
Olancha
CHARCOAL KILNS
GOLDEN CANYON
DARWIN FALLS
Trona Wildrose Road
MAHOGANY FLAT CAMPGROUND
ARTISTS PALETTE
395
DEVILS GOLF COURSE
TELESCOPE PEAK 11,049'
DANTES VIEW
14
Ridgecrest
BADWATER
Garlock Cutoff
395
TRONA PINNACLES
To L.A.
Randsburg

ABOUT THE DEATH VALLEY AREA

Death Valley is a land of extremes; it is the largest national park in the continental United States, is home to the lowest point in the western hemisphere, and has recorded one of the highest temperatures in the world—an astounding 134-degrees Fahrenheit!

Park elevations range from nearly 300-feet below sea level to snow capped peaks more than 11,000-feet high. In between are scattered mines & ghost towns, a castle, extensive sand dune complexes, hidden waterfalls & oases, fascinating archaeological sites, beautiful multi-colored canyons & cliffs, dense pinion pine forests, extinct volcanoes, interesting plant life, and salt flats & formations many thousands of feet thick.

Sunrises are magnificent, the night sky is indescribable, and solitude abounds. You're going to love it here!

Getting There

Get to the Furnace Creek area of Death Valley, from Los Angeles, by taking Interstate 5 north to CA 14 north, for about 95-miles beyond the town of Mojave (CA 14 eventually becomes CA 395). At the junction of CA 395/CA 190, in the Town of Olancha, gas up (last gas for some distance), and then turn right (east) onto CA 190 and stay on it for about 100-miles to Furnace Creek.

Lodging, Supplies, Maps, and Information

There are two primary locations to lodge within Death Valley National Park—Furnace Creek and Stovepipe Wells. Both of these locations, about 26-miles apart, have gas, supplies, motel rooms, campgrounds, and restaurants.

Furnace Creek can be considered the center of activity in Death Valley; Furnace Creek Inn, Furnace Creek Ranch, the main campgrounds, and the National Park Service headquarters are all located here. The Furnace Creek Ranch has small cabins, motel rooms, a store, and two restaurants. The campground is behind the Visitors Center, and a gas station (with limited operating hours) is nearby too. Be sure to take a dip in Furnace Creek's spring fed swimming pool.

Across the road from Furnace Creek Ranch is the Furnace Creek Inn, a luxury hotel built in the late 1920's using local stone and travertine deposited by the nearby springs. Behind the walls of this hotel are beautiful grounds laced by streams and ponds. The phone number for Furnace Creek Ranch and Furnace Creek Inn are the same: 760.786.2345.

Stove Pipe Wells also has a motel, a restaurant, a small store, a campground, and a gas station. Though the store & gas station operate under limited hours and the campground is closed during the summer, we have found the motel at Stovepipe Wells to be, for the most part, a better deal. It is quieter, a bit less expensive, and more likely to have a vacancy. The phone number for Stovepipe Wells is: 760.786.2387.

Mahogany Flats Campground (8,100ft), located high in the Panamint Mountains, is a wonderful summer base-camp with awesome views of Death Valley. This is also the launching point for the traditional route to Telescope Peak (11,049ft), Death Valley's highest point.

One other note about camping in Death Valley National Park; it's legal to primitively camp as long as you remain at least 5-miles from a campground and 0.25-mile from any water source. This last requirement is especially important because, as stated earlier, your presence may prevent shy animals from coming in for a life saving drink of water. Contact Death Valley National Park regarding camping at Mahogany Flats, or primitively in the backcountry.

There are many good maps for Death Valley National Park, but the one that I recommend is Tom Harrison's map titled, appropriately, "Death Valley." It can be picked up at most outdoor gear/sporting goods stores, at locations throughout the park, or direct via the web at: www.tomharrisonmaps.com. DeLorme's, "Southern & Central California Atlas & Gazetteer" and "Northern California Atlas & Gazetteer" are always handy, as are the

American Automobile Association's (AAA) "San Bernardino County" & "Inyo County" maps.

I can also recommend two great sources of information to aid you with your trip planning: The first is a book by T. Scott Bryan & Betty Tucker-Bryan titled, *The Explorer's Guide To Death Valley National Park*. Its nearly 400 pages are packed with enough material to keep you busy for years.

The other great source of information is the Death Valley Visitors Center in Furnace Creek. It's loaded with great interpretive displays, books, maps, and a huge relief map of the park. The National Park Service can be contacted at: Death Valley National Park, PO Box 579, Death Valley, CA 92328-0579, or by phone at 760.786.3200, or via the web at www. nps.gov/deva.

In order to organize these awesome adventures, I have divided them into five separate 'Journeys'. The directions for these tours assume that the reader is base-camped at Furnace Creek, but they can be easily modified to fit any starting point in the park. Also, be sure that your vehicle is in decent shape, carry lots of water with you, and gas up whenever possible; distances out here are extreme and you don't want to miss out on an adventure—or get stuck somewhere—because you are low on fuel.

JOURNEY #1

Golden Canyon

From Furnace Creek, turn right (south) on CA 190, and then at 1.3-miles turn right again, towards Badwater. At just over 3-miles (from Furnace Creek) turn left into the Golden Canyon parking lot.

The 1.5-mile hike up the canyon is an easy stroll through some fascinating geology. In fact, Golden Canyon is named after the yellow canyon walls, which in some light almost appear to glow. If you have time, hike to Red Cathedral, an interesting formation at the head of the canyon.

Retrace your steps to your vehicle when you've finished this fun walk.

Devils Golf Course

From the Golden Canyon parking area, turn left (South) and continue for about 12-miles from Furnace Creek (9-miles from Golden Canyon) to the turnoff for the Devil's Golf Course. Turn right here and continue for about 1.5-miles to the parking area.

The fantastic formations that you see around you are 95% pure table salt, having been created as the salt crystallizes, expands, and then is influenced by the heat, cold, rain, and wind found here. Beneath this area are thousands of feet of alternating layers of salt and sediments from ancient lakes; some say these layers are as much as 15,000 feet thick!

Badwater

Back out on the main highway (CA 190), turn right (still heading south) and continue for another 8-miles to the parking area at Badwater, so named because an early surveyor who noticed that his mule wouldn't drink from the pool of water here made the notation, "bad water", on his map. You are now at about 280 feet below sea level. Due west of you, out on the salt flat, is the lowest point in the western hemisphere...282 feet below sea level!

Across this salt flat, to the west, are the Panamint Mountains. The high point, a bit south of west, is Telescope Peak (11,049ft), the highest point in the park. If possible, take the time to walk out on the salt flats, *beyond* where the trail runs out and the tourists turn back. This is where the most interesting salt formations are and where you'll get the greatest perspective on the grandeur of this valley…and the grandeur of our God.

A fun hike for a *very strong*, *very capable* group begins here at Badwater, crosses the salt flat, climbs a ridge to Telescope Peak and ends at the Mahogany Flat Trailhead. You'll need good route finding skills, cached water, transportation at Mahogany Flats and the ability to walk about 30 or so, mostly cross-country miles, through extreme temperature ranges, while accumulating about 12,000 feet of elevation gain. Contact park rangers for more information if you believe that you're up to it.

Artist's Palette

Get back on the main highway, this time heading north, back towards Furnace Creek. At about 8-miles, from Badwater, turn right onto a one-way road marked Artist Drive and follow it for about 4-miles to the parking area.

Take some time here to check out the magnificent geology and the brilliant colors; red, pink, yellow, orange, and brown. Explore the area, meditate on our God, or practice some of the spiritual exercises in this book.

Back in your car, the one-way road twists and turns through the low, narrow canyons of the Black Mountains until you again reach the main highway. Turn right to return to Furnace Creek.

JOURNEY #2

Zabriskie Point

From Furnace Creek, turn right (south) on to the main road (CA 190). At just about 1.3-miles you'll reach the junction with the turnoff to Badwater. Do not turn here; instead continue straight ahead on CA 190 for about 4.8-miles (from Furnace Creek) to the Zabriskie Point parking lot.

From the parking area, walk up a short trail to the badlands overlook. This place is an amazing geological wonderland…it is beautiful. The higher point between where you stand and the valley below is 'Manley Beacon', named after one of the early pioneers who drifted into Death Valley in 1849. If you have time, walk over to this peak and scramble to the top. It's a blast!

Another way to see this area is to leave a car at the Golden Canyon parking area, then return to Zabriskie Point and walk the 2.5-downhill miles back to Golden Canyon.

This is a great full moon hike too.

Dante's View (5,475ft)

Turn right (south) out of the Zabriskie Point parking area and then, in about 7 miles, turn right onto the road to Dante's View, about 13-miles further on.

The panorama from Dante's View is awesome! To the west, the Panamint Mountains rise more then 11,000ft above the valley floor—about 5,600ft higher then where you now stand. Below—almost 6,000ft lower and 25 degrees warmer—the bed of ancient Manley Lake, including Badwater and the salt flats, stretches for miles and miles. Enjoy the views, take photographs, and worship the Lord who created all of this.

When you are finished, return to Furnace Creek the same way that you came up.

Journey #3

Bailey's Hot Springs

Fill your tank in Furnace Creek, and then turn left (north) on CA190. At about 11-miles, turn right on the Daylight Pass Cutoff (the Beatty Cutoff). In about 10-miles you'll again bear right (northeast) onto Hwy 374, towards Beatty, Nevada, 20-miles away. Once in Beatty, from the streetlight, travel 5.5-miles north on Hwy 95, and then watch for a large sign on the right (east) side of the road. This is a private campground, but the hot springs are open to the public for a small fee.

The hot springs bubble up into three large indoor pools, which actually used to be water reservoirs for the railroad. The pools temperatures range from 101 to 108 degrees Fahrenheit and are very clean. I've been here several times (this is a great place to soak after a long hike), and we've always had these pools to ourselves.

Beatty has restaurants, gas (probably cheaper than in Death Valley), and supplies.

Ryholite Ghost Town

Fill your tank in Furnace Creek, and then turn left (north) on CA190. At about 11-miles, turn right on the Daylight Pass Cutoff (the Beatty Cutoff) and then, about 10-miles beyond, bear right (northeast) onto Hwy 374, towards Beatty, Nevada. Continue on Hwy 374 for about 16-miles (4-miles shy of Beatty, Nevada), and turn left (north) onto the road to the ghost town of Ryholite, about 2-miles further on.

If you're coming from Bailey's Hot Springs, head south 5.5-miles to the junction of US 95/Hwy 374. Turn right (southwest) on Hwy 374 and then, in about 4-miles, turn right (north) again onto the road to the ghost town of Ryholite, about 2-miles further on.

Try to imagine a town of 10,000 people, 3 railroads, a telephone & telegraph office, 3 newspapers, an opera house, a symphony, baseball teams, tennis courts, 3 swimming pools, 2 undertakers, 2 hospitals, 8 physicians, 2 dentists, 18 grocery stores, and at least 53 saloons. Check out the bank and the bottle house too, and, if your visit is in the cooler months, look for the Bureau of Land Management (BLM) ranger; he or she will be glad to give you the scoop on the history of this fascinating place.

When your visit is over, head back to Hwy 374 and turn left, northeast, towards Beatty where you can grab lunch, gas up and buy any supplies that you may need.

Or turn right for 2-miles to the cutoff for the road to Titus Canyon.

Titus Canyon

Fill your tank in Furnace Creek, and then turn left (north) on CA 190. At 11-miles turn right (northeast) on the Daylight Pass Cutoff, and then in about 10-miles again bear right (northeast) onto Hwy 374, towards Beatty, Nevada. Continue on Hwy 374 for about 14-miles to the turnoff for Titus Canyon. Turn left (west) onto this road.

If you're coming from Beatty, at the junction of US 95/Hwy 374, head southwest on Hwy 374 for about 6-miles (about 2-miles beyond Ryholite), and then turn right (west) onto the road to Titus Canyon. This one-way—from east to west—dirt road is a bit washboardy for the first few miles, but is suitable for any vehicle in decent shape.

The road winds into Grapevine Canyon, and then crosses Red Pass at 5,240ft above sea level. A couple of miles beyond Red Pass you'll come to the ghost town of Leadville with its old cabins and other remains to explore.

Beyond Leadville, Titus Canyon narrows and becomes even more dramatic and fascinating. Notice the palm trees about 2.4-miles beyond Leadville (about 18.4-miles from Hwy 374); they mark the location of Klare Spring. Ancient Shoshone or Western Paiute Indians left their mark, in the form of petroglyphs, on a large gray boulder alongside this spring. Also keep an eye out for the Bighorn Sheep that can often be found in this area.

The stretch of canyon below Klare Spring is very narrow and dramatic; indeed, it's been called one of the most picturesque in the state. Enjoy it for the 8.6-miles beyond the springs, before hitting North Highway, turning left (south), and following the signs back to Furnace Creek, somewhere over 40-miles away.

Titus Canyon floods very easily and may be closed if a heavy storm is expected or has passed by within a few days of your visit. Check the canyons' status with park rangers before heading out on this trip, and save it for another day if weather threatens.

JOURNEY #4

Scotty's Castle

Fill your tank in Furnace Creek, and then turn left (north) on CA 190. At about 17.5-miles from Furnace Creek you'll come to a junction; turn right here (north), towards Scotty's Castle. At about 50-miles (from Furnace Creek) you'll pass the Grapevine entrance station; Scotty's Castle is a right turn just to the north of this station.

Albert Johnson was an insurance executive from Chicago who made his way to Southern California in the mid-1920's after having been advised by his doctor to move to a warmer, drier, climate. While searching around the California desert for a place to settle down he met one of Death Valley's most colorful characters, Walter "Death Valley Scotty" Scott. Scotty was an occasional prospector, a former trick rider for Buffalo Bill's Wild West Show, a fanciful storyteller, and an aggressive promoter of his own self-interests. The two became fast friends and together came up with the idea for the Death Valley Ranch, later known as Scotty's Castle. Using Johnson's money, construction started on the 2 million dollar mansion in 1925 and continued until 1931, when the Depression took a large bite out of Johnson's portfolio and brought the building to a halt.

The mansion boasts, in addition to a fantastic setting, eighteen fireplaces, an 185ft swimming pool, an indoor waterfall, a pipe organ, and antiques galore.

The desert air must have agreed with Johnson, because he lived to be 75 years old. Death Valley Scotty died in 1954, at the ripe age of 81.

Guided tours of Scotty's Castle are offered every day from 9am to 5 P.M.

Ubehebe Crater

From Scotty's Castle, backtrack to the main road and turn right, following the signs to the half-mile wide, 600-foot deep, Ubehebe Crater.

Only the main crater is visible from the parking area, but if you hike the rim trail you'll see that there are actually several distinct craters. Notice, too, the dark gray soil that surrounds the craters. This is actually cinder, which was strewn over a six square-mile area by the fierce explosions that formed these cavities.

For a good challenge, make your way down the natural ramp that leads to the bottom, and then hike back up the scree…it's harder than it looks.

JOURNEY #5

Sand Dunes

These sand dunes, located about 24-miles west of Furnace Creek on CA 190 (2-miles east of Stovepipe Wells), cover an area about 14-miles square. You can pull off anywhere along the road, although one wider than average area has some interesting interpretive displays describing the creation and ecology of the dunes.

After you've read up on the dunes, go out there and feel them under your feet. Climb to the highest point and run (or roll) down, look for animal tracks, pray together, and enjoy a sunset from among them.

One evening a beautiful walk on these dunes degenerated into a huge sand fight, after which we headed back to Furnace Creek Ranch for dinner. We had sand in our ears, our noses, our mouths, our hair, on the table, under our chairs, and in our food…it was awesome!

Mosaic Canyon

Mosaic Canyon is about 25-miles from Furnace Creek, and a short hop west of Stove Pipe Wells. Take the dirt road heading south from CA 190, just to the west of Stove Pipe Wells, and in about 2.5-miles you'll reach the mouth of the canyon. Park here and walk into the gorge.

The first 0.5-mile of Mosaic Canyon is deep and narrow, and then the canyon widens over the following 1-mile or so. Look closely at the rock walls through here; they're fascinating. Look high, too, as this is prime Bighorn Sheep country.

Depending on your level of ambition, this hike can be as much as 5-miles in length with the first 1.5-miles being the most interesting in terms of geology, and the last 3.5-miles the most difficult.

Turn back at any time and retrace your route back to your vehicle.

Charcoal Kilns

These fascinating charcoal kilns are high up in the Juniper and Pinion Pines of the Panamint Mountains. The kilns, which are 30 feet high by 30 feet wide and look like giant beehives, kept the mines across the Panamint Valley going strong by producing charcoal, which was used in the smelting process.

From CA 190 & Wildrose Road, about 9-miles west of Stove Pipe Wells, take Wildrose Road north for about 18-miles to a junction in the Wildrose area. Turn left here (in Wildrose) for about 8-miles to the Charcoal Kilns.

Mahogany Flat (8,100 feet)

From the Charcoal Kilns, continue up the road for about 2-miles, passing the Thorndike Campground, to the Mahogany Flat campground.

Mahogany Flat, and its amazing views of Death Valley more then 8,000 feet below, is a comfortable elevation for summer camping. Winter here can be rough, however; it's not unusual for this area to be under several feet of snow from November through March.

Mahogany Flat is also the trailhead for the traditional route to Telescope Peak.

Telescope Peak (11,049ft)

This wonderful hike to the highest point in the park is highly recommended; the view and the "above the world" feel is fantastic.

You'll find the beginning of this outstanding trail at the south end of the Mahogany Flats Campground. The route winds around Rogers and Bennett Peaks, with the views becoming more and more awesome as you progress; Badwater, in Death Valley, is more then 11,000 feet below you to the east, while the Panamint Valley lays about 8,000 feet below you to the west. The summit is home to ancient Bristlecone Pines and, on a clear day, has views that reach from Charleston Peak (near Las Vegas) to the southeast, the White Mountains to the north, the Sierra Nevada's to the west and the San Gabriel and San Bernardino Mountains (near Los Angeles) to the south.

The best time to climb Telescope Peak is May through October, with June and July being the best for wildflower viewing; a full moon ascent would be wonderful too. Winter, however, can bring fierce storms, deep snow, severe winds and the need for ice axes, crampons, and proper training in their use.

Anticipate a hike of 14-miles (round-trip), with about 3,000 feet of elevation gain. Bring plenty of water, sunscreen, a hat and a camera for this hike; save it for another day if electrical storms threaten.

OTHER ADVENTURES

The following three adventures, along an alternative driving route, are a great way to break up the long drive to Death Valley:

Randsburg

From the town of Mojave, travel north on CA 14 for about 20-miles, to the Red Rock-Randsburg Road. Take the Red Rock-Randsburg Road east for 21-miles (bearing right at 12-miles) to the town of Randsburg.

Randsburg is one of the few mining communities of California that exists today not as a ghost town, but instead as a, "living ghost town." That is, it has a great mix of the old and the new, with several year-round residents. Stop here and visit the antique stores and the Randsburg Desert Museum, then grab a malt at the original, old-fashioned, soda fountain located in the general store. This fountain was originally shipped by boat from Europe, around the tip of South America to Los Angeles, and then hauled by wagon to Randsburg where it's been ever since. Get with the proprietors for more about the history of this wonderful place.

Trona Pinnacles National Natural Landmark

From Randsburg, take US 395 north for about 13.5-miles to South China Lake Blvd, in Ridgecrest. Turn right on South China Lake Blvd for 6-miles to the junction of CA 178 (be sure to gas up before you leave Ridgecrest). Turn right (east) on CA 178 and stay on it for about 17-miles, or so, to a marked dirt road. Turn right (south) on this dirt road, and in 0.5-mile you'll reach a junction; bear right, cross a set of railroad tracks and continue on for about 5-miles to the formations (Note: Wet weather can make this road a quagmire).

The more than 500 pinnacles—some as tall as 140 feet and spread out over 13 square miles—were created when calcium released by hot springs at the bottom of the now-dry Searles Lake was combined with the carbonates found within the lake itself. This matter built up around the springs until it reached the surface of the lake and now, while the lake has dried up, what are reportedly the best examples of Tufa towers in the United States remain.

Plan to spend a night in this surreal place, it's a wonderful setting to meditate on the Lord. While there are no official campgrounds here, primitive camping is allowed; bring everything that you'll need, including lots of water.

Continuing on towards Death Valley, from the pinnacles, return to CA 178 and turn right (north) into the town of Trona (limited gas and supplies). Continue north on CA 178 beyond Trona (where the road is called 'Trona-Wildrose Road') for about 31-miles. At the Y, bear left (west) for 14.5-miles to CA 190. Turn right (east) on CA 190 to Furnace Creek, or left to Darwin Falls (described below).

Darwin Falls

This is an easy 1.5-mile round trip hike to a hidden desert oasis. From the town of Trona, take Hwy 178 (Trona-Wildrose Road) north for about 31-miles. At the Y, bear left (west) for 14.5-miles to CA 190. Turn left (west) on CA 190 for 3.2-miles

(1-mile beyond Panamint Springs Resort), and then turn left again onto the dirt road. Continue ahead for 2.5 miles, and then bear right at the fork for 0.30-mile to the parking area.

If you're coming from the junction of US 395/CA 190, in the town of Olancha, travel east on CA 190 for about 44-miles to the turnoff for Darwin Falls on the right (south) almost exactly 1-mile before you reach the Panamint Springs Resort. Turn right onto the dirt road for 2.5-miles, and then bear right again at the fork for 0.30-mile to the parking area.

From the parking area, head up-canyon following a tiny trickle of water which continues to grow as you make your way upstream, crossing and recrossing the creek. The trail is not well defined, but as long as you stay in the canyon bottom and follow the creek you can't go wrong.

The vegetation increases as you continue upstream; cottonwoods, willows, colorful mosses, ferns, and more then 80 species of birds call this oasis home. In a short time you'll come to a fantastic series of falls, each higher and more beautiful then the last. This is an awesome place.

This is a pretty straightforward walk, almost a stroll, but it can be very hot here in the summer. For this reason, and because you may have a better chance of seeing wildlife, this is a great early morning walk.

Be sure to carry plenty of water and sunblock.

The Kern River Valley Area

Walk among huge Sequoia trees on the "Trail of 100 Giants"; Swim, kayak or float a high mountain river or lake; Hike to, and explore, an interesting cave, a fire tower, and a great swimming hole; Search for wildlife at an awesome nature preserve; Stand atop a waterfall; Learn about village life for ancient Native Americans…and more!

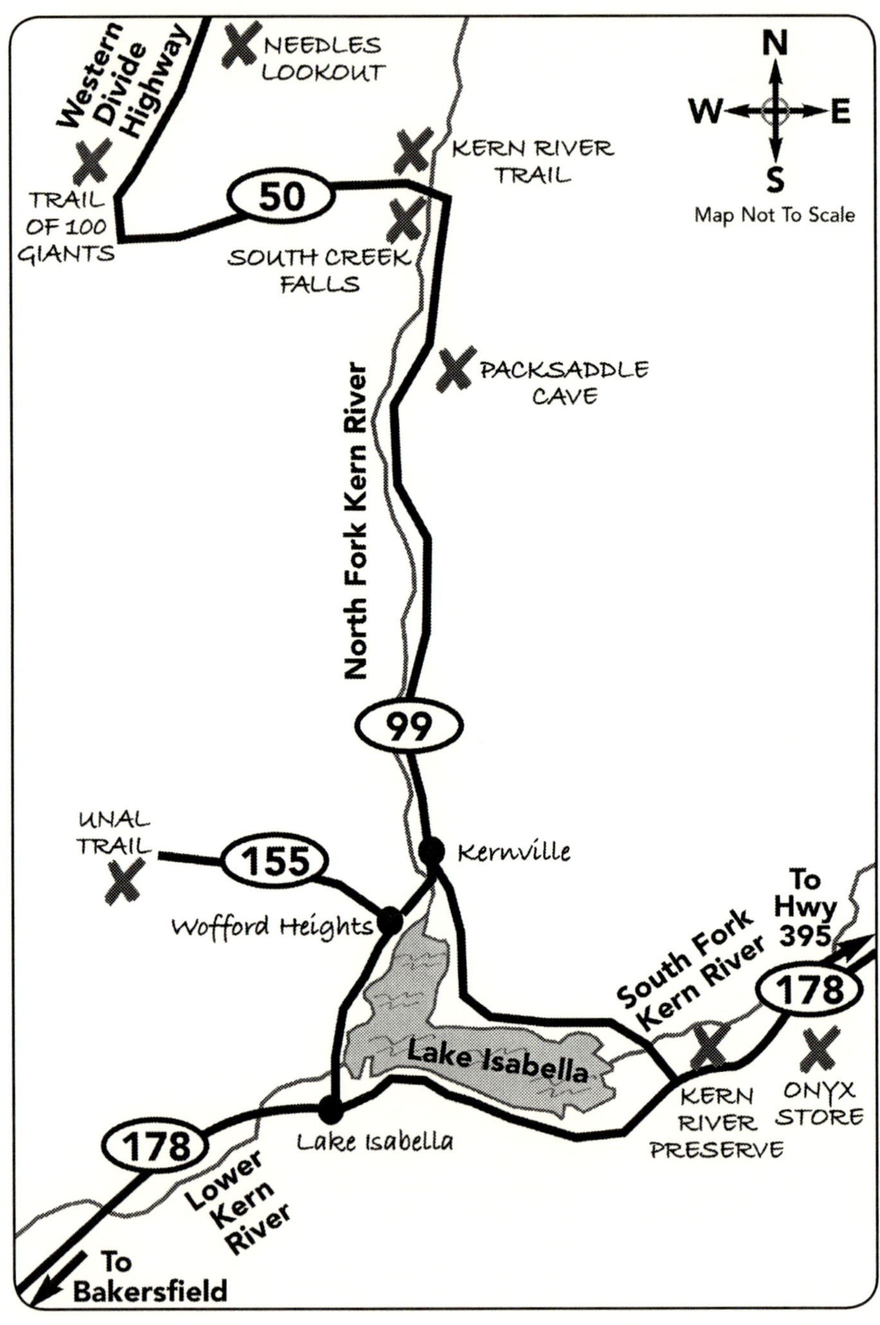

Western Divide Highway
NEEDLES LOOKOUT
N
W E
S
Map Not To Scale
TRAIL OF 100 GIANTS
50
KERN RIVER TRAIL
SOUTH CREEK FALLS
North Fork Kern River
PACKSADDLE CAVE
99
UNAL TRAIL
155
Kernville
To Hwy 395
Wofford Heights
South Fork Kern River
178
Lake Isabella
Lake Isabella
KERN RIVER PRESERVE
ONYX STORE
178
Lower Kern River
To Bakersfield

ABOUT THE KERN RIVER VALLEY AREA

The Kern River Valley area is fantastic! Five of California's six bioregions—ranging from the gnarled Joshua tree of the high desert to the majestic giant Sequoia of the high mountains—converge here, creating homes for wildlife as varied as road runners, quail, black bear, beaver, deer, and mountain lions.

From its birthplace high in the Sierra Nevada Mountains, the Kern River tumbles into the valley to fill Lake Isabella, one of the state's largest reservoirs. This river, the Kern, is the longest whitewater river in California and has more protected miles of Wild & Scenic designation than any other river in the continental United States.

Come out to the Kern Valley for great hiking, whitewater rafting & kayaking, wildlife watching, mountain biking, and spring wildflowers…you'll love it!

Getting There

There are a couple of ways to approach the Kern River Valley from the south. The first option is to head north on Interstate 5, cross over the Tejon Pass into the San Joaquin Valley, and then take CA 99 north to Bakersfield. In Bakersfield, take Hwy 58 east for about 11.5-miles and exit at Comanche Drive. Turn left (north), over the freeway, and follow Comanche Drive for about 5.5-miles, to the junction of Hwy 178. Turn right (east) on Hwy 178, which soon parallels the lower Kern River and enters the Kern River Canyon. Stay on Hwy 178 to the town of Lake Isabella.

The second option is to head north on Hwy 14, from the Santa Clarita Valley, to the town of Mojave. From Mojave, continue north for about 37-miles (passing through the beautiful Red Rock Canyon area) to the intersection of Hwy 178 West. Head west on Hwy 178, climbing through a wonderful forest of Joshua Trees before crossing over Walker Pass (the Pacific Crest Trail, stretching from Mexico to Canada, crosses the highway here at Walker Pass) and descending into the South Fork Valley.

Continuing west on Hwy 178, towards Lake Isabella, you'll first pass the Onyx Store—built in 1861 and thought to be the oldest continuously operated store in California—and then a few miles further on, The Nature Conservancy's 'Kern River Preserve', where the South Fork of the Kern River winds through a stunning mix of cottonwoods, willow, and other riparian vegetation.

Early one winter morning I was at this preserve photographing the sunrise when I heard a loud splash behind me. Turning, I caught sight of a deer leaping out of the river onto the opposite bank. The sun, filtered through the heavy morning mist, cast a warm, yellowish, glow that accentuated the yellowed leaves and grasses. With every bound, first onto the shore, and then towards the sheltering cottonwoods, a shower of golden-yellow droplets exploded from this animal. I will never forget the thrill that I felt at that sight.

Lodging, Supplies, Maps, and Information

The towns of Lake Isabella and Kernville both have grocery stores, restaurants, gas stations and motels. In addition, a Sequoia National Forest ranger station is located in Kernville, where you can find books, maps, permits and a staff who can answer all of your questions. The folks at the ranger station can be reached at: Cannell Meadow Ranger District, 105 Whitney Road, PO Box 9, Kernville, CA 93238, or by phone at: 760.376.3781.

For more information about the area's many, many campgrounds, both public and private, contact the above ranger station or the Kern River Valley Chamber of Commerce at: PO Box 567, 6048 Lake Isabella Blvd, Suite B, Lake Isabella, CA 93240, or by phone, toll free, at 866.KRV.4FUN, or online at: www.kernrivervalley.com. Another website that you might want to check out is www.kernvalley.net.

Another really cool option for lodging is to stay in one of the refurbished fire lookout towers or guard cabins that are available for rent in the nearby Sequoia National Forest. For more information, including photographs, go to www.fs.fed.us/r5/sequoia/ and click on "Cabin and Fire Lookout Tower Rentals."

Finally, when is the best time to go? Depends on what you are looking for: April, May & June are the best months for floating the river, Spring and Fall are the best seasons for hiking; long summer weekends & holidays are the most crowded.

Be sure that you have DeLorme's, "Southern & Central California Atlas & Gazetteer", or its equivalent, and a good Sequoia National Forest map; you can pick up the latter from virtually any Southern California outdoor gear store or directly from the ranger station.

Additionally, I highly recommend two books that are packed with lots of great adventures throughout this area: *Exploring the Southern Sierra: East Side* and *Exploring the Southern Sierra: West Side* (J.C Jenkins & Ruby Johnson Jenkins)

Lake Isabella

With approximately 38-miles of shoreline and more then 11,200 acres of surface area, Lake Isabella is one of the largest reservoirs in California. It has three marinas and eight campgrounds along its shore, including three (Hungry Gulch, Boulder Gulch and Tillie Creek) that are handicap accessible. Tillie Creek Campground also has an amphitheater with ranger-led talks and slideshows scheduled throughout the summer.

Floating The River

The months of April, May and June find the Kern River running wild from the melting snows of the Sierra Nevada. This is the optimum time for the whitewater kayaking and rafting offered by the many local commercial outfitters; request a list of outfitters from the Kern River Valley Chamber of Commerce.

Later in the summer, as the river mellows, tubing & swimming are the way to go.

Because of its challenging and deceptive currents, eddies, boulders, and underwater snags the Kern River can be very dangerous—particularly the Lower Kern, below the dam. Check with the Forest Service for safe places and times to swim & tube along the river; if in doubt, or if you have young children, head over to the safer swimming beaches of Lake Isabella.

I mention very few private outfitters in this book, but I do want to make an exception here: Mountain & River Adventures (in Kernville) took great care of one of our groups of more then 60 people. They have their own campground along the river with BBQ's, hammocks, a volleyball court, and a climbing wall. They have buses to haul your group to various points along the river or lake, and they offer rafting, whitewater & flatwater kayaking, mountain biking and hiking excursions. Best of all, though, they were very pleasant to deal with and bent over backwards to accommodate our needs. Contact Mountain & River Adventures by phone at 760.376.6553 or online at: www.mtnriver.com.

Kern River Preserve

The Kern River Preserve embraces a part of the largest contiguous cottonwood/willow forest remaining in California. The South Fork of the Kern River meanders through this 1,127-acre preserve where more then 315 species of birds have been observed, including 74 species of neotropical birds that migrate from as far away as southern South America. Mammals at the preserve include, mule deer, black bear, coyote, gray fox, bobcats, beaver and raccoons.

The preserve is open every day from dawn to dusk. Larger groups are asked to make advanced arrangements by contacting: Kern River Preserve, PO Box 1662, 18747 Highway 178, Weldon, CA 93283 or by phone at: 760.378.3044 or online at: <u>kern.audubon.org.</u>

Hike To Pack Saddle Cave

From Kernville, drive north on Sierra Way Road (Kern River Hwy/Hwy 99) for about 16-miles. Park in the lot marked by a small Forest Service bulletin board, on the left, just beyond the entrance to Fairview Campground.

This moderately steep, 5-miles round-trip trip hike, starts across the highway at the old jeep trail. Head up the jeep road for about 1.8-miles where you'll first cross Packsaddle Creek, and then parallel it for about 0.6-miles to a junction with a small spur trail coming in from the left; follow this spur 100 yards up the hill to the cave.

The fascinating features of most caves (stalagmites, stalactites, etc.) were vandalized long ago, but it's a fun cave anyway. Bring your headlamp, a snack, and plenty of water; the trail can be very hot in the summer.

The Kern River Trail & Swim

From Kernville, drive north on Sierra Way Road (Kern River Hwy/Hwy 99) for about 23-miles; cross the Johnsondale Bridge and park in the lot on the far side of it.

Walk back across the old bridge and descend the nearly 60 steps to the Kern River Trail, which travels north (upstream) along the river for about 3.5-miles before turning east to join up with the Rincon Trail. There is a great swimming hole here, just below the bridge, and many more waiting to be discovered upstream, along with many wonderful campsites and sandy riverbanks from which to sunbathe, journal, read & relax.

Watch for small clumps of Poison Oak along this riverside trail—remember, "Leaves of three, let it be"—and if the river is running too swiftly, head over to one of the safer swimming beaches at Lake Isabella.

South Creek Falls

This pretty waterfall is visible from the highway, exactly 0.5-mile north of the Johnsondale Bridge (about 23-miles north of Kernville). Look for the small, partially fenced, parking pullout just above the falls, and then walk back down the road for the best views.

Please observe the Forest Service sign warning against climbing beyond the fence.

Trail Of 100 Giants

From Kernville, drive north on Sierra Way Road (Kern River Hwy/Hwy 99) for about 33-miles, passing Johnsondale R-Ranch (where the road becomes Highway 50) to the junction of Western Divide Highway. Turn right on Western Divide Highway and continue for 2.5-miles to the trailhead parking area on the right, just before Redwood Meadow Campground. The trail begins across the highway.

Giant Sequoia's are an amazing tree: By volume they are the largest living organism in the world, they have an amazing resistance to fire, insects & disease, and they are endowed with an unusually high amount of Tannic Acid, which prevents the growth of algae and bacteria, thus retarding decay. In fact, a fallen Sequoia can show little evidence of decomposition, sometimes for centuries, until the Tannin leaches out or the loss of moisture makes the tree vulnerable to fire. Take a look at some of the fallen giants in this grove; they're fantastic.

This is a wonderful place; the 125 beautiful giants mixed in among the pines and cedars are monuments to God's creative glory, the trail is maintained and nearly flat (suitable for wheelchairs and baby strollers), and there's a good chance that you'll have it all to yourselves.

The elevation here is about 6,400ft, so plan for great summer weather, chilly nights and snow in the winter. Check out your Sequoia National Forest map for other nearby groves of Sequoia trees.

I think that you'll agree that this grove is a natural cathedral, solemn & majestic, created by our Lord as a witness to His Glory. Please don't leave this place without acknowledging Him.

Hike To Needles Lookout

From Kernville, drive north on Sierra Way Road (Kern River Hwy/Hwy 99) for about 33-miles, passing Johnsondale R-Ranch (where the road become Highway 50) to the junction of Western Divide Highway. Turn right on Western Divide Highway and continue for approximately 13.5-miles (about 11-miles beyond the *Trail of 100 Giants*) to Forest Service Road 21S05, the Needles Road. (If you get to the Quaking Aspen Campground, you've gone about 0.5-mile too far). Turn right (east) on the Needles Road and drive about 2.8-miles to the trailhead.

The Needles Lookout is located high on a rocky pinnacle endowed with fantastic views that reach (on a clear day) as far away as Mount Whitney to the northeast and the San Joaquin Valley to the west. Built in 1938, the lookout is still manned during the fire season and is an integral part of the Forest Service's wildfire early warning system.

This 4-mile (roundtrip) hike begins at the east end of the parking area where the trail climbs slightly, rounds a pair of hills, and then switchbacks down to a saddle and back up (the steepest part of the hike) to a small rock cove. From there a steep and very exposed staircase leads to a pinnacle, and then across a boardwalk and up another steep staircase—189 steps in all—to the highest point, the walkway of the lookout.

A sign will tell you if the tower is open; it is closed during fires and lightning storms so that the lookout employee can focus on his or her responsibilities. If it's open, go on in, introduce yourself, and ask the spotter any questions you can think of, including how the tower handles lightning strikes (the answer is quite interesting). Also, look for the stool with the glass insulators that the spotter sits on to ride out such storms.

No matter whether the tower is open or closed, the views are magnificent and can be enjoyed from any place on the pinnacle. When you're finished, retrace your route back to the parking area.

Bring plenty of water, a snack, sunscreen, and a jacket—the pinnacle is exposed and the winds can be pretty strong. Save this hike for another day if electrical storms threaten.

Unal: The Trail Of The Bear

From Wofford Heights, on the western shore of Lake Isabella, take Hwy 155 west for about 8-miles to Greenhorn Summit. Turn left at the sign for Shirley Meadows Ski Area and drive 100 yards to the Greenhorn Fire Station. The Unal Trailhead is on the right side of the road, just beyond the fire station.

This pleasant, 3-mile loop trail, meanders through cool pines & cedars, and across a small stream before coming to a Tubatulabal house, and a few artifacts & grinding slicks that illustrate how these area Native Americans lived centuries ago.

Twenty-five points of interest along the trail correspond to an interpretive brochure— available at the trailhead—that is written as if through the eyes of a young Tubatulabal lad.

This area, the Shirley Meadows Ski Area in Alta Vista, is also a wonderful place to ski & snowboard if the snowfall has been good; a lack of snowmaking equipment, though, handicaps it in drier winters.

CHAPTER NINE

The Red Rock Canyon State Park Area

Camp among brilliantly colored and textured rock formations; Hike to a Native American rock art site; Visit a 'living' ghost town replete with mining relics, antique stores, and a historic soda fountain; Wander among fantastic wildflowers; Learn about a colorful desert character & see his life's 'work'; Search for Desert Tortoises among the Creosote; Explore giant Tufa towers…and more!

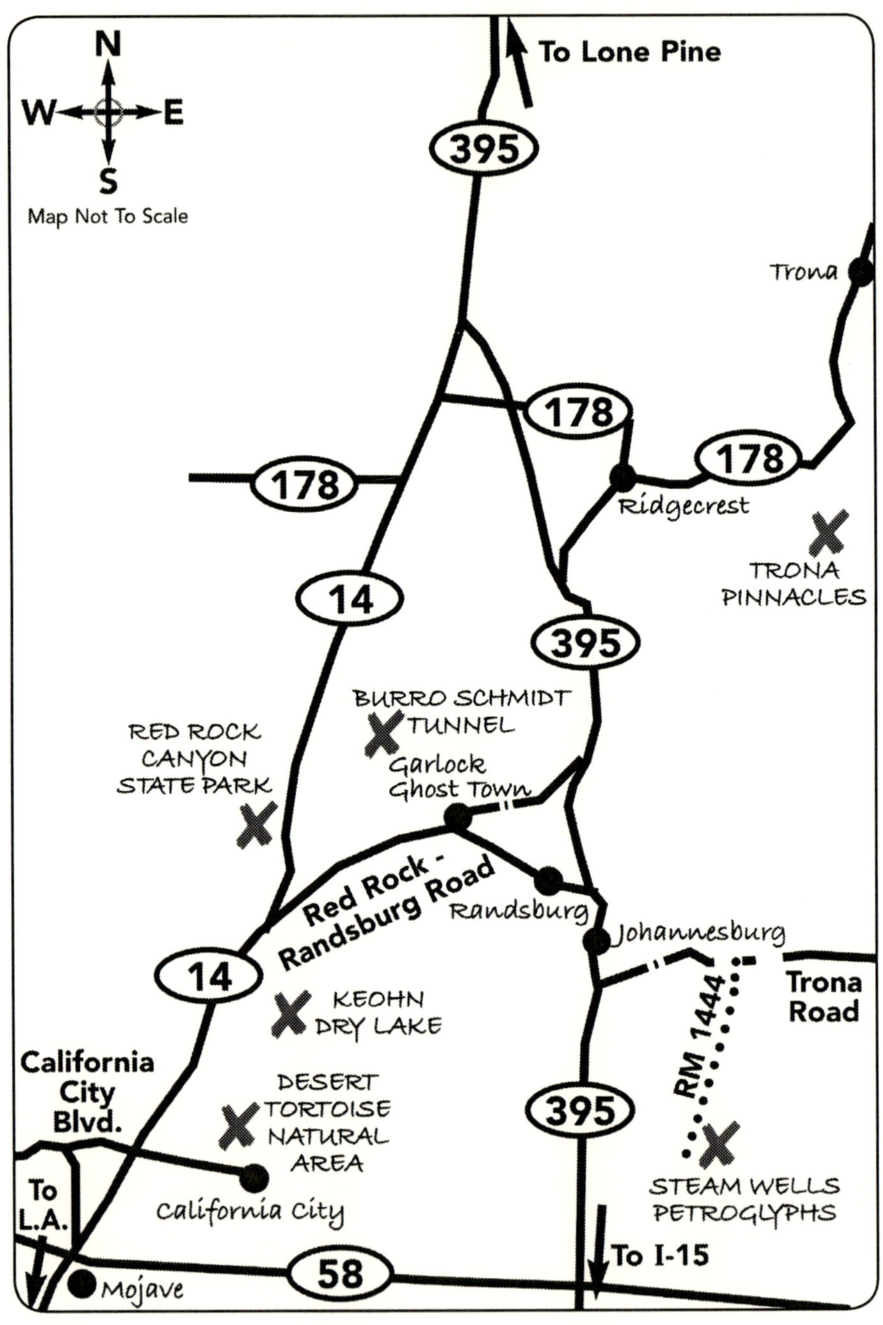

N
W E
S
Map Not To Scale
To Lone Pine
395
Trona
178
178
178
Ridgecrest
TRONA PINNACLES
14
395
BURRO SCHMIDT TUNNEL
RED ROCK CANYON STATE PARK
Garlock Ghost Town
Red Rock - Randsburg Road
Randsburg
Johannesburg
Trona Road
14
KEOHN DRY LAKE
California City Blvd.
DESERT TORTOISE NATURAL AREA
RM 1444
395
To L.A.
California City
STEAM WELLS PETROGLYPHS
To I-15
58
Mojave

ABOUT THE RED ROCK STATE PARK AREA

The highlight of this beautiful 30,000-acre park is its incredible geological wonders, which include pink, red, gray & white banded walls eroded into beautiful columns, red caprocks balancing precariously on soft clay pedestals, and arid basins peppered with stands of Joshua trees.

The surrounding desert is awash in fascinating history, scenery, and wildlife. Ancient petroglyphs, ghost towns, giant mineral towers, and the endangered desert tortoise await discovery. The star-filled night sky is a bonus.

One trip out here and you won't want to go home.

Getting There

From Los Angeles head north on Interstate 5 to CA 14 north, 25-miles beyond the town of Mojave, to Red Rock Canyon State Park, which straddles both sides of the highway. Turn left on Abbott Drive, and follow it about 0.75-miles to the Ranger Station/Visitors Center/Campground.

Supplies, Lodging, Maps & Information

Supplies, gas and motels are available in the towns of Ridgecrest and Mojave, both about 30 minutes from the park.

Red Rock Canyon Campground, located in a wide basin studded with Joshua trees, is open year-round with 50 sites, running water and pit toilets. Information about Red Rock State Park is available through the primary headquarters in the city of Lancaster. Contact: The Mojave Desert Information Center, 43779 15th Street West, Lancaster, CA 93534, or by phone at: 661.942.0662.

Primitive camping is allowed on the BLM administered lands that surround the state park. For more information, contact: Bureau of Land Management Ridgecrest Resource Area, 300 South Richmond Road, Ridgecrest, CA 93555, or by phone at: 760.384.5400.

Jawbone Station, just south of Red Rock Canyon on Hwy 14, also has a Visitors Center with well-informed staff. If during the course of your trip you have any questions at all, pop in and talk with them. Besides having intimate knowledge of the area, they also have books and local maps. Get there from Red Rock Canyon State Park by traveling south on Hwy 14 for about 3.75-miles. Turn right (west) on Jawbone Canyon Road, then immediately right again into the Visitors Center parking area.

As far as maps go, be sure that you have DeLorme's, "Southern & Central California Atlas & Gazetteer", or its equivalent, and AAA's "Kern County" & "San Bernardino County" maps. Contact the BLM for a map of the El Paso/Rand Mountains (for the Burro Schmidt Tunnel adventure).

Springtime, with its explosion of as many as 150 species of wildflowers, is the most beautiful time to make this trip.

Desert Tortoise Natural Area

From Red Rock Canyon, head south on Hwy 14 for about 19.5-miles to California City Boulevard. Turn left (east) on California City Boulevard for about 9-miles to 20 Mule Team Parkway. Turn left (north) on 20 Mule Team Parkway for about 1-mile to Randsburg-Mojave Road, and then bear left for another 3-miles to the parking area and kiosk.

Though it is possible to see them as late as September, the very best time of year to spot the Desert Tortoise is from early March through late May. Shy and reclusive, tortoises spend all winter, and the hottest part of summer days, in underground burrows.

If you do see a tortoise, please observe it from a discreet distance; it's not only illegal to harass them, but the stress from an encounter with you would likely result in the shortening of its life through the loss of irreplaceable water. If you don't happen to see a tortoise on this trip, no worries; there are always plenty of wonderful things to discover in the desert, especially during the riotous springtime wildflower bloom.

A second, and more primitive, location to search for the Desert Tortoise is nearer to Red Rock Canyon. Get there, from Red Rock Canyon, by heading south on Hwy 14 for about 5-miles to Rogers Road. Turn left on Rogers Road for 0.7-mile to Neuralia Road. Turn right (south) on Neuralia Road and drive about 0.9-miles to Munsey Road. Turn left (east) on Munsey road and then, at about 5.6-miles from the junction of Neuralia/Munsey Roads, look for a spur on the right that leads about 0.25-mile to the natural area. Leave your vehicle at the boundary (no vehicles are allowed into the natural area), and set out across the open desert to see what you can see.

If you continue east on Munsey Road, beyond this spur, the route swings northeast to follow the ancient shoreline of Koehn Lake. No vehicles are allowed onto the lakebed, but it's a wonderful place for a hike.

Bring a hat, sunscreen and plenty of water. Contact the Bureau of Land Management for more information regarding the Desert Tortoise Natural Area.

Randsburg

From Red Rock Canyon, head south on Hwy 14 for about 3.5-miles to the Red Rock-Randsburg Road. Turn left (east) on the Red Rock-Randsburg Road for about 21-miles (bearing right at about 12-miles) to the town of Randsburg.

Randsburg is one of the few mining communities of California that exists not as a ghost town, but instead as a, "living ghost town." That is, it's a great mix of old and new, and boasts several year-round residents. Explore the antique stores and the Randsburg Desert Museum and try to imagine what it was like here during the boom years, when more than 14,000 people made this their home. Grab a malt at the original, old-fashioned, soda fountain located in the general store and ask the proprietors to tell you some stories about the history of this wonderful place.

Steam Wells Petroglyph Site

From Red Rock Canyon State Park, head south on Hwy 14 for about 3.5-miles to the Red Rock-Randsburg Road. Turn left (east) onto Red Rock-Randsburg road and continue driving for about 21-miles (bearing right at about 12-miles) to the town of Randsburg. Go through Randsburg for 1-mile to US 395. Turn right (south) on US 395 for about 2-miles to Trona Road, and then turn left (east) for about 1.4-miles to BLM road RM1444. Turn right onto RM1444—this dirt road may or may not be well marked, but you should see a BLM plastic fence-post type of sign at some point along the way.

As you travel along, ignore the roads coming in from both the left and the right, but instead stay on the most obviously traveled route—and keep an eye out for road markers. At about 3.8-miles you should pass a sign that says, "Golden Valley Wilderness Area" and then, in another 1.2-mile (4-miles total from Trona Road), a wide spot just before the road drops back into the bottom of a wash.

Park here, at this wide spot, grab your gear and, on foot now, head up another wash that comes in from the north. At about 0.4-miles, where the wash splits, stick to the left (west) and head for a small arroyo in the hills another 0.2-miles away. The photo above shows the mouth of that arroyo; the petroglyphs are on the rock outcroppings on both sides.

Contact the Bureau of Land Management for more information regarding the Steam Wells Petroglyph site or the 1.2-miles round trip hike.

Trona Pinnacles National Natural Landmark

From Red Rock Canyon State Park, head south on Hwy 14 for about 3.5-miles to the Red Rock-Randsburg Road. Turn left (east) onto Red Rock-Randsburg Road for about 12.5-miles, and then bear left onto the Garlock Road for another 9-miles (passing the remains of the town of Garlock) to US 395. Turn left (north) on US 395, for about 9.5-miles, to South China Lake Blvd in Ridgecrest. Turn right on South China Lake Blvd for 6-miles to the junction of CA 178 (be sure to gas up before you leave Ridgecrest). Turn right (east) on CA 178 and stay on it for about 17-miles to a dirt road marked as, 'Trona Pinnacles National Natural Landmark.' Turn right (south) on this dirt road and in 0.5-miles you'll reach a junction; bear right, cross a set of railroad tracks and continue on for about 5-miles to the formations (Note: Wet weather can make this road a quagmire).

These pinnacles—more then 500 of them as much as 140 feet high and spread out over 13 square miles—are reportedly the best examples of Tufa towers in the United States. The pinnacles were created when calcium released by hot springs at the bottom of the now-dry Searles Lake combined with the carbonates found within the lake itself, eventually building up around the springs until it reached the surface of the lake. While the lake dried up, the towers remain.

You may recognize this place as the backdrop for several commercials and science fiction movies, including the 2001 remake of the Planet of the Apes.

There are no official campgrounds here—and no amenities of any kind—but primitive camping is allowed; bring everything you'll need, including lots of water. Contact the Bureau of Land Management for more information regarding the Trona Pinnacles National Natural Landmark.

Burro Schmidt's Tunnel

From Red Rock Canyon State Park, take CA Hwy 14 north for about 9.5-miles, and then turn right (southeast) onto a graded BLM road marked '*EP15*' (look for the small wooden sign here declaring, 'Schmidt Tunnel'). You'll remain on this road, EP15, for the next 8.4-miles:

- About 1.6-miles, from Hwy 14, you'll cross over Red Rock-Inyokern Road.
- At about 4.6-miles there will be a cutoff to the right leading to the remains and artifacts of the Holly Ash Mine (definitely worth exploring).
- At about 4.7-miles you'll come to a 2-way intersection; bear left here, still remaining on the marked 'EP15'.
- In about 1 more mile you'll pass a rusty iron cabin on the right—the former Bonanza Gulch Post Office—and then drop into Bonanza Gulch itself.
- Remain on road EP15 and over the next 1-mile you'll see several old cabins on both sides of the road, the remnants of the old mining community of Bonanza Gulch.
- At about 8.4-miles from Hwy 14 you'll reach another junction; the road to Burro Schmidt's Tunnel continues southeast, up the wash, while EP15 turns northeast. Follow the signs up the wash to Burro Schmidt's Tunnel, about 9.3 miles from Hwy 14
- Note: While EP15 is very well marked and suitable for most vehicles, it does have a couple of stretches that require higher clearance than my recently rented Dodge Neon had to offer. In fact, if you come across any Neon parts while driving this road, please contact me at www. Godgrowthandgreatadventure.com to arrange their return.

Burro Schmidt, aka William Henry Schmidt, was born in Rhode Island in 1871. He moved from the east while he was in his twenties, following medical advice he had received about seeking a better climate—several members of his family had died of tuberculosis and he had been told that he probably wouldn't live very long himself.

Schmidt fell into a pattern of working summers in the Kern Valley region, and then returning in the winter to work his own claims here in the Last Chance Canyon area. During this period he had a few small successes, enough to keep him hopeful, and so he toiled away.

At some point he decided that when he did strike it big he would need an efficient way to transport his wealth out, and so he began tunneling a 'shortcut' through the mountain. He tunneled, and he tunneled, and he tunneled, and he tunneled. For about 30 years he dug this tunnel—all 1,872 feet of it—using only a pick, a four-pound hammer and a hand drill. Occasionally he was able to supplement this with a bit of dynamite, a wheelbarrow and, after the tunnel was fairly long, a set of rails and an ore cart.

Schmidt became more and more reclusive, eventually earning the nickname Burro Schmidt because of the company that he kept. Ultimately he sold this claim, along with the tunnel, and moved to other area claims that he held. When he finally died in 1954, at the age of 83 he had outlived, by decades, the predictions of his eastern doctors. Interestingly, Burro Schmidt sold his tunnel to another man who has also been advised to come west for health reasons. That fellow's widow—in her 90's when I last saw her—continued to live on site, dispensing first hand history of the area to anybody interested enough to ask. She passed on in 2003.

There are two cabins at the site; the first is the caretakers, and the second Burro Schmidt's. Like a sort of open-air museum, Schmidt's one-room shack has interesting artifacts scattered all about the front of it and the interior is papered with magazine and newspaper pages dating back to the 1920's. Since the death of the widow, however, there is no longer a caretaker on-site and the homes have suffered some vandalism.

Bring your headlamp to explore the tunnel, and watch your head; I'm guessing that Burro Schmidt was a fairly short guy. After taking in the fantastic views from the far end of the tunnel you can retrace your steps, or return to the cabins by hiking up and over the mountain.

For more information regarding Burro Schmidt, his tunnel, or attempts to preserve this jewel, contact the Bureau of Land Management or go to www.burroschmidttunnel.org.

154

CHAPTER TEN

The Devils Punchbowl Area

Wander among fascinating rock formations, a forest of Joshua Trees, and 2,000 year old Limber Pines; Climb a desert butte; Discover a mine, soak under a waterfall, and 'bag' the highest peak in the San Gabriel Mountains; Stand in awe of an ocean of wildflowers; Practice the 'grand silence' at a monastery; Visit a chalet built into a rock outcrop; Traverse a mountain river, by foot, from the high pines to the desert sage; Watch for Bighorn Sheep… and more!

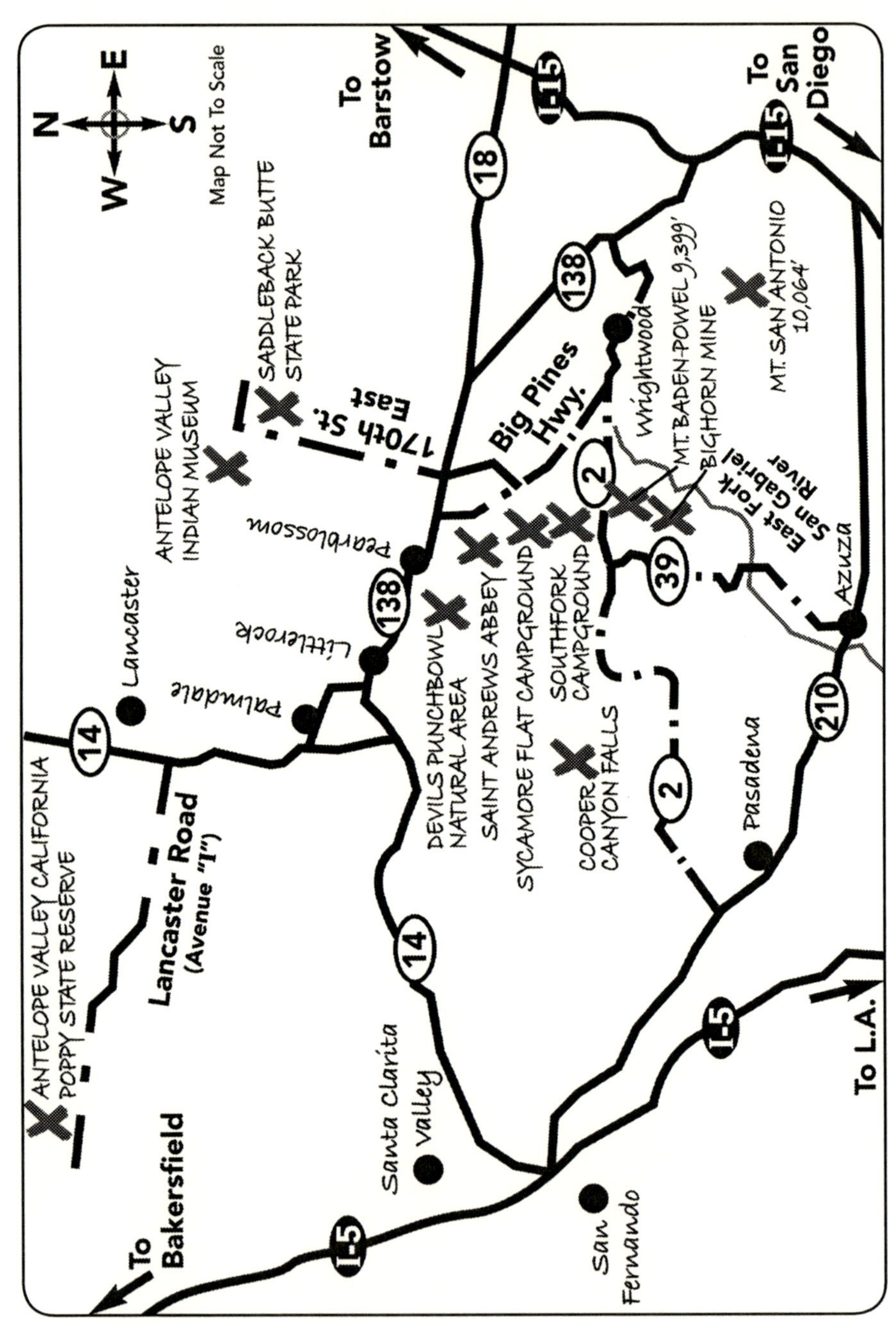
N
E
S
W
Map Not To Scale
To Barstow
To San Diego
I-15
18
138
Antelope Valley Indian Museum
Saddleback Butte State Park
170th St. East
Big Pines Hwy.
Wrightwood
Mt. Baden-Powell 9,399'
Bighorn Mine
Mt. San Antonio 10,064'
2
East Fork San Gabriel River
Pearblossom
Azuza
Lancaster
Littlerock
138
Devils Punchbowl Natural Area
Saint Andrews Abbey
Sycamore Flat Campground
Southfork Campground
39
Palmdale
Cooper Canyon Falls
Pasadena
210
14
Antelope Valley California Poppy State Reserve
Lancaster Road (Avenue "I")
2
To Bakersfield
14
Santa Clarita Valley
I-5
To L.A.
San Fernando
I-5

ABOUT THE DEVILS PUNCHBOWL AREA

The centerpiece attraction of the Devils Punchbowl County Natural Park is the bizarre, steeply tilted 300 foot-high rock formations. These formations, evidence of the San Andreas Fault that sits under the park, are an awesome playground for rock climbers, hikers and photographers.

To the north of the park, lower down on the flats of the Antelope Valley, the landscape is high desert—highlighted by junipers and Joshua trees, fantastic buttes and glorious spring wildflowers. To the south the pine covered San Gabriel Mountains rise to heights of more then 10,000ft and are home to beautiful streams of water, groves of 2000-year-old limber pines, Black Bears, Mountain Lions and Bighorn Sheep.

There is something for everybody here…you're going to have a fantastic time!

Getting There

The *Sycamore Flat Campground* and *Southfork Campground* are located just a few minutes away from the Devils Punchbowl County Natural Park. Get there…

From Interstate 15

Get to these Campgrounds, from Interstate 15, by exiting at Hwy 138 (Pearblossom Highway), just north of the city of San Bernardino, and heading west for approximately 27-miles to 165th Street East. Turn left (south) on 165th Street East for about 6.25-miles to Big Pines Highway (after a short distance, 165th Street East becomes Bob's Gap Road and angles east then back west). Turn left onto Big Pines Highway (Valyermo Rd) and then a pretty quick right onto Big Rock Creek Road. Stay on Big Rock Creek Road for about 2.5-miles, passing Sycamore Campground, then turn right on a marked dirt road to Southfork Creek Campground.

From California Highway 14

Get to the Sycamore Flat & Southfork Campgrounds, from California Highway 14, by exiting at Highway 138 (Pearblossom Highway) in the Antelope Valley and heading east for about 5.75-miles to the intersection of Hwy 138 and Avenue T. Turn right (south) here, continuing on Highway 138 for about 12.25-miles more, through the towns of Littlerock and Pearblossom, to 165th Street East. Turn right (south) on 165th Street East for about 6.25-miles to Big Pines Highway (after a short distance, 165th Street East becomes Bob's Gap Road and angles east then back west). Turn left onto Big Pines Highway (Valyermo Rd) and then a pretty quick right onto Big Rock Creek Road. Stay on Big Rock Creek Road for about 2.5-miles, passing Sycamore Campground, and then turn right onto a marked dirt road to Southfork Creek Campground.

Supplies, Lodging, Maps & Information

Supplies, gas and lodging are available in the Palmdale area and, to a limited degree, Pearblossom, Little Rock and the small mountain town of Wrightwood, which also offers cabins for rent. Contact the Wrightwood Chamber of Commerce online at www.wrightwoodchamber.org for more information regarding such lodging.

Of the several campgrounds in the area, most are in the San Gabriel Mountains, but at least one is out on the desert, at Saddleback Butte State Park. The campgrounds discussed in this chapter, Southfork & Sycamore Flat, have been featured because of their moderate elevation and proximity to some fantastic adventures. These campgrounds, however, can be uncomfortable during the hottest times of the year and closed during the coldest (it snows here!). During these periods you may want to camp higher up in the pines (summer) or among the Joshua Trees of Saddleback Butte State Park (winter).

The Southfork Campground, located at about 4,500ft, has 21 first come, first served sites. There is no drinking water here, but in a pinch you can shoot over to Sycamore Flat which does have piped-in water (shut off in the winter). Several great trails pass through this campground, as does the South Fork of Big Rock Creek. Southfork is closed from about November to May.

The Sycamore Flat campground, located at about 4,200ft, has 11 first come, first served sites and is open year round. There is a small fee to camp at Sycamore Flats. For more information regarding either of these campgrounds, contact the Angeles National Forest at the number below.

Be sure that you have DeLorme's, "Southern & Central California Atlas & Gazetteer", or its equivalent, and the American Automobile Association's (AAA) "Los Angeles County" & "San Bernardino County" maps. Additionally, Tom Harrison (www.tomharrisonmaps.com) puts out a wonderful series of topo maps that cover the entire San Gabriel Mountains area: 'Angeles High Country', 'Angeles Front Country', 'Mount Wilson', and 'Mount Baldy/Cucamonga Wilderness.'

Two great area hiking guides are: *"Trails of the Angeles: 100 Hikes in the San Gabriel's"* (John W. Robinson) and, *"Afoot & Afield in Los Angeles County"* (Jerry Schmidt)

For more information regarding maps, road & trail conditions, alternate campgrounds, or any necessary permits, contact the Angeles National Forest at: Mount Baldy Visitors Center, PO Box 592, Mount Baldy Road, Mount Baldy Village, California, 91759, or by phone at 909.982.2829.

National Forest Adventure Pass

In 1997, as a way of raising much needed revenue to help defray the costs of recreation on their respective lands, the Angeles, San Bernardino, Los Padres, and Cleveland National Forests instituted a fee policy. This policy calls for each and every vehicle parked on land within these forests (including campgrounds) to display a "National Forest Adventure Pass." Visitors may travel through national forest lands without an adventure pass, but every parked vehicle must display one.

Both day and yearly passes can be purchased for a very nominal fee and are valid at all four national forests. Passes are available at the ranger stations and Visitors Centers of these forests, as well as most outdoor stores in Southern California, and many convenience-type stores near or within these national forests.

Having the combination of spontaneity and absent-mindedness means that I have the unique ability to plan things at the last minute while leaving behind essential items. After receiving several tickets for not having an Adventure Pass, I found it to be much easier to just purchase the one-year pass and keep it in my glove box where it's always handy.

Contact the Angeles National Forest, at the above phone number, for more information regarding the National Forest Adventure Pass.

Devil's Punchbowl Natural Area

This rugged wilderness park lies in a fascinating transition zone between the pine-covered San Gabriel Mountains to the south, and the Joshua trees of the Mojave Desert to the north. It is 1,310-acres in size, sits between 4,200ft and 6,500ft in elevation, and features unusual rock formations that have been forced as much as 300 feet into the air by the movement of the San Andreas Fault.

The park has several miles of hiking trails, rock climbing opportunities, a picnic area & restrooms, and a great Visitors Center. The park is open seven days a week, from sunrise to sunset, while the Visitors Center is open from 9 A.M. to 4 P.M.

Get to the Devils Punchbowl, from the Sycamore Flat/Southfork Campgrounds, by heading north on Big Rock Creek Road to Big Pines Highway (Valyermo Rd). Turn left onto Big Pines Highway for about 2-miles to the intersection of Fort Tejon Road/Pallett Circle, and then turn left onto Pallett Circle for perhaps another 2-miles, to Longview Road (N6 or "Tumbleweed Road"). Turn left (south) on Longview Road to Devils Punchbowl.

Look for Devils Perch, a prominent natural rock arch that is visible from the road beginning about 0.25-mile from the park entrance.

For more information regarding the Devils Punchbowl County Natural Area, contact: Devils Punchbowl Nature Center, 28000 Devils Punchbowl Road, Pearblossom, CA 93553, or by phone at: 661.944.2743 or on the web at: www.parks.co.la. us/devil_narea.html.

Devils Punchbowl Loop Trail

The loop trail is an easy, 1-mile long introduction to the punchbowl area. It begins just behind the Visitors Center, switchbacks down into Punchbowl Canyon, and then climbs back out near some of the highest formations in the park.

Soon after starting down the trail you'll intersect another path; the Pinyon Pathway is a shorter (0.3-mile), self-guided hike, which loops through the Pinyon-juniper zone along the Punchbowls' rim. Grab a brochure for this one.

Devils Chair Hike

The route for this hike stretches between the Devils Punchbowl parking area, and the Southfork Campground. A great way to do this roughly 5.5-mile hike, if you can arrange a shuttle, is to have your group dropped off at the Devils Punchbowl and then walk back to camp. That's how I'll describe this hike—from the Devils Punchbowl back to the Southfork Campground:

Catch the Burkhart Trail at the south end of the Devils Punchbowl parking lot and climb northwest along the rim of the Punchbowl. At 0.5-mile the trail joins an old road and then, at 0.8-mile, arrives at a junction. Bear left (east) here, now on the Punchbowl Trail, and continue meandering along the rim before descending in a series of steep switchbacks to another junction, about 3-miles from the parking area. At this junction, follow this short (0.1-mile) spur west and then north, to catch the not-to-be-missed views from the Devils Chair overlook.

After you've taken in the view, backtrack to the junction, turn left (east), and continue descending until, at 3.7-miles from the parking area, you reach the oaks, pines and small creek at the bottom of Holcomb Canyon (There are some great areas for primitive camping along here; contact the park rangers regarding necessary permits).

The trail, continuing east out of Holcomb Canyon, climbs a short distance to a saddle, and then descends for about 1-mile to the Southfork Campground.

It can be very hot here in the summer; be sure to bring plenty of water & sunscreen.

Blue Ridge To Mount San Antonio (Old Baldy)

This fairly strenuous hike, with more then 3,000ft of elevation gain in a short 10 round trip miles, undulates across an alpine ridge, just skirts two of the highest points in the San Gabriel Mountains, and then ascends a steep incline to the summit of Mt Baldy (10,064ft), the highest point in the San Gabriel Mountains.

Get to the trailhead, from the Southfork Campground, by heading north on Big Rock Creek to Big Pines Highway (Valyermo Rd). Turn right onto Big Pines Highway and follow it for about 10.5-miles to its intersection with Highway 2 (Angeles Crest Highway). Turn right onto Highway 2 for approximately 2-miles to a dirt road on the left. This is the Blue Ridge road, heading to Guffy Campground and Prairie Fork. Stay on this road and in about 6-miles you'll hit a junction, stay left (the track to the right goes to Prairie Fork) for about another 1.7-miles to a trail sign for Devil's Backbone.

The route for this hike begins on the south side of the road where the trail descends steeply for a short distance to a narrow ridge (Devil's Backbone), and then meanders up and down this ridge, just skirting Pine Mountain (9648ft) and Dawson Peak (9575ft), before climbing steeply to the summit of Old Baldy.

Along the way, watch for Nelson's Bighorn Sheep—there are upwards of 700 of these wonderful animals within the San Gabriel Mountains—and then, on the summit, enjoy your lunch and the views, sign the register (and the ones on Pine Mountain & Dawson Peak if you decide to bag those too), and then retrace your steps back to the trailhead.

Note: Any lingering late-season snow on the north side of Baldy can make the stretch just below the summit rather icy and treacherous.

Mt. Baden-Powell Hike

Mount Baden-Powell (9399ft), one of my favorite hikes, is an aggressive lung & thigh burner featuring twisted 2,000 year-old Limber Pines, Bighorn Sheep, and astounding views.

Get to the trailhead at Vincent Gap, from the Southfork Campground, by heading north on Big Rock Creek Road to Big Pines Highway (Valyermo Rd). Turn right (southeast) onto Big Pines Highway and follow it for about 10.5-miles to the intersection with Highway 2 (Angeles Crest Highway). Turn right onto Highway 2 for about 5.5-miles, to the parking area at Vincent Gap (6,565ft).

The trail to the summit of Baden-Powell is pretty straightforward; it starts near a large sign, heads up a short wooden staircase, and then climbs about 41 switchbacks to gain 2,800 feet over 4-miles (8-miles round trip). At about 1.5-miles into the hike a side trail leads 200 yards east to a dribbling pipe at

Lamel Springs. At about 3.5-miles another short spur trail leads 300 yards southwest to an ancient grove of Limber Pines.

The summit also has several weather beaten Limber & Lodgepole Pines—the former up to 20 centuries old—as well as awesome views of Mt Baldy, the inner San Gabriel Mountains, the Mojave Desert and, if the air quality is decent, even the far off Channel Islands. Watch too for Nelson's Bighorn Sheep; they can be found on the summit and the flanks of this beautiful mountain.

Sign the register, check out the monument to the Boy Scouts (Lord Baden-Powell, this mountains namesake, was the founder of the Boy Scouts), have lunch and a nap and then, when finished, retrace your steps to the trailhead.

If you decide to do this hike by moonlight, stick around for the sunrise too— Baden-Powell casts a really cool miles-long shadow across the Antelope Valley. Also, be sure to bring plenty of warm clothes—the winds blowing across the summit can be fast and cold—and then top this adventure off with a post-hike hot chocolate in the nearby mountain town of Wrightwood.

Note: Winter ascents on Baden-Powell can become icy and snowy technical climbs requiring crampons, an ice ax, and proper training in their use.

Bighorn Mine Hike

This is a fun, fairly short hike to an old mining complex and a stamp mill located on the flank of Mount Baden-Powell. The trail starts at the Vincent Gap Trailhead (6,565ft), the same one described above for the Mount Baden-Powell hike, and is about 4-miles (round-trip) in length with about 500 feet of elevation gain.

From the Vincent Gap parking area, walk around the "road closed" sign and follow the dirt road—actually the remains of an old wagon road—as it drops about 60 feet and contours southeast around Mt. Baden-Powell. Negotiate a washed out section, at just over 1-mile into the hike, and then pass the first mine tunnel in this complex. The trail shortly climbs about 300 feet, passing the foundations of some old mine buildings, before coming to the stamp mill and the end of the wagon road.

There is a bit of old equipment around the area and several very unsafe mineshafts, including a large one behind the stamp mill. Please be very careful while exploring this area and stay out of the shafts themselves.

When you've finished with this adventure, retrace your steps to the parking area.

East Fork Traverse

This fantastic 14.5-mile hike begins in the pines & cedars of Vincent Gap, follows the East Fork of the San Gabriel River through the rugged Narrows, and finishes up in the desert-like environment of the East Fork Trailhead. Along the way you'll traverse a narrow canyon, experience some interesting history & wildlife, and cross the river at least thirty times.

The Car Shuttle

This hike requires a long car shuttle: Get to the start of the hike at the Vincent Gap Trailhead, from the South Fork Campground, by heading north on Big Rock Creek Road to Big Pines Highway (Valyermo Rd). Turn right (southeast) onto Big Pines Highway and follow it for about 10.5-miles to its intersection with

Highway 2 (Angeles Crest Highway). Turn right onto Highway 2 for about 5.5-miles, to the parking area at Vincent Gap.

The hike ends at the East Fork parking area. To get to the East Fork parking area from the Vincent Gap Trailhead, drive east on Angeles Crest Highway (Hwy 2) for about 14.5-miles, through the small town of Wrightwood, to Highway 138 (the Pearblossom Highway). Turn right (east) onto Highway 138 for about 8.5-miles to Interstate 15. Head south on Interstate 15 for about 19-miles to Highway 210. Take Highway 210 west for about 24-miles to Hwy 39 (San Gabriel Canyon Road), in the city of Azusa. Take Hwy 39 north, through Azusa, for about 10-miles, and then turn right (east) onto the East Fork Road and continue for about 8-miles more to the parking area at the end of the road. You'll want to leave a vehicle(s) here (with the appropriate number of Adventure Passes), and then return to Vincent Gap to begin the hike.

Another much more preferred option is to have others, who do not wish to spend the day walking in water, drop the hikers off at the Vincent Gap trailhead, and then drive around to the East Fork parking area to meet them when they've finished with the walk.

The Hike

From the Vincent Gap parking area, walk around the 'Road Closed' sign and start down the old dirt wagon road that leads to the Bighorn Mine. After a short distance, perhaps 200 yards, catch the path coming in from the left and head down into Vincent Gulch and the Sheep Mountain Wilderness area, home to a fairly large number of Nelson Bighorn Sheep, as well as bears and mountain lions. At about 0.7-mile into the hike you'll see a faint spur trail coming in from the right; follow this for about 100 yards to the site of an old cabin that was home to Tom Vincent; hunter, hermit, founder of the Bighorn Mine, and resident of the San Gabriel Mountains from the 1870's to the 1920s.

Back on the main route, the trail continues to switchback steeply downhill, crossing Vincent Gulch at about 1.6-miles, and then remaining on the east bank until, at about 3.8-miles, it reaches Prairie Fork. Here, at Prairie Fork, a second trail drops in from the Cabin Flat Campground; avoid that trail and instead bear right (west) for a short distance down a gravel wash to the Mine Gulch Junction, a flat area of sand and rock. Here, at 4,500ft, the Vincent Gulch, Mine Gulch, and Prairie Forks' come together to form the East Fork of the San Gabriel River.

Following the river downstream now, be aware that you may need to pick your own route over the next 1-mile or so, as the river regularly floods and obliterates the trail. Notice too, as you travel along, that the river is becoming larger, the mountains higher, the canyon deeper and the terrain more rugged.

At about 5-miles into the hike, the canyon narrows for a short while and the water crossings become more challenging. At about 7.3-miles Fish Fork (3,400ft) enters from the east and then, at 8.3-miles, Iron Fork (3,200ft) enters the canyon from the west.

For about the next 1-mile or so, beyond Iron Fork, the canyon really closes in as you traverse an area called The Narrows, the deepest gorge in southern California. It is an area chock-full of cascades, deep swimming holes, and high rock walls.

As a 14 year-old boy, I often made solo trips out here to swim in the beautiful pools, lie on the sun-warmed sand, and watch the stars through a narrow sliver of sky. My favorite place to spend the night was on a small, sandy beach just across the river from a rock wall many hundreds of feet high. Every afternoon, like clockwork, Bighorn Sheep would begin to make their way down this high cliff. They would descend slowly for several hours, feeding along the way, before reaching the river and a drink of water just at dusk. For the rest of the evening I would listen as these beautiful animals made their way back up the cliff, charting their progress by the rocks kicked loose to tumble to the river below.

On one occasion, a red fox in panicked flight dashed through my camp here, coming between me and the fire that I was be-

ing warmed by. I thought it better that I never knew what was out there that terrified him more than I did.

Continuing on through the Narrows, be sure to keep your eye out for the rough trail that crosses and re-crosses the river. Several times this trail climbs above the river on the right (west) side of the canyon to skirt cascades and waterfalls; the going will be a lot tougher if you miss these stretches of trail. At the lower end of The Narrows, about 9.7-miles into the walk, you'll make a sharp turn to the right and come upon *The Bridge To Nowhere*.

In the 1920's, a road was planned that would reach all the way up the San Gabriel Canyon to Mine Gulch, and then over Blue Ridge to the town of Wrightwood. By the mid-1930's, with the project pushed all the way to this point, a bridge was built and a tunnel carved out of solid rock. The next winter, however, an especially fierce rainstorm caused a tremendous flood that washed out more then five miles of the road, leaving behind only this bridge—the Bridge to Nowhere—high up and out of reach of the waters.

The Bridge to Nowhere is the uppermost terminus for most people heading up canyon, so be prepared to run into more and more hikers, fishermen, prospectors, and bungee jumpers (clients of a licensed company) as you cover the final 4.8-miles, and 14 or so river crossings, of this hike.

After crossing over the bridge, continue on the now well-worn trail first passing, at about 12-miles into the hike (2.3-miles from the bridge), Allison Gulch dumping into the river from the left, and then about 300 yards further on Swan Rock on the right; the light colored swan is on the huge, dark colored, rock wall.

Finally, about 2-miles beyond Swan Rock you'll pass the Heaton Flat campground and, a short 0.5-mile further on, come to the end of the hike at the East Fork parking area.

More thoughts regarding this wonderful hike:

- This hike—14.5-mile long with about 400 feet of elevation gain and 4,800 feet of loss—begins high in the pines & cedars of Vincent Gap (6,565ft), is almost all downhill, and because of the 30 or more river crossings should definitely *not* be done during periods of high water.
- Although this route basically follows the river drainage the entire way, you'll still need to study the maps before heading out.
- Put all of your gear and food into a dry-sack, or a plastic garbage-type bag, and then put that into your pack. This will help keep it dry as you spend the day crossing and re-crossing the river.
- You will be required to have a permit to pass through the 44,000-acre Sheep Mountain Wilderness. For permit information, contact the Mount Baldy Visitors Center by phone at 909.982.2829.

Cooper Canyon Falls

Get to the trailhead for the hike to this sweet waterfall, from the Southfork Campground, by heading north on Big Rock Creek Road to Big Pines Highway (Valyermo Rd). Turn right (southeast) onto Big Pines Highway and follow it for about 10.5-miles to its intersection with Highway 2 (Angeles Crest Highway). Turn right onto Highway 2 for about 30.5-miles, to the Buckhorn Campground (6,400ft) near mile-marker 58.33. Drive all the way through the campground and catch the short dirt road leading to the trailhead for the Burkhart Trail.

On foot now, head down the Burkhardt Trail paralleling, but remaining high above, Buckhorn Creek. At about 0.5-mile from the campground, look for a large rock outcrop across the canyon; a couple of nice swimming holes and 10-foot high waterfalls lie along the creek between this rock outcrop and the campground. These waterfalls, however, are not as nice as the one that you're headed towards.

Continue down the trail, through the pine and cedar, descending through a couple of long switchbacks to a trail junction at about 1.75-miles. This junction is the intersection of the Burkhardt/Pacific Crest & Silver Moccasin trails; turn right here, toward Eagles Roost and Burkhardt Saddle. The waterfalls are a short 0.10-mile beyond the trail junction.

Continue down the trail for about 30-yards beyond the waterfalls, to a spur leading steeply down to their base. The lower fall is about 35 feet high, the upper is about 15 feet high, and there's a great little swimming hole at the base.

Enjoy a nice swim here, soak in the sun, take some photos, have a snack and then, when you're ready, retrace your steps back to the trailhead.

This hike—about 3.75-miles round trip with about 850 feet of elevation loss/gain—is best done in the spring and early summer, when snowmelt and rainwater make the cascade more dramatic.

Saddleback Butte State Park

Three thousand acre Saddleback Butte State Park is a great fall-through-spring destination, when skies are blue, temperatures are mild, and sunsets are awesome. Among the highlights of this park are wonderful 360-degree views from the summit of Saddleback Butte (3,651ft), a fantastic Joshua tree forest, and dazzling springtime wildflower displays.

Get to the park, from the South Fork Campground, by heading northwest on Big Rock Creek Road to its intersection with Big Pines Hwy. Turn left onto Big Pines Hwy (Valyermo Rd), and then almost immediately turn right (north) onto Bob's Gap Road. Bob's Gap Road angles east, and then back west, and in about 4.75-miles becomes 165th Street East. Continue north on 165th Street East for about 4.5-miles, until it angles east and becomes 170th Street East. Continue north on 170th Street East for about 10-miles to Avenue J. Turn right (east) on Avenue J; the park entrance will be on your right.

Joshua Trail Loop

Catch the easy, 0.5-mile long, Joshua Trail near the park Visitors Center and follow the yellow-capped posts towards the west where the trail first ascends, and then circles around, a small rock outcrop.

The nine interpretive stops along the route correspond to a brochure available at the Visitors Center.

Saddleback-Little Butte Loop

The 5.2-mile Saddleback-Little Butte Loop trail begins at the campground and follows yellow-capped posts east to a junction, at about the 1-mile mark, where the Little Butte Trail breaks off to the left. Continuing east, the trail climbs to a saddle, about 1.7-miles from the campground, and then climbs steeply for 0.3 mile to the summit of the butte.

Sign the register, enjoy the views and your lunch, and then descend the butte the way you came, returning to the 1-mile junction. At this point you can either retrace your route back to the campground, for a 4-mile hike, or you can turn right onto the Little Butte Trail and make this hike a loop.

If you opt for the loop, turn right (north) onto the Little Butte Trail for 0.5-mile to the top of the aptly named, "Little Butte." Another 1-mile (4.5-miles from the campground) will bring you to the road near the picnic area; turn left here to tie the loop together at the campground.

Saddleback Butte State Park has 50 campsites (some with verandas for shade), restrooms, water, and a picnic area. For more information contact the park through the Mojave Desert Information Center at 661.942.0662, or online at www.parks. ca.gov.

Antelope Valley Indian Museum

From Saddleback Butte State Park it's a short hop to the nearby Antelope Valley Indian Museum, an extraordinary pale-green Swiss chalet built right into Paiute Butte.

Self-taught artist Howard Arden Edwards, collector of many of the artifacts on display, homesteaded these 160 acres before beginning construction of this building in about 1928. The property was later purchased by Grace Oliver, an anthropologist who greatly increased the collection and eventually opened it as a museum, a job now overseen by the State of California.

The various rooms within the museum are built around the rocks & fissures of the butte, and are loaded with artifacts. There is also a nature trail, bookstore, and a building, *The*

Joshua Cottage, where visitors and their children can actually try their hands at grinding corn, building a fire with a bow, and other cool things.

Get to the Antelope Valley Indian Museum, from Saddleback Butte State Park (at the intersection of Avenue J & 170th Street East), by heading south on 170th Street East for about 3-miles to Avenue M. Turn right (west) on Avenue M for about 1-mile or so; the park entrance is on the right (north).

The museum operates under limited hours, generally on weekends from 11am to 4pm, October to June. For more information contact the Mojave Desert Information Center by phone at: 661.942.0662 or via the web at: www.avim.av.org.

Antelope Valley California Poppy State Reserve

I definitely recommend a side trip to this world-class preserve where, when the right season combines with the right conditions, the hillsides literally explode with color. I mean it, the wildflower display in this area can be just staggering.

The wildflowers are not exceptional every year, and the season is not long, but when the conditions are right you'll want to be ready. The reserve has a "poppy-hotline" that will assist you in this; begin calling it sometime in mid-to-late February and head out as soon as they tell you the bloom is on. Don't wait more then a few days or you'll miss it.

Although the preserve is open to the public year round, the Visitors Center is only open from about mid-March to about mid-May to coincide with the blooming season. The rest of the year the preserve is a dry, rolling grassland.

The preserve has restrooms, water, and several loop trails to explore. Springtime wildflower updates can be heard by calling the poppy hotline at 661.724.1180. For other trip-planning information contact the Jane S. Pinheiro Interpretive Center, between about mid-march to mid-may: Antelope Valley California Poppy Reserve, 15101 West Lancaster Road, Lancaster, CA 93536, or by phone at 661.942.0662, or on the web at: www.parks.ca.gov.

Get to the Antelope Valley California Poppy State Reserve, from the Southfork Campground, by heading north on Big Rock Creek Road to its intersection with Big Pines Highway. Turn left onto Big Pines Highway (Valyermo Rd), and then almost immediately go right onto Bob's Gap Road. Bob's Gap Road angles east, and then back west, becoming 165th Street East before reaching Highway 138 (Pearblossom Highway), about 6.25-miles from Big Pines Highway/Valyermo Rd.

Turn left (west) on Highway 138 for about 12.25-miles, to the junction of Hwy 138 and Avenue T. Continue northwest through the intersection for about 1.5-miles to 'Avenue S'. Turn left (west) onto 'Avenue S' for about 5-miles to California Highway 14. Hop on Hwy 14 and head north for about 10.75-miles and exit at 'Avenue I' in Lancaster.

Head west on Avenue I (which soon becomes 'Lancaster Road) for about 13-miles as the road curves north, then back west; the poppy preserve is on the right.

Charlie Brown Farms

As you travel back and forth on the Pearblossom Highway (Hwy 138), take a few minutes and swing into Charlie Brown Farms for a buffalo or ostrich burger, or one of (I said one!) more than 100 different kinds of milk shakes. They have other things on their menu too, as well as locally produced fruits, vegetables, honey, and a million different kinds of knick-knacks, trinkets, and souvenirs.

Charlie Brown Farms is located on the north side of Pearblossom Highway, in the small town of Little Rock. Contact them at: Charlie Brown Farms, 8317 Pearblossom Highway (Hwy 138), Little Rock, California 93543, or by phone at 661.944.2606 or on the web at: www.charliebrownfarms.com.

Saint Andrew's Abbey

Saint Andrew's Abbey is a Roman Catholic Benedictine community made up of men who have committed themselves to following the cycle of prayer and work set down by Saint Benedict centuries ago. This cycle is comprised of periods of individual & corporate prayer, manual labor, and a deep, contemplative reading of the Scriptures (Lectio Divina), which are woven together to produce a day of worship and praise.

The monks welcome men and women seeking to connect more deeply with God to do so at the abbey, where they can pray, rest, read, write, walk, and experience silence. These kinds of personal retreats can be achieved through simple day trips, through overnight stays, or by attending one of the many retreats/workshops held throughout the year.

For an overnight, self-directed type of retreat you'll want to stay in one of the 17 rooms available within the Retreat House. They're reasonably priced, and include three home-style meals per day that are shared communally with the monks and other guests. The entire environment is conducive to worship; the grounds are peaceful, the chapel is open 24-hours for prayer & meditation, and there is a period between about 9pm and 9am called the Grand Silence. A time without busyness and noise; a time to just meditate on the treasure that we have in our Savior.

The Abbey is a great place in which to creatively worship God (to read, to write stories, poetry or music, to paint, etc.), to study His Word, to listen to Him in divine silence, and to meditate on the precept that the monks of Saint Andrew's Abbey live by—"Prefer nothing to the love of Christ."

Visit the abbey, from the Southfork Campground, by heading north on Big Rock Creek Road to its intersection with Big Pines Highway (Valyermo Rd). Turn left onto Big Pines Highway/Valyermo Road for approximately 2-miles. The entrance to the abbey is on the left, just before the intersection of Fort Tejon Road.

For directions from other locations, information about their fantastic workshops, or to reserve a room for a personal retreat, contact the abbey at: Saint Andrew's Abbey, 31001 North Valyermo Road, Valyermo, CA 93563 or by phone at 661.944.2178. The abbeys website also has a tremendous amount of information: www.valyermo.com.

CHAPTER ELEVEN

The Mojave Desert National Preserve Area

Check out an amazing cave complex, a lava tube, and "singing" sand dunes; Wonder at fascinating fossils embedded in the walls of a canyon; Walk among incredible spring wildflowers, a Joshua tree forest, and colorful volcanic craters & lava flows; Discover historic towns, mining artifacts, and a railroad depot; Descend a cliff using iron rings embedded in the rock; Discover life and beauty where a subterranean desert river rises to the surface… and more!

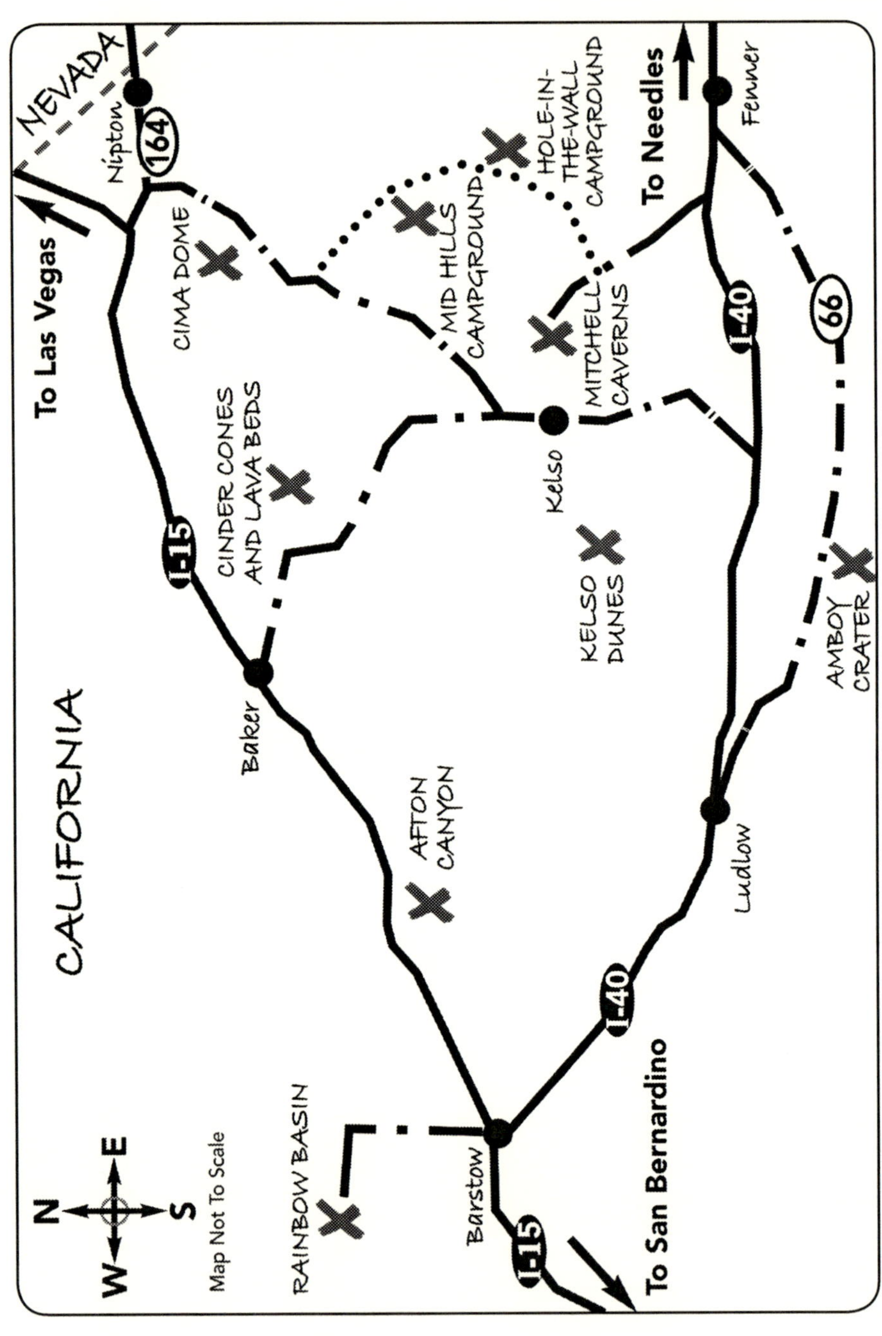

NEVADA
CALIFORNIA
To Las Vegas
To Needles
To San Bernardino
Nipton
164
CIMA DOME
MID HILLS CAMPGROUND
HOLE-IN-THE-WALL CAMPGROUND
Fenner
CINDER CONES AND LAVA BEDS
MITCHELL CAVERNS
I-40
66
I-15
Kelso
KELSO DUNES
AMBOY CRATER
Baker
AFTON CANYON
Ludlow
I-40
RAINBOW BASIN
Barstow
I-15
N
E
S
W
Map Not To Scale

About the Mojave National Preserve Area

The 1.6 million-acre Mojave National Preserve is situated in an area known as the Lonesome Triangle; a place where California's three desert regions (the Mojave, Sonoran, and Great Basin) come together to create one of the most diverse environments in the world. The elevations at the preserve range to nearly 8,000 feet above sea level, encompassing Creosote dominated flats, pinion/juniper highlands, and the world's largest and densest Joshua tree forest. Other awesome sites here include huge sand dune complexes, dry lakebeds, cinder cones & lava tubes, limestone caves, colorful geology, ghost towns, Bighorn Sheep, and fantastic history.

The Mojave Preserve is amazing!

Getting There

From the south (L.A., San Bernardino, San Diego, etc.), take Interstate 15 north to the city of Barstow. From Barstow you have the option of continuing north on I-15, or heading east on I-40. If you choose to continue north on I-15, traveling about 90-miles to the Cima Road turnoff will put you in a good position to hit the campgrounds from the north.

Traveling east on I-40 for about 101-miles will bring you to Essex Road, the southern entrance to the preserve and campgrounds

Supplies, Lodging, Maps and Information

Supplies, gas and motels are available in the city of Barstow and the towns of Baker (on I-15) and Needles (on I-40). Gas and limited supplies are available at Ludlow and Fenner, both on I-40. Be sure to gas up at every opportunity.

As far as lodging goes, aside from the motels available at Baker, Barstow, and Needles, there are two developed campgrounds in the preserve—Mid-Hills and Hole-in-the-Wall—and one campground within the Providence Mountains State Recreation Area, a small, fascinating area encircled by the preserve.

Mid-Hills Campground—so named because of its location mid way between the Providence and New York Mountains—is a great place to base camp in the summer; its 5,200ft elevation places you above the most intense heat (summer daytime temps average about 90-degrees, verses more then 110-degrees at lower elevations), and the area is covered in shade-providing junipers & Pinion Pines. A short 0.5-mile walk west from the campground will bring you to some wonderful granite minarets and fantastic views of Kelso Valley, and Cima Dome beyond. Note that winter often brings snowstorms at this elevation.

Mid-Hills has 26 sites, restrooms, running water, fire rings (be sure to bring your own wood and charcoal), and tables. The campsites here are first come, first served and there is a small fee.

Nearby Hole-In-the-Wall Campground (4,200ft) has 35 campsites, restrooms, running water, tables, and accommodations for large RV's. There is also a seasonal ranger station/Visitors Center and an equestrian campsite & corral. One of the highlights of this area is an interesting hike that involves lowering yourself down a pockmarked cliff using iron rings set into the rock. Find this trail, the Hole-in-the-Wall Trail, by following the dirt road past the Visitors Center to the parking area at the picnic ground. The trail proceeds into a wall of rocks where you'll find the iron rings; use these to lower yourself into Banshee Canyon and continue walking through the canyon bottom towards Wild Horse Canyon. Turn around at any time and retrace your steps back to the campground.

All campsites here are first come, first served with the exception of a group site. For more information about this site contact the Mojave National Preserve at the address below.

To get to the Mid-Hills & Hole-in-the-Wall Campgrounds from the north, take I-15 north from Barstow for about 90 miles to the Cima Road exit. Go south on Cima Road for about 17-miles, and then take a right on Kelso-Cima Road and continue south for about 4.4-miles to Cedar Canyon Road (signed for

Mid-Hills and Hole-in-Wall Campgrounds). Go left (east) on Cedar Canyon Road to Black Canyon Road (also signed):

- *For Mid-Hills Campground*: Head south on Black Canyon Road for just under 5 miles to Wild Horse Canyon Road and turn right (west); Mid-Hills Campground is 2 miles ahead.
- *For Hole-In-The-Wall Campground*: Go south on Black Canyon Road for about 8.3 miles to Hole-in-the-Wall Campground.

To get to the Mid-Hills & Hole-in-the-Wall Campgrounds from the south, take Interstate 40 about 101-miles east from its intersection with Interstate 15 in Barstow. Exit I-40 at Essex Road and head north for about 9.7-miles to Black Canyon Road:

- *For Hole-In-The-Wall Campground*: Head north (right) on Black Canyon road for about 8.5-miles to Hole-in-the-Wall Campground.
- *For Mid-Hills Campground*: Take Black Canyon Road north for just over 8.5-miles to Wild Horse Canyon Road. Turn left (north-west) on Wild Horse Canyon Road and follow it for just over 9-miles to Mid-Hills Campground.

Apart from these campgrounds, primitive camping is allowed throughout the preserve, but try to choose sites that have traditionally been used for camping to avoid further scarring the land. Also, try to stay away from roads and day use areas and at least 0.25-mile from any water source—to protect shy wildlife. Oh, and don't forget to protect scarce natural resources, too, by bringing your own firewood and kindling.

For more information, the National Park Service maintains two Visitors Centers that are staffed by informed rangers and loaded with books and maps for purchase. The first Visitor Center, the primary one for the preserve, is located in the historic Kelso Railroad Depot located at 1924 Kelso-Cima Road, Kelso, California 92332 or by phone at 760.252.6161. This sweet depot is described in more detail below.

The second Visitors Center is in Baker. Contact: Mojave Desert Information Center, 72157 Baker Boulevard, PO Box 241, Baker, CA 92309, or by phone at 760.733.4040.

As far as maps go, be sure that you have DeLorme's, "Southern & Central California Atlas & Gazetteer", or its equivalent, and a copy of the National Geographic, "Mojave National Preserve" topo map (www.trailsillustrated.com). A book that may be helpful is, "Mojave National Preserve: A Visitors Guide" (Cheri Rae & John McKinney).

The Bureau of Land Management administers most of the land surrounding the preserve. Contact them at: BLM Needles Resource Office, 101 West Spikes Road, Needles, CA 92363 or by phone at: 760.326.7000.

In order to organize the preserve's various activities in a logical sequence, I've begun at Providence Mountains State Recreation Area and worked around in a clock-wise direction, finishing out the chapter with a couple of cool sites for the drive up from the city.

Providence Mountains State Recreation Area

Providence Mountains State Recreation Area is a small jewel encircled by the Mojave National Preserve. This recreation area has a great little Visitors Center, a small campground with six sites & running water, several nice nature trails, one of the greatest drive-to desert views you'll find anywhere, and the awesome Mitchell Cavern complex.

The complex, really two fascinating caves linked by a tunnel, has chambers with names like Bottomless Pit, Queen's Chamber, and Hollow Floor Room. The formations within this system are world class and include, aside from the customary stalactites, stalagmites & columns, coral pipes—existing in only six other U.S. caverns—and three cave shields, one of which has been declared the finest to be found anywhere.

Flowstone, soda straws, bell canopies, and popcorn round out the fascinating formations here.

There is another cave here, the Winding Stair Cave, just to the north of Mitchell Cavern, but it is restricted to experienced caving groups with a special entry permit. This sweet cave has a 320-foot drop vertical drop that is pulled off through a series of rappels ranging in length from 50 to 180 feet.

Contact the park for more information, including times and fees, for the ranger led tour of Mitchell Caverns: Providence Mountains State Recreation Area, Mitchell Caverns Natural Preserve, PO Box 1, Essex, CA 92332, or by phone at: 760.928.2586.

Get there by heading east on Interstate 40 for about 101-miles from its intersection with Interstate 15 in Barstow. Exit at Essex Road and head north for about 15.3-miles to the Visitors Center and campground.

Note: Check '*The Resources*' section of this book for more information on caving clubs, classes & instruction.

Kelso Dunes

Kelso Dunes, at more then 45 miles square and piled in places over 700 feet high, is one of the most extensive, and one of the most beautiful, dune systems in the west. It also sings…sort of.

To get to the Kelso Dunes, from the south, take the Kelbaker Road exit from Interstate 40, and head north for about 14-miles, to a signed dirt road. Turn left (west) onto this road and follow it for about 3-miles to a parking area with interpretive signs.

From the north, at Kelso Depot, head south on Kelbaker Road for about 7-miles to the signed dirt road, and turn right (west) for about 3-miles to the parking area. The trail to the dunes begins near the interpretive signs.

The 3-mile round-trip hike to the top of the dunes is a must do, and a bit more challenging then it appears. Take the short (0.25-mile) trail that heads out from the parking area and disappears at the base of the dunes. The best route to the top,

I think, is to angle towards the low saddle just to the right of the highest dune and then, when you've reached it, climb the crest to the summit.

Walking along you'll notice that, as your feet cause mini-avalanches and slides, you can hear the dunes singing, "sha-boom, sha-boom." This is caused by the highly polished grains of rose quartz sliding over the underlying surface of sand, causing vibrations that are felt as much as heard.

Once atop the highest dune, take in the view—the Granite Mountains are to the south, the Providence Mountains to the east, the Kelso Mountains to the north, and the Bristol Mountains to the southwest—and then, when you've finished, surf, slide and somersault your way back to the parking lot, all while being serenaded by the sliding sand…sha-boom, sha-boom.

Midday heat on the dunes can be brutal so try to plan for an early morning or late afternoon visit, when the sun is low, the shadows long, and the colors awesome. Also, on your hike keep an eye out for the more then 100 varieties of plants that live on or near the dunes, as well as sidewinders, kit foxes and other fascinating animals.

Kelso Railroad Depot

Kelso—with her deep, dependable wells that were so vital to the operation of old fashioned steam engines—came into her own in 1906 with the completion of the Los Angeles and Salt Lake Railroad.

Later, during the early 1940's while the Second World War was raging, Kelso's population boomed to about 2,000 souls, but the closing of area mines and the decline of the railroad caused her to bust. Today, Kelso's population stands at about two dozen.

The beautiful Spanish style train depot was built in 1924 and, amazingly, remained open until about 1985, serving meals to hungry visitors driving (the railroad had long ceased passenger service) through the desert. The depot has been renovated for use as the Mojave National Preserve Headquarters and Visitors Center and has museum exhibits, a theater, and bookstore.

Photo credit: National Park Service

To get to the Kelso Depot from Interstate 40 to the south, drive north on Kelbaker Road for about 21-miles to the intersection of Kelbaker Road & Kelso-Cima Road.

From the north, on Interstate 15 in Baker, take Kelbaker Road south for about 34.5-miles to the intersection of Kelbaker Road & Kelso-Cima Road.

You can't miss the depot.

Cinder Cones National Natural Landmark

The 25,600 acres of this awesome, otherworldly place contain 32 colorful, rounded cinder cones (extinct volcanoes), more then 60 flows, and at least one very cool lava tube.

To get to the Cinder Cones National Natural Landmark from Interstate 15, gas up in Baker and then take Kelbaker Road south for about 18-miles to Aiken Mine Road (dirt). Head north (left) on Aiken Mine Road into the Cinder Cones.

From the south, on Interstate 40, take Kelbaker Road north for about 36-miles (15-miles beyond Kelso) to Aiken Mine Road (dirt). Turn right (north) and head into the cinder cone area.

The lava tube, created when lava hardened on the outside and the liquid lava inside drained out, is along Aiken Mine Road, about 5-miles north of its junction with Kelbaker Road. Look for a large, cave-like hole into the earth. Descend a ladder and explore the tube, enjoy the cool air, watch for bats, and enter the great chamber, further down the tube, by stretching out on your belly and wiggling into it.

Be sure to bring your headlamp for this.

Cima Dome

Cima Dome—about 75 miles square and rising more then 1,500 feet above the desert floor—is the single most symmetrical natural dome in the United States. Because the dome is so immense, and its slopes are so gentle, its symmetrical shape is not always apparent from close up, but it can be clearly seen from either the town of Baker, on I-15, or from the northern section of the Mid-Hills Campground. The perfect contour lines on your topographical map also give it away.

The Joshua tree forest atop Cima Dome—said to be the largest and densest in the world—is a great place for photographers to catch the early morning or late afternoon light.

The Teutonia Hike (described below) will take you into this forest.

Teutonia Peak Hike

The trailhead is located on the west side of Cima Road, about 11-miles south of Interstate 15.

This easy trail wanders through the Joshua tree forest, passes an old mining operation, and then climbs a ridge and clambers over some boulders to the summit of the 5,755ft peak. Take in the views, have a snack, and then retrace your steps back to the trailhead.

This is a 4-mile round trip hike with about 600 feet of elevation gain.

Nipton

In 1904, just as the San Pedro, Salt Lake and Los Angeles Railroad was nearing completion, the small hamlet of Nipton sprang to life to serve the needs of the areas miners, railroad workers, and ranchers. A century later life here is very different; there is but a single hotel, a general store, and a campground.

The quaint Hotel Nipton, completed in 1910, today functions as a southwestern-style bed and breakfast, replete with a hot tub. This would be an awesome place to bring your sweetheart, or to hold a spiritual or creative retreat.

Nipton's small campground has picnic tables, fire rings and four RV sites with hook-ups; the Trading Post stocks cold drinks.

From Interstate 15, exit at Wheaton Springs and take Nipton Springs Road east for about 10.5-miles to Nipton.

For more information, contact: Nipton Station, Route #1, PO Box 357, Nipton, CA 92364, or by phone at 760.856.2335.

ADVENTURES OUTSIDE THE PRESERVE

The following interesting sites would make great side trips on the way to, or from, the preserve:

Rainbow Basin National Natural Landmark

Rainbow basin is made up of fascinating sedimentary layers with a wide range of colors: orange, white, pink, green, black, brown, and red. Entombed within these layers are the remains of rhinos, mastodons, camels and 'dog-bears', as well as some of the most well preserved (fossilized) insects in the world.

As you drive the scenic 3-mile long road through the badlands of Rainbow Basin, be sure to stop along the way for a closer look at the geology and fossils—but be aware that their collection is illegal. Leave anything that you may find for others to enjoy too.

Get to Rainbow Basin, from Old Highway 58 in Barstow, by taking the Fort Irwin Road north 5.5-miles to Fossil Bed Road. Go left (northwest) on Fossil Bed Road for about 3-miles to Rainbow Basin National Natural Landmark.

Afton Canyon Natural Area

This eight mile long, 600 foot deep, wonderfully colored chasm has often been described as the Grand Canyon of the Mojave. The usually subterranean Mojave River is forced to the surface here, providing prime habitat for many varieties of plants and animals, including cottonwoods, willows, rabbit bush, egrets, herons, turtles, and frogs.

Afton Canyon has also been called Cave Canyon because of the presence of a large cave once used by pre-historic Native Americans (and later, settlers) traveling the Mojave Trail between the Colorado River and the coast of California.

Get to this wonderful desert canyon, from Interstates 15 & 40 in Barstow, by taking Interstate 15 north for 33-miles to the Afton turnoff. Follow a dirt road southwest for about 3-miles to the Afton Campground & parking area.

Amboy Crater

Get to this cool little volcano, from Barstow, by taking Interstate 40 east for a bit more then 50-miles to the Ludlow exit. Top off your tank here in Ludlow, then take the National Trails Highway (Old Route 66) southeast for 28-miles and turn right (south) on a signed dirt road. Follow this road for a short 0.4-mile to the parking area and trailhead.

From there, follow the well-marked 3-mile round-trip trail as it meanders upward to the rim of the cinder cone, and then check out the great views of the surrounding desert, including some interesting volcanic flows and formations.

Walk around the rim, take it all in and then, when you're finished, retrace your steps to the parking area.

From the Amboy Crater parking area, backtrack 0.4-mile to the National Trails Highway (Old Route 66). If you are headed to the preserve, turn right (east) and stay on the National Trails Highway for approximately 30-miles to the junction of Essex Road. Turn left here (north) and in about 7-miles, or so, you'll hit Interstate 40 again. Continue north on Essex Road to enter the preserve.

If you are headed home, turn left (west) onto the National Trails Highway and backtrack to Interstate 40.

CHAPTER TWELVE

The Joshua Tree National Park Area

Wander through fabulous forests of twisted Joshua trees, diverse cactus gardens, and jumbled boulder piles; Wonder at Native American petroglyphs; Tour an historic ranch house and an ancient Serrano Indian village site; Hike to several hidden oases, a cattle rustlers hideout, a volcanic crater, and an old mine, complete with its massive stamp mill; Take rock climbing lessons and tackle routes with names like, 'Tiers for Fears' and 'Mind Over Splatter'; Explore fantastic sand dunes; Revel at the 100-mile views from 'Inspiration Point'; Be amazed at the beautiful spring wildflowers…and more!

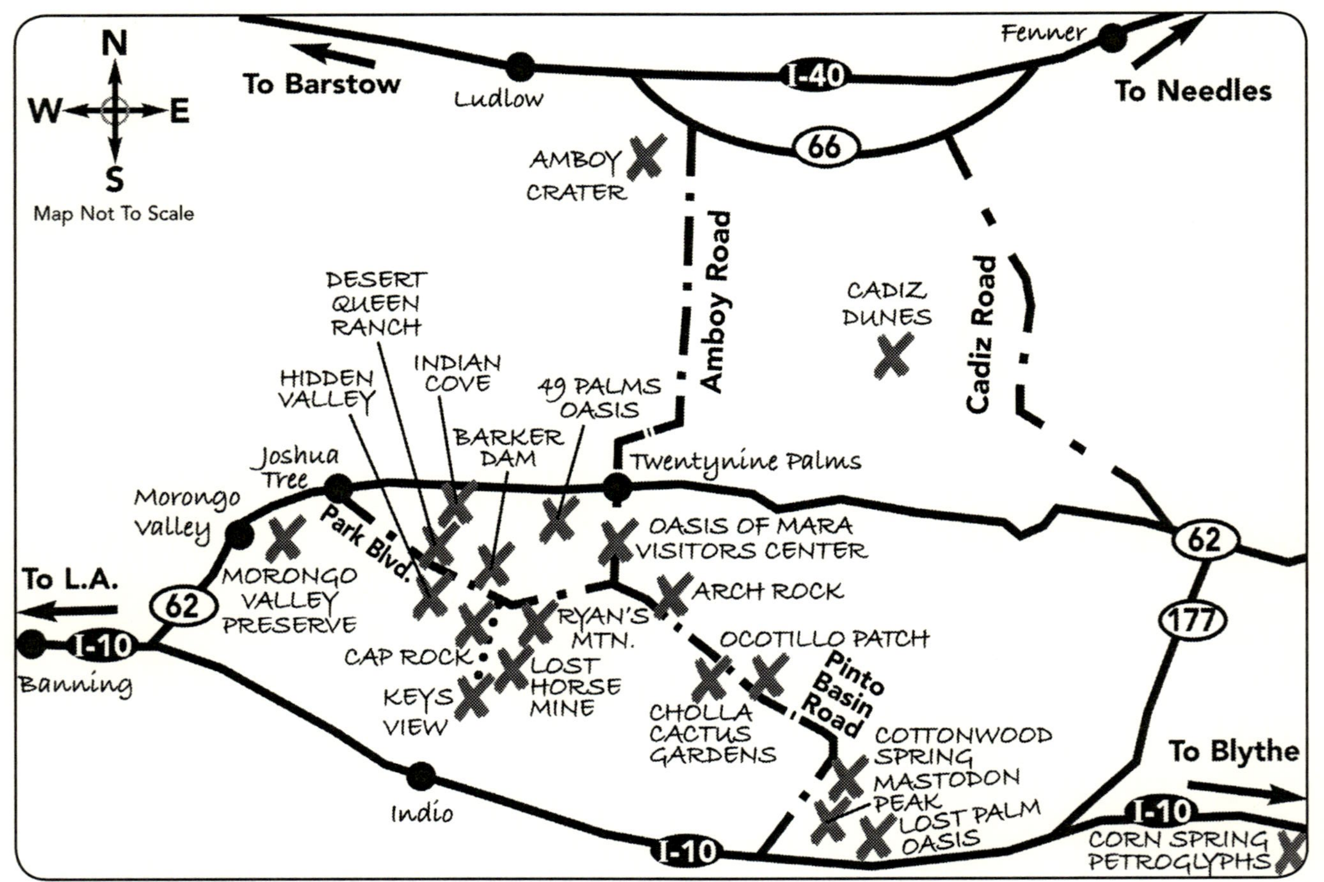

N
E
S
W
Map Not To Scale
To Barstow
Ludlow
I-40
Fenner
To Needles
66
AMBOY CRATER
Amboy Road
CADIZ DUNES
Cadiz Road
DESERT QUEEN RANCH
HIDDEN VALLEY
INDIAN COVE
49 PALMS OASIS
BARKER DAM
Twentynine Palms
Joshua Tree
Morongo valley
Park Blvd.
OASIS OF MARA VISITORS CENTER
To L.A.
62
MORONGO VALLEY PRESERVE
ARCH ROCK
I-10
Banning
CAP ROCK
RYAN'S MTN.
OCOTILLO PATCH
177
KEYS VIEW
LOST HORSE MINE
Pinto Basin Road
CHOLLA CACTUS GARDENS
COTTONWOOD SPRING
MASTODON PEAK
LOST PALM OASIS
To Blythe
Indio
I-10
I-10
CORN SPRING PETROGLYPHS
62

ABOUT THE JOSHUA TREE NATIONAL PARK AREA

The fantastic Joshua Tree National Park encompasses more then 794,000 acres, is home to six distinct mountain ranges, and straddles two separate deserts—the Sonoran and the Mojave.

The Sonoran Desert is lower, hotter and dryer, with summertime temperatures that can reach 120 degrees. The massive Pinto Basin, surrounded by five of the parks six mountain ranges, is in the Sonoran Desert.

The higher desert, the Mojave, is home to Joshua Trees, Pinion Pines, and Junipers. The cooler temperatures and towering boulder piles & formations—known the world over for their more then 5000 rock climbing routes—are a big draw during the spring and fall. The Mojave Desert makes up the western half of the park.

The park, located just northeast of Palm Springs, has fantastic springtime wildflower displays, beautiful palm oases, Native American village & rock art sites, awesome views, cactus gardens, 52 species of mammals, 45 species of reptiles, and 250 species of birds.

It is a beautiful place and you're going to love it.

Getting There

Get to Twentynine Palms entrance station, from the Los Angeles basin, by heading east on Interstate 10 to Hwy 62, about 16-miles east of Banning. Take Hwy 62 northeast for about 43-miles (passing the small towns of Yucca Valley and Joshua Tree) to Utah Trail, which is signed for Joshua Tree National Park. Head south on Utah Trail for about 1-mile to the Oasis Visitors Center and, just beyond, the park entrance.

The southern entrance to the park is through the Cottonwood Spring Entrance Station. Get there by taking Interstate 10 east, 25-miles east of the town of Indio, and exiting at Cottonwood Spring Road. Head north on Cottonwood Spring Road for about 7-miles to the entrance station.

Supplies, Lodging, Maps & Information

Supplies, gas, and motels are available in the towns of Twentynine Palms, Joshua Tree, Yucca Valley, and Indio. Twentynine Palms would probably be the best place to lodge if you intended to stay the night in a motel and explore the park by day. For a listing of area motels contact the Twentynine Palms Chamber of Commerce & Visitors Center by phone at 760.367.3445, or online at www.visit29.org.

The main Visitors Center/Park Headquarters is at the Oasis of Mara, located in Twentynine Palms. The other Visitors Center is located at the Cottonwood Spring entrance, north of Interstate 10 and east of the town of Indio. Both of these centers are goldmines in terms of gathering information and orienting ones-self to the park. They both feature informative displays, stores, restrooms, and running water.

As far as camping goes, there are nine year round campgrounds in the park, six of which are available on a first-come, first-served basis. These campgrounds—allowing two cars, two tents and up to six people per site—fill very early on spring and fall weekends.

The group campsites—Cottonwood, Sheep Pass, and Indian Cove—have a capacity of from 10 to 70 people and can be reserved by calling 800.365.2267.

All of the campgrounds have tables and fire rings but, of course, you'll need to bring your own wood as all of the vegetation within the park is protected. You'll also need to bring plenty of containers to hold your water; it is only available at the Oasis Visitors Center, the Indian Cove Ranger Station, the West Entrance Station, and the Black Rock and Cottonwood Campgrounds.

Primitive backcountry camping is allowed within the park, as long as you are at least 1-mile from any road, 500 feet from any trail, and 0.25-mile from any water source. If you choose this option you'll need to have an overnight permit, which can be self-issued from any one of the 12-backcountry boards placed at trailheads throughout the park.

For more information, contact: Joshua Tree National Park, 74485 National Park Drive, Twentynine Palms, CA 92277, or by phone at 760.367.5500. The following websites have some good information as well: www.nps.gov/jotr or www.joshua-tree.national-park.com.

Joshua Tree: The Complete Guide (Destination Press), would be a handy guide to the park and, as far as maps go, be sure that you have DeLorme's, "Southern & Central California Atlas & Gazetteer", or its equivalent, AAA's "San Bernardino County" map, and a copy of Tom Harrison's "Joshua Tree National Park Recreation Map" (www.tomharrisonmaps.com).

The springtime wildflower show at the park can be so magnificent that a wildflower hotline has been established to let visitors know how the blooms are coming along. Contact the park for the hotline number, and then prepare for a long weekend trip—or a one-day mad dash—to view and photograph these beauties.

Rock Climbing

The park is known the world over for its more then 5000 established rock climbing routes. In fact, climbing actually put Joshua Tree National Park on the map long before President Clinton did.

The following private rock climbing organizations are licensed to guide and teach lessons within Joshua Tree National Park. There are others, too; contact the park for a complete list:

Joshua Tree Rock Climbing School
800.890.4745
www.rockclimbingschool.com
Uprising Adventure Guides
888.CLIMBON
www.uprising.com
Vertical Adventures
800.514.8785
www.vertical-adventures.com

A Note About Directions

All of the directions to the various sites listed below are figured from the park's Oasis Visitors Center, in the town of Twentynine Palms. As always, all mileage is approximate.

The Oasis Of Mara

The Oasis of Mara, located behind the main Visitors Center in Twentynine Palms, was for centuries a home to the Serrano Indians (*Mara* is a Serrano Indian word that means, *"much grass"*). Take a bit of time to learn about the history of this area, and to explore the nature trail that weaves through the Fan Palms.

Fortynine Palms Oasis Dayhike

From the Oasis Visitors Center, head north for 1-mile to Hwy 62 and then take Hwy 62 west for about 5-miles to Canyon Road. Head south on Canyon Road for about 1.8-miles, bearing left where the road forks. The pavement ends at the trailhead for this roughly 3-miles (round trip) hike with about 400 feet of elevation gain.

This ancient, but well maintained, Indian trail weaves around, and up and over a small ridge before reaching a small hidden valley with about, well, 49 palms.

As you explore the oasis you'll notice that many of the palms have been blackened by fire. The reason is this: When the dead fronds (leaves) of palm trees fold downward they form a sort of hula skirt that becomes a haven for bugs, rats, and other parasites. Burning this 'skirt' away makes for a much healthier tree. In fact, area Native Americans used to burn these fronds to prompt the tree to produce a larger crop of fruit.

Watch for birds & Bighorn Sheep, read, pray, journal, have lunch, and enjoy the water and palms of this cool canyon. When you're finished retrace your route to the trailhead.

Arch Rock

This very short loop hike—perhaps 0.3-mile long—starts at the White Tank Campground and meanders past a beautiful 25ft long natural arch.

From the Oasis Visitors Center, drive south on Utah Trail (becoming Park Boulevard) for about 9-miles to the junction with Pinto Basin Road. Bear left (southeast) onto Pinto Basin Road for about 2-miles, or so, to White Tank Campground. Turn left into White Tank Campground, and then bear left until you reach the parking area and the start of the hike near campsite #9.

Cholla Cactus Garden

From the Oasis Visitors Center, drive south on Utah Trail (becoming Park Boulevard when it enters the park) for about 9-miles, to a junction with Pinto Basin Road. Go southeast on Pinto Basin Road for about 9 more miles to the Cholla Cactus Garden. The Garden is on the south (right) side of the road.

Cholla Cacti are fascinating, and very photogenic. Catch this garden in the morning or early evening when it's backlit by low angle light—it is beautiful!

Be sure to grab a brochure either at the Visitors Center or at the start of the 0.3-mile trail that ambles through this awesome place.

The Ocotillo Patch

Continuing on for about 2-miles southeast of the Cholla Cactus Garden, Pinto Basin Road passes through a short sliver of desert sprinkled with tall, spindly plants called Ocotillo. These plants, capable of growing to heights of perhaps 30ft, are masters at conserving energy and appear to be dead for most of the year; as soon as a good rain materializes, however, bright green leaves almost immediately appear. In the spring beautiful little red flowers decorate the tips of the ocotillo's branches.

Mastodon Peak (3,371ft)

From the Ocotillo Patch, continue southeast on Pinto Basin Road for about 20-miles to Cottonwood Spring Ranger Station, Visitors Center & Campground. Turn left (east) and drive about 0.5-mile beyond the campground entrance to the day use parking area. If you have time, stop in at the Visitors Center and check out the interpretive displays, as well as the spring and the ancient Native American bedrock mortars (grinding holes) around the area.

Catch the trail for this hike at the day use parking area, and follow the signs for Lost Palms Oasis and Mastodon Peak. At about 0.5-mile you'll reach a junction, bear left here towards Mastodon Peak, which is about 1-mile further on ahead.

Mastodon Peak takes its name from its resemblance to that prehistoric creature; reach the top from its base by bearing right (east) to the rear of the hill (actually, more of an interesting boulder outcrop), and scrambling over the large boulders to the summit.

After enjoying the views you have two options: Either retrace your steps to the parking area—making this a 3-mile roundtrip hike with about 400ft of elevation gain—or backtrack 1-mile to the main trail and hike to Lost Palms Oasis (described below) for a 9.5-mile round-trip hike.

Lost Palms Oasis Hike

The trailhead for the Lost Palms Oasis Dayhike is the same as for Mastodon Peak, described above. From the parking area, head out on a trail signed for Lost Palms Oasis/Mastodon Peak. You'll reach a junction about 0.5-mile beyond the parking area; bear right here towards Lost Palms Oasis, about 3.75-miles away.

You'll want to have a desert plant identification book with you on this hike; the trail sweeps through a beautiful Sonoran Desert community before swinging past an overlook and descending to the oasis itself. As with all desert oases, keep an eye out for Bighorn Sheep, particularly along the canyon walls.

Enjoy this desert jewel or, if you still feel like walking, continue south beyond Lost Palms Canyon for another 1-mile, or so, to the even more secluded Victory Palms Oasis.

From the parking area, the trail to Lost Palms is about 8.5-miles in length, round trip, with about 450ft of elevation gain. Be sure to bring plenty of water, sunscreen and a hat; this trail is virtually shade-less.

Ryan Mountain Hike

From the Oasis Visitors Center in Twentynine Palms, drive south on Utah Trail (becoming Park Boulevard) for about 9-miles to the junction with Pinto Basin Road. Bear right (west) here, still on Park Boulevard, for about 9 more miles, to the Ryan Mountain trailhead parking area on the south side of the road.

The view from the 5,457ft summit is said to be the best in the park; 360-degrees of wonder take in the Queen Valley, the Wonderland of Rocks, Lost Horse Valley, Pleasant Valley, and the far off peaks of San Gorgonio and San Jacinto.

This well traveled trail heads south from the Ryan Mountain parking area and climbs about 700 vertical feet in a short 1.5-miles (one-way). Enjoy the awesome views, sign the register (you sometimes really have to search for it), and share lunch together. When you're finished retrace your steps back to the trailhead.

Before leaving the parking area, follow the signs to a rock-shelter used for centuries by area Native Americans.

Cap Rock Nature Trail

This very cool handicapped accessible nature trail is a great walk for those who don't want to wander far from the road. Check out the interpretive displays, signs, and the namesake, "Cap Rock."

Get to the Cap Rock parking area from the Ryan Mountain Trailhead by continuing west on Park Boulevard, for a little more than 2-miles, to the junction of Park Boulevard & Keys View Road.

Lost Horse Mine Hike

This hike takes you to the remains of the once prosperous Lost Horse Mine, abandoned when a fault was struck and the gold played out.

Little remains of this operation today but the 10-stamp mill that once processed the ore, a few building foundations, and treeless slopes—the stamp mill's steam driven engines required a lot of fuel! There are also quite a few open shafts, so be careful when you poke around.

The trail—4-miles round-trip with about 500ft of elevation gain—leaves the Lost Horse parking area and follows the abandoned mining road for most of the way. From the 10-stamp mill, follow a short, steep trail to the views from Lost Horse Point and then, after you've explored the area, retrace your route back to the trailhead.

To get to the Lost Horse Mine trailhead from the Cap Rock Nature Trail (Park Boulevard & Keys View Road), head south on Key's View Road for about 2.5-miles and then take the dirt road heading southeast for 1-mile.

Key's View

From the Lost Horse Mine trailhead, backtrack northwest on the dirt road for 1-mile to Key's View Road; turn left (south) here for about 3-miles to Key's View.

The vista from Keys View (5,185ft) is awesome and takes in the Salton Sea, the Coachella Valley, and the San Jacinto, Santa Rosa & San Bernardino Mountains. Look especially for beautiful Mount San Jacinto, the featured peak of Trip Number 8 of this book.

For even more spectacular views than you now behold, head up the steep 1.5-mile round-trip trail that switchbacks northwest from the overlook. This route sort of fades at the first summit (a false one), descends slightly to a westward saddle, and then climbs past the park service's wildlife blind and on up to Inspiration Point (5,575ft) and its fabulous 360-degree views.

Hidden Valley Nature Trail

From Key's Overlook, backtrack north on Key's View Road for about 5-miles to its junction with Park Boulevard & Quail Springs Road; continue north on Quail Springs Road for about 3-more miles to the Hidden Valley Campground. The trail begins to the left of the restrooms in the Hidden Valley parking area.

A 1-mile long loop trail meanders through the interior of this fascinating little valley where, in the 1880's, cattle that were stolen in Arizona were held to allow their new brands to heal before being sold in California.

Barker Dam Petroglyph Hike

From the Hidden Valley Campground, head northeast on the signed Barker Dam Road (dirt), to the Barker Dam Trailhead.

From the parking area, follow the signed trail into the Wonderland of Rock for about 1.1-miles, and then squeeze through a passage, wind through dramatic canyons, and scramble over some boulders to reach Barker Lake. Continuing on, past the man-made dam, you'll come to some brilliantly colored pictographs; in the 1960's a movie crew painted these over the existing, genuine, Native American rock art so that they would better stand out for a picture they were shooting. Look through the paint for the petroglyphs—the true art.

Desert Queen Ranch

This rustic ranch—home to Bill Keys for more then 50 years—has been well preserved and now provides visitors a glimpse of early settler life in this desert.

In order to maintain the historical integrity of this site, and to protect it from vandals, the National Park Service requires visitors to be chaperoned/guided by rangers. The tour is about 1.5 hours in length and includes the layout of the ranch, information about Keys day-to-day activities, a discussion of his equipment (scattered about the property), and a visit to both a Serrano Indian village and an early schoolhouse used by local children.

Contact the park rangers for more information regarding this fantastic tour.

Boy Scout Trail/Wonderland Of Rocks Traverse

This great walk can either be done as a 5.7-mile car shuttle, or an 11.4-mile round trip hike.

To set up the car shuttle, drop off a vehicle(s) at the backcountry board at the Indian Cove Canyon parking/camping area. Get there from the Oasis Visitors Center by driving north for about 1-mile to Hwy 62, and then heading west on Hwy 62 for about 8.5-miles to Indian Cove Road. Turn left (south) on Indian Cove Road for about 1.5-miles to the picnic area and the backcountry board (kiosk).

Leave a vehicle(s) here, then return to Hwy 62 and turn left (west) for about 11-miles to the town of Joshua Tree. In the town of Joshua Tree, turn left (southeast) onto Park Boulevard/Quail Springs Road for about 10.3-miles to the Quail Springs Picnic Area. The Wonderland of Rocks backcountry board (kiosk), the beginning of the hike, is on the north side of Park Boulevard, 0.7-mile east of the Quail Springs Picnic Area.

On foot now, from the Wonderland of Rocks backcountry board head northeast on the Boy Scout Trail (a dirt road) for about 1.4-miles, to the Willow Hole Trail coming in from the right. Take the Willow Hole Trail northeast to where it enters a dry wash, and then continue downhill in this wash, which eventually opens up into a canyon bottom lined with mounds of boulders.

At about 3.5-miles from the trailhead you'll arrive at Willow Hole and, bearing to the right, follow a well-trod path through the willows, then over a low ridge and across a saddle between two piles of boulders. From here, follow the narrow canyon below you; the one that drains Willow Hole.

At about 0.7-mile below Willow Hole, a large canyon comes in from the right; make sure that you stay in the main canyon bottom, which veers north here and descends about 0.3-mile to join with Rattlesnake Canyon.

From Rattlesnake Canyon it's only about 1-mile to the Indian Cove parking area, but there's still a decent amount of scrambling to do; the canyon angles left prior to dropping into Indian Cove, keep to the left to avoid the most difficult navigating.

Once at Indian Cove continue on to the vehicle(s) that you left at the picnic area, or turn around and retrace your steps to the Wonderland of Rocks backcountry board.

This traverse of the Wonderland of Rocks area is a great walk, but it's not a pushover; the later part of this hike requires a fair amount of scrambling, boulder hopping, and route finding. Because of this route finding component, you may want to bring along the USGS topographic map titled, *Indian Cove*. You may also want to pick up a copy of, "*On Foot in Joshua Tree*

National Park" (Patty Furbush). She has a great description of this walk, including a small topo map.

ADVENTURE OUTSIDE THE PARK

The following great adventures are located within a short hop of Joshua Tree National Park:

Big Morongo Canyon Preserve

Big Morongo Canyon, home to a wonderful year-round high desert oasis, was used for centuries by ancient peoples as a stopping place on the journey between the Mojave and Colorado deserts. At least five archaeological sites attesting to this have been identified within the canyon, including fire rings, pottery shards, and mortar holes.

This oasis, one of the ten largest in California, is nationally recognized for its bird watching potential, as more then 235 species have been spotted here. Other animals that inhabit this 4,500-acre preserve include Mule deer, mountain lions, bobcats, raccoons, ringtail cats, and Bighorn Sheep.

Get to the Big Morongo Canyon Preserve from the junction of Interstate 10 & Hwy 62, about 16-miles east of Banning, by driving 11-miles north on Highway 62 to Morongo Valley. Turn right on East Drive (located just beyond the business district) and look for the preserve's entrance station on the left.

Once there, check out the interpretive displays, grab a checklist of canyon birds, and choose a trail to explore. The *Desert Wash*, *Yucca Ridge*, *Willow*, and *Mesquite* trails are shorter; the *Canyon Trail* is the longest. To catch this one, take the main trail out of the parking area, past a Sycamore tree-lined field and some park buildings, to the Mesquite Trail. Stay on the Mesquite Trail for about 0.35-mile to a wooden boardwalk that crosses a spring-fed marsh in an awesome riparian area comprised of willows, cottonwoods, alders, and fan palms.

When you arrive at the junction of the Yucca Ridge & Canyon Trails, turn right onto Canyon Trail—and the oasis at the canyons' mouth. You can continue on this trail for as much as

5.5-more miles (making this about a 12-mile round-trip hike) or, of course, turn back anytime.

For more information, including preserve hours, contact: Big Morongo Canyon Preserve, PO Box 780, Morongo Valley, CA 92256 or by phone at 760.363.7190 or online at: www. bigmorongo.org.

Amboy Crater

To get to this cool extinct volcano, from the Oasis Visitors Center in Twentynine Palms, head north for about 3-miles (crossing Hwy 62) to Amboy Road. Turn right (east) and stay on Amboy Road for about 45-miles (Amboy Road eventually turns north) to the National Trails Highway (Old Route 66). Turn left (west) on the National Trails Highway for about 1.2-miles, and then turn left again (south) onto a signed dirt road. Follow this road for a short 0.4-mile to a dirt parking area.

The 3-mile round-trip walk to the cinder cone begins at the parking area and follows a well-marked trail that meanders to the rim and some great views of the local volcanic action (lava flows, etc.) and the surrounding desert.

Walk around the rim, take it all in and then, when you're finished, retrace your steps to the parking area.

Cadiz Dunes Wilderness

To catch these cool dunes from the Amboy Crater parking area, backtrack to National Trails Hwy (Old Route 66) and turn right (east), where you'll remain for about 13.5-miles to Cadiz Road. Turn right (south) on Cadiz Road which, in about 3.3-miles, jogs east for about 0.8-mile before crossing some railroad tracks and heading south again. At this point the pavement ends, the road becomes graded dirt, and the tracks are on the west side of the road. In another 2-miles, or so, the road re-crosses the tracks (the tracks are on the east now) and then, in about 6.5-more miles, look for a dirt road heading south into the dunes. Follow this road into the dunes for about 2.5-miles to an informal camping area (without facilities).

This 19,300-acres wilderness area is a favorite of photographers, particularly over a full moon or during the springtime when unique desert plants and flowers make a showing.

Learn more about these dunes, and the life they contain, by contacting the BLM for maps, brochures, and information: Bureau of Land Management Needles Field Office, 101 West Spikes Road, Needles, CA 92363, or by phone at 760.326.7000.

Corn Spring Petroglyphs

Get to this cool petroglyph site, from the Cottonwood Spring Entrance Station, by traveling east on Interstate 10 for 32-miles to the Corn Spring exit. At the Corn Spring exit, turn right (south) and catch the frontage road heading east for about 0.6-mile, and then turn right (south) onto the dirt road marked "Corn Spring." Head south for about 7-miles (from the frontage road) to the campground, where a sign just before its entrance marks the petroglyph site.

Though the sign directs you to the panels on the north side of this desert wash, the most elaborate elements are on the south side.

CHAPTER THIRTEEN

The San Jacinto Mountains Area

Ascend nearly a vertical mile in an alpine tram; Take in astounding views over dinner; Hike, backpack, or snowshoe in an alpine world; 'Bag' a beautiful 10,000ft peak; Hike to a desert oasis with wonderful Native American rock art, waterfalls, and possibly, Bighorn Sheep; Journey through a desert preserve; Tackle the "Palms-to-Pines" extreme hike…and more!

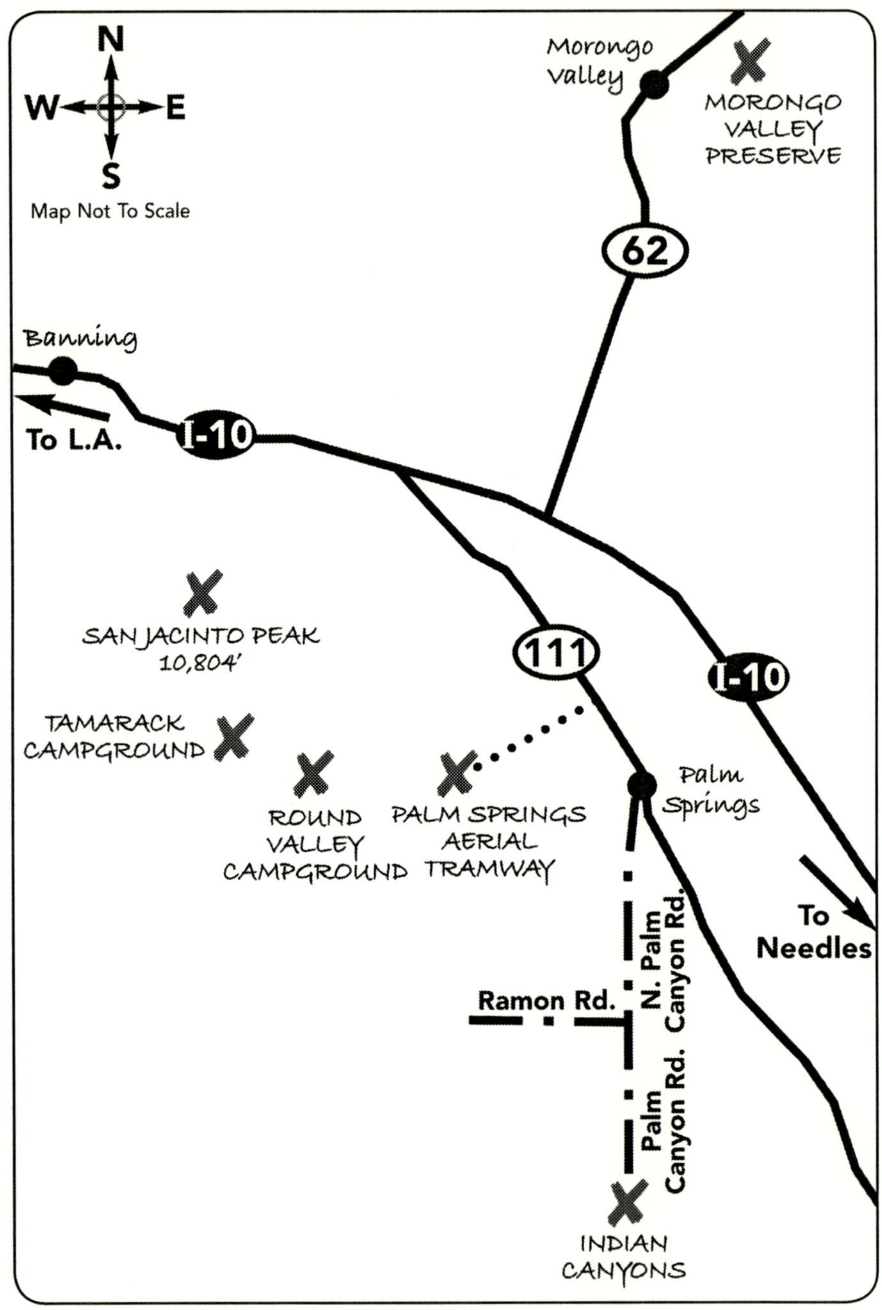

N
W
E
S
Map Not To Scale
Morongo Valley
MORONGO VALLEY PRESERVE
62
Banning
To L.A.
I-10
SAN JACINTO PEAK 10,804'
TAMARACK CAMPGROUND
111
I-10
ROUND VALLEY CAMPGROUND
PALM SPRINGS AERIAL TRAMWAY
Palm Springs
To Needles
Ramon Rd.
N. Palm Canyon Rd.
Palm Canyon Rd.
INDIAN CANYONS

ABOUT THE MOUNT SAN JACINTO AREA

The San Jacinto Mountains area is fantastically diverse; the city of Palm Springs lies in the low desert at the base of the mountains, while almost directly above, shrouded in a pine forest, is the summit of Mount San Jacinto (10,804ft), the second highest point in Southern California.

The 14,000 acre 'Mount San Jacinto State Park' surrounding the peak sits entirely in an alpine setting above 6,000 feet, and is accessed by a gondola that is lifted nearly a vertical mile from the low desert.

Near Palm Springs, along the eastern flank of the San Jacinto Mountains, are desert canyons that are home to three of the largest palm oases in the world, as well as bedrock mortars, rock art, and other fascinating archaeological sites.

There is so much to see here; you're going to have a blast!

Getting There

From Los Angeles, head east on Interstate 10 for about 95-miles to Highway 111 (about 12-miles east of Banning). Take Hwy 111 south for 9-miles to Tramway Road, and then turn right for about 3.8-miles to the parking area at the Palm Springs Aerial Tramway's 'Valley Station'.

Palm Springs Aerial Tramway

This experience is worth the trip alone as the world's largest rotating gondola—swept along on a system of towers and cables—carries you almost a vertical mile in about fourteen minutes. You'll find the nearly 40-degree difference in temperatures between the tram's lower terminus (the Valley Station 2,643ft) and its upper one (the Mountain Station, 8,516ft) to be as exhilarating as the far-reaching views.

Photo Credit: Palm Springs Aerial Tramway

Once at the Mountain Station, check out the gift shop, the snack bar, the State Park Visitors Center, and the restaurant. Walk out the east-facing doors onto the deck to catch panoramic views of the desert and the Salton Sea. Exit through the back door into a world of giant pines, grassy meadows, and fresh air.

Hike to the Desert View overlook, check out the self-guided nature trail, or begin your backpacking trip here. In the evening, sit out on the deck & enjoy a bowl of chili, more than 6,000 feet above the lights of Palm Springs and Palm Desert. It is awesome!

Contact the Palm Springs Aerial Tramway for more information regarding schedules, fees, and special deals: One Tramway Road, Palm Springs, CA 92262, or by phone (toll free) at 888.515.TRAM, or online at www.pstramway.com.

The Palm Springs Aerial Tramway is open 7 days a week, year round, except for the first 10 days or so in August when it's shut down for maintenance.

Supplies, Lodging, Maps & Information

All supplies, gas, and lodging for this trip are available in the Palm Springs area. Although I encourage people to sleep out under the stars whenever possible, a group so desiring could easily base camp at a Palm Springs motel and visit the mountains and the desert oases by day.

For more information about lodging and area sights, contact the Palm Springs Bureau of Tourism: 777 North Palm Canyon Drive, Suite 201, Palm Springs CA, 92262, or by phone at 800.927.7256, or online at: www.palm-springs.org.

With more then 20 million people living within 150-miles of the San Jacinto Mountains, it became necessary, in order to preserve both the land and the wilderness experience, to establish a quota/permit system limiting the number of visitors into the wilderness areas.

There are four designated backpacking campgrounds within the state park/ wilderness area that are sited well away from easily damaged meadows and streams. Two of those four campgrounds are the most suitable for a climb of Mount San Jacinto—Round Valley and Tamarack Valley.

Directions to the Round Valley and Tamarack Valley Campgrounds are as follows: With permit in hand (we'll discuss permits in greater detail in a few moments), take the Palm Springs Aerial Tramway up to the Mountain Station. Go through the back doors of the Mountain Station, and down the paved path for 0.25-miles to the Long Valley Trail (towards Round Valley). At about 0.6-miles the trail crosses a creek and begins climbing, and then at about 1.7-miles you'll come to a junction; bear right here towards Round Valley. At 2-miles you'll pass by a couple of pit toilets and then, in another 0.1-mile, a water spigot (last dependable water) and a junction post. Camping is allowed here in designated areas on the fringe of Round Valley, or 0.5-mile north in Tamarack Valley. For more information regarding camping, recreating, or traveling across state park/state wilderness land, contact: Mount San Jacinto State Park, PO Box 308, Idyllwild, CA 92549, or by phone at

951.659.2607, or on the web at: www.sanjac.statepark.org or, www.parks.ca.gov.

If the Round Valley or Tamarack Campgrounds are full, or if you only wish to backpack into the forest without climbing Mount San Jacinto, look into camping options on the National Forest land surrounding the park. You may have to walk farther, but their overnight requirements are definitely more liberal. For more information regarding camping, recreating or traveling across this national forest land, contact: San Jacinto District Office, USDA Forest Service, 54270 Pinecrest, PO Box 518, Idyllwild, CA 92349, or by phone at 909.382.2921.

For the trips in this chapter you'll need to have DeLorme's, "Southern & Central California Atlas & Gazetteer", or its equivalent, a copy of the Forest Service map titled, "A Guide to the San Jacinto Wilderness", or its equivalent (to help make sense of the various bureaucratic boundaries), and Tom Harrison's great map titled, "San Jacinto Wilderness" (www.tomharrison-maps.com).

Permits

In order to insure the preservation of the natural environment, and to assure the visitor a quality wilderness experience, the state and the Forest Service have both instituted wilderness permit systems for the San Jacinto Mountains Wilderness area;

everyone entering, whether for one day or several, is required to have a permit in their possession.

A permit is *not* necessary, however, if you only plan to visit the Mountain Station or hike the Desert View Trail.

Dayhiking: If you plan to visit the mountain during the day but intend to sleep elsewhere, perhaps in Palm Springs or Idyllwild, you can issue yourself a wilderness permit at the Long Valley Ranger Station. This is what you would do, say, if you wanted to ride the tram up early in the morning, climb Mount San Jacinto, and then take the tram back down in the evening, after a great post-hike dinner at the Mountain Station.

First, get to the Long Valley Ranger Station by taking the Palm Springs Aerial Tramway to the Mountain Station. Exit through the rear doors of the Mountain Station and take the paved path 0.25-miles to the ranger station. Find the self-issue permits and follow the instructions, making sure to leave one copy for the rangers while retaining the other copy in your possession. This permit is only good for the issuing day, if you return the following day you'll need to issue yourself another permit.

Remember, these self-issue permits are *NOT* valid for overnight stays in the forest.

Backpacking: If your group wants to sleep among the pines and under the stars you'll need to apply for an overnight permit, which can be done up to 8 weeks in advance by contacting Mount San Jacinto State Park at the above address. If you mail in your request (the best way), be sure to send it in at least 10 days in advance, try to have alternative dates in case your primary dates are unavailable, and be aware that groups are limited to 15 persons within the wilderness area.

In the summertime, wilderness area campgrounds are often booked solid as early as four weeks in advance, so be sure to get your reservation in as soon as possible.

San Jacinto State Park & Wilderness Area

The 14,000-acre Mount San Jacinto State Park, sitting entirely above 6,000ft, is home to granite peaks, pine forests, high mountain meadows, and Mount San Jacinto, which at 10,804ft is the second highest summit in Southern California.

The northeast face of this mountain drops 9,000ft in less then four miles, making it one of the steepest and most spectacular ranges in North America. Famed conservationist John Muir, upon witnessing a sunrise from the summit of Mount San Jacinto, was inspired to write, "The view from San Jacinto is the most sublime spectacle to be found anywhere on this earth." This magnificent view, when not marred by smog and haze, extends from the Channel Islands to the mountains of Northern Baja.

As previously mentioned, a wilderness permit is necessary for travel and camping in the wilderness area.

Desert View Trail

This easy walk takes you to wonderful views of Palm Springs, the Salton Sea, and the surrounding desert—more then 6,000 vertical feet below!

Catch this 2-mile round trip trail by following the paved path downhill from the rear of the Mountain Station, and then turning left at the bottom of the ramp onto the trail signed, "Nature Trail." This trail eventually joins the Desert View Trail, which you'll follow to the 270-degree vista.

'Bagging' Mount San Jacinto

Tall pines, crisp air and amazing views make a climb of Mount San Jacinto an absolutely unforgettable endeavor.

From the ranger station, with permit in hand, head right on the Long Valley Trail towards Round Valley. At about 0.6-miles the trail crosses a creek and begins climbing. At about 1.7-miles you'll come to a junction; bear right here, towards Round Valley. At 2-miles you'll pass by a couple of pit toilets and then, in another 0.1-mile, a water spigot (last dependable water) and a junction post. Camp here in designated areas on the fringe of Round Valley or 0.5-mile north in Tamarack Valley.

From Round Valley, climb for about 1-mile to Wellmans Divide, then head right (north) to a saddle just south of the summit and angle right towards the peak. Pass a historic stone hut and then scramble from boulder to boulder to the summit block itself at 10,804ft.

Enjoy the views, snap a few photos, sign the register, and share lunch. Look to the northwest for Mount San Gorgonio (Old Greyback), which at 11,500ft is the highest point in Southern California; further west, probably poking out of the haze, is Mount Baldy (10,064ft). These are both great walks, too.

When you're ready, retrace your steps to your campground, or continue on to the Mountain Station to complete this roughly 12-mile round-trip, 2,600ft of elevation gain, hike.

Winter Activities

The San Jacinto Mountains are a fantastic winter wonderland. You can snowshoe, Nordic-ski & snow camp here, the restaurant is open year round with chili and hot chocolate to cap a day (or days) spent in the snow, and you don't have to mess with putting chains on your tires; simply drive to the desert station parking area, step into the tram and emerge, fourteen minutes later, into a world at least 40-degrees colder than the one you left. It's a wonderful way to enjoy the snow.

The Palms-To-Pines Extreme Hike

This hike, also known as the Cactus-to-Clouds Strut, is extremely challenging, potentially very dangerous, and only suitable for a very strong and very capable group. If, for example, you only climb the shortest route, just to the Mountain Station, you still will have climbed nearly 8,000 vertical feet in about 9-miles. The longer route, to the summit of Mount San Jacinto and then back to the Mountain Station for the ride down, will require you to climb more than 10,600 vertical feet in about 20-miles! This is not an easy walk.

To prepare for this walk you'll want to train as a group on hikes that will take you above 9,000ft, with at least 4,000-5,000ft of accumulated elevation gain. Mount Baldy and Mount San Gorgonio, located in the nearby Angeles and San Bernardino National Forests, are great for this type of work out; check your local outdoor store for guidebooks & maps to these mountains.

You'll also want to take into consideration the time of year you'll be doing this walk; because the trailhead is in the low desert and the highpoint is in an alpine forest you'll experience an extremely wide range of temperatures. For this reason the best times to attempt this walk, to avoid contending with blazing heat, ice, or snow, is during the months of April-May or October-early November.

Also, because it can be very cold here overnight, you'll want to be sure that you plan your trip so that you make it to the Mountain Station before the last tram departs for the evening. One way to accomplish this, while also avoiding the desert heat of the lower elevations, is to get a pre-dawn start. I once started out from here at midnight and walked by the light of a beautiful full moon.

Finally, be sure to carry your Ten Essentials and more water then you think you'll need—there is no dependable water at all on the first leg of this route.

Get to the trailhead by taking Interstate 10 to Hwy 111, about 12-miles east of Banning, and then heading south on Highway 111 into Palm Springs, where it becomes Palm Canyon Road. Stay on Palm Canyon Road, through downtown Palm Springs, to Ramon Road. Turn right on Ramon Road to the end of the street; parking can be found in the surrounding residential neighborhood.

From the very end of Ramon Road, follow a dirt road north to an intersection about 1-mile away. Many spaghetti-like trails thread through this area, but the intersection that you seek has a boulder spray painted with words advising that Long Valley is 8-miles away. This very good route really begins climbing at this point, and in a very short while you'll reach a sign that states, in part:

"CAUTION! Before continuing further, please consider your preparedness for undertaking this hike. There have been fatalities & many rescues of injured & lost persons attempting to complete this extremely difficult route! Don't be next! Know your limitations! Be prepared!"

Continue scrambling up the trail, from the low desert through the high desert and eventually into pine and fir zones; every step taking you higher and unfolding a more and more fabulous panorama of the city of Palm Springs and the surrounding desert.

About 5-miles from Ramon Road the trail begins to thread through Manzanita chaparral—make sure that you don't lose the route here, you must be on it to negotiate the coming terrain—and then, at about 6-miles (close to 5,800ft), you'll cross a shallow ravine, pass under some nice oak trees, and begin climbing a ridge.

At about 7,600ft the trail veers from the ridge and traverses several steep, deeply shaded gullies where ice or hard packed snow can be a serious threat in the late winter & early spring;

if necessary, be sure that you have an ice ax, crampons, and proper training in their use.

From this point the trail nears a large rock outcropping, then veers sharply left (southwest) and switchbacks almost straight up to the lip of Long Meadow/Long Valley. The Mountain Station is to the right, through the trees, but you'll have to go left and around the hill to get there.

If the Mountain Station is as far as you plan to go…congratulations! You just climbed about 8,000ft in a mere 9-miles. Celebrate over a bowl of chili and a glass of lemonade, and then take the tram down the hill and a cab back to your vehicle(s).

If you're continuing on to the summit of Mount San Jacinto, fill up your water bottles here in Long Valley, issue yourself a wilderness permit at the ranger station, and follow the above directions to the summit about 12 round-trip miles away.

Oh, and don't forget that you need to make it back to the Mountain Station before the last tram departs…or be prepared for a very cold night on the mountain.

The Waterfalls & Bighorn Sheep Of Indian Canyons

Home to the first (Palm Canyon), second (Andreas Canyon) and fourth (Murray Canyon) largest California Fan Palm oases in the world, and inhabited for centuries by the Cahuilla (Kaw-we-ah) Indians, these canyons are, today, fantastic places to explore, to swim in, to photograph, and to be fascinated by.

Get to the Indian Canyons, from Los Angeles, by heading east on Interstate 10 to Highway 111, about 12-miles east of Banning. Take Hwy 111 south to Palm Springs where it eventually becomes Palm Canyon Drive (through town) and then changes again to South Palm Canyon Drive. Remain on South Palm Canyon Drive for about 3 more miles to the Indian Canyons entrance station.

After entering the reservation, drive for a couple of hundred yards to the first junction, and then turn right to the Andreas Canyon parking area, noting as you do so the prominent ridge of rock adjacent to the northeast corner; it has many fine petroglyphs (engravings) scattered about it. Signs warn against climbing on the rocks themselves, but no worries, several fine elements are visible from ground level.

After you have checked out the rock art, explore the canyon for a short distance upstream; there are bedrock mortars and metates along the creek, as well as interpretive signs loaded with cultural information. When you reach the fence, about 0.25-mile from the parking area, cross the creek and return from the other side.

When you have returned to the parking lot, follow the signs south to the picnic area, located between Murray and Andreas Canyons, where you'll find another sign marked, "Murray Canyon, 20 minutes." The 20 minutes that this sign refers to will get you to the first of the palms, but the good stuff—the waterfalls and dramatic scenery—are somewhat further up the canyon.

This well-marked trail leads you into a canyon with a small stream that flows heavier and heavier as you advance into the canyon. As you continue to walk, the growth of palms (nearly 1,000 in this canyon), willows, and reeds grow denser too. Check out the fantastic formations of red rock, the thousands of Barrel Cacti and, potentially, the Peninsula Bighorn Sheep that make this area home.

You'll soon come to the first waterfall, actually a cascade; the second is a few hundred yards beyond. Both falls have nice pools where you can picnic, swim, and nap. When you're ready, retrace your steps to the parking area; the round trip mileage for both of these hikes, as described, is about 5.1-miles.

There is an entrance fee for the Indian Canyons, as well as limited operating hours during the summer. For more information regarding other canyons, the trading post or visitation times, contact the Agua Caliente Band of Cahuilla Indians/Indian Canyons at 800.790.3398 or 760.325.3400.

Big Morongo Canyon Preserve

Big Morongo Canyon contains a wonderful year round high desert oasis with fire rings, pottery shards & mortar holes that attest to its use by ancient cultures.

This canyon, home to one of the ten largest desert oases in California, is nationally recognized for its bird watching potential; more then 235 species have been spotted here. Other animals that inhabit this 4,500-acre preserve include Mule deer, mountain lions, bobcats, raccoons and ringtail cats. During the summer months look for Bighorn Sheep in the cooler hours of dawn and dusk.

From the parking lot, check out the interpretive displays, grab a checklist of canyon birds, and choose a trail to explore. *Desert Wash, Yucca Ridge, Willow* and *Mesquite* trails are shorter, while the *Canyon Trail* is the longest. To catch this one take the main trail out of the parking area, past a field lined by Sycamore trees and some park buildings, to the Mesquite Trail, which you'll stay on for 0.35-miles to a wooden boardwalk crossing a spring-fed marsh and meandering through an awesome riparian area.

At the junction of Yucca Ridge & Canyon Trails, turn right onto the Canyon Trail and the oasis at the canyon's mouth. The route extends for as much as 5.5-miles more miles, making this about a 12-mile (round trip) hike. Walk as far as you want and turn back anytime.

Get to the preserve, from the Los Angeles area by heading east on Interstate 10 to Highway 62, about 16-miles east of Banning, and then driving 11-miles north on Highway 62 to Morongo Valley. Turn right on East Drive and look for the preserve's entrance station on the left.

For more information, including preserve hours, contact: Big Morongo Canyon Preserve, PO Box 780, Morongo Valley, CA 92256, or by phone at 760.363.7190, or online at <u>www.bigmorongo.org</u>.

CHAPTER FOURTEEN

The Anza-Borrego Desert State Park Area

Wander through awesome badlands; Rest under an elephant tree; Hike to several native palm oases & waterfalls; Be amazed at awesome wildflower displays; Explore Native American rock art, village sites, and 'fish traps'; Search for Bighorn Sheep; Squeeze through a slot canyon; Prowl wind eroded caves; Stand atop an ancient oyster bed; Soak your cares away in a hot spring; Search for wildlife at a fresh-water marsh; Enjoy a piece of the best apple pie you'll ever eat; Swim in the Salton Sea…and more!

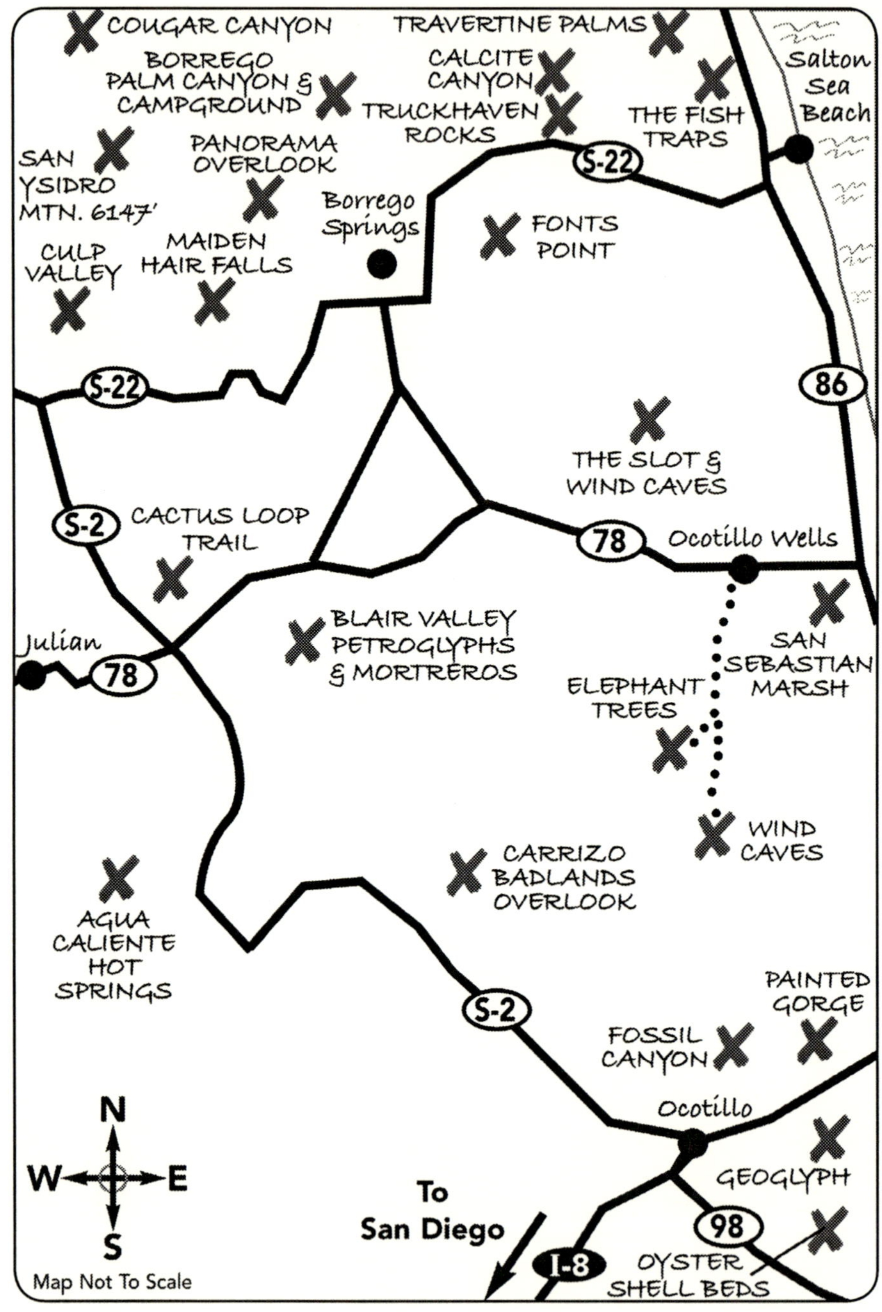
COUGAR CANYON
TRAVERTINE PALMS
BORREGO PALM CANYON & CAMPGROUND
CALCITE CANYON
Salton Sea Beach
TRUCKHAVEN ROCKS
THE FISH TRAPS
SAN YSIDRO MTN. 6147'
PANORAMA OVERLOOK
S-22
Borrego Springs
FONTS POINT
CULP VALLEY
MAIDEN HAIR FALLS
S-22
86
THE SLOT & WIND CAVES
S-2
CACTUS LOOP TRAIL
78
Ocotillo Wells
Julian
78
BLAIR VALLEY PETROGLYPHS & MORTREROS
SAN SEBASTIAN MARSH
ELEPHANT TREES
WIND CAVES
CARRIZO BADLANDS OVERLOOK
AGUA CALIENTE HOT SPRINGS
PAINTED GORGE
S-2
FOSSIL CANYON
N
W   E
S
Ocotillo
To San Diego
GEOGLYPH
98
I-8
OYSTER SHELL BEDS
Map Not To Scale

ABOUT THE ANZA-BORREGO DESERT AREA

Anza-Borrego Desert State Park—named for Anza, the explorer who traversed the area in 1774, and Borrego, the Spanish name for Bighorn Sheep—is, at more than 600,000 acres, the largest state park in the lower 48 states. With elevations that range from a mere 15-feet above sea level to more than 6,000ft above, this great park encompasses rugged canyons, sculpted badlands, high mountains ranges, 25 beautiful palm oases, several year-round streams, and phenomenal springtime wildflower displays.

Native life within the park includes the pygmy palm, the elephant tree, 22 species of cacti, more then 60 species of mammals (including about 300 Peninsular Bighorn Sheep), 270 types of birds, somewhere around 60 species of reptiles and, for centuries, man. Evidence of ancient peoples abounds in the form of village sites, pictographs, grinding holes, and fascinating geoglyphs.

Anza-Borrego Desert State Park is a place of great beauty and solitude. You're going to have a great time here!

Getting There

Get to Anza-Borrego Desert State Park, in eastern San Diego County, from the Los Angeles area, by traveling south on Interstate 15 to Temecula. In Temecula, take the Highway 79 exit south towards Indio/Warner Springs. About 5-miles beyond Warner Springs, turn left onto Highway S-2 and then, in another 5-miles, turn left onto Highway S-22 (signed for Anza-Borrego Desert State Park). Pass through the small town of Ranchita and descend a very steep, 12-mile grade. At the stop sign (Palm Canyon Drive) turn left to the Park Headquarters/Visitors Center and Borrego Palm Canyon Campground.

Get to the Anza-Borrego Desert State Park, from the San Diego area, by traveling east on Interstate 8 to Highway 79. Take Highway 79 north, about 18-miles beyond Julian, to Highway S-2; turn right onto Hwy S-2 and then, in 5-miles, turn left onto Highway S-22 (signed for Anza-Borrego Desert State Park). Pass through the small town of Ranchita and descend the very steep, 12-mile grade. At the stop sign (Palm Canyon Drive) turn left to the Park Headquarters/Visitors Center and Borrego Palm Canyon Campground.

The parks primary Visitors Center is located about 2-miles west of downtown Borrego Springs, at the west end of Palm Canyon Drive, just off of Highway S-22.

Lodging, Supplies, Maps & Information

Lodging (hotels, motels, and resorts), restaurants, supplies and gasoline are available in the small town of Borrego Springs, an island of private land in the middle of the park. Contact the Borrego Springs Chamber of Commerce for more information: PO Box 420, Borrego Springs, CA 92004, by phone at 800.559.5524, or online at www.borregosprings. org. Limited supplies are also available in the towns of Julian, Ocotillo Wells, and Ocotillo.

The three developed campgrounds in the park are *Borrego Palm Canyon*, *Tamarisk Grove*, and *The Vern Whitaker Equestrian Campground*.

Borrego Palm Canyon Campground has 65 tent sites, 52 RV sites, and 5 group sites that can accommodate up to 24 people per site. The campground has flush toilets, showers, drinking water, and fire rings and is located near the Visitors Center, 2.5-miles west of Borrego Springs, on the west end of Palm Canyon Drive.

Tamarisk Grove Campground has 27 sites with flush toilets, showers, drinking water, and fire rings as well as a kiosk with maps, brochures and park information. Get to the Tamarisk Grove Campground, from Borrego Springs, by traveling south on Borrego Springs Road for about 5.5-miles, to County Road S-3. Turn right (south) on County Road S-3 for somewhere around 6-miles; Tamarisk Grove Campground is on the right, just before Highway 78.

The Vern Whitaker Equestrian Campground has 10 developed sites, flush toilets, solar heated showers, and fire rings. This campground, complete with corrals, is for campers with horses only. The Vern Whitaker Equestrian Campground is located 8-miles north of Borrego Springs, off Borrego Springs Road.

Make your reservations for one of these three campgrounds by contacting Reserve America at 800.444.7275 or www.reserveusa.com. Note: The group sites at Borrego Palm Canyon require six months advance reservations.

There are several other, much more primitive, campgrounds in the park. These are undeveloped, first come, first served with tables, chemical toilets and, occasionally, fire rings, but no running water or showers. Backcountry camping is also available with the purchase of a very inexpensive day permit. Check with the park staff for more information regarding primitive campsites or backcountry permits & regulations.

Partially buried under a native garden, the park's impressive Visitors Center offers a museum, video programs, a bookstore, current road & trail conditions and knowledgeable staff to answer all of your questions. Just outside the doors is a short (0.6-mile), self-guided, nature trail that meanders through a cactus garden and past a pupfish pond.

The Visitors Center is open every day from October through May—when daytime highs are in the 70's and 80's—but is only staffed on weekends and holidays from June to September, when temperatures can reach as much as 125-degrees! For park information contact: Anza-Borrego Desert State Park, 200 Palm Canyon Drive, Borrego Springs, CA 92004, or by phone at 760.767.5311, or via the web at: www.anzaborrego.statepark.org.

As far as maps go, I recommend, of course, Delorme's Southern & Central Atlas & Gazetteer, as well as Tom Harrison's "San Diego Backcountry" map (www.tomharrisonmaps.com). The American Automobile Association's, "San Diego County" and "Imperial County" maps would be good to have, too.

I also highly recommend the book, "*The Anza-Borrego Desert Region: A Guide to the State Park and Adjacent Areas of the Western Colorado Desert*" (Lowell & Diana Lindsay); it's jam packed full of great area adventures and natural history.

Wildflowers

Although certain factors (wind, rain, temperatures, etc.) influence the outcome, the spring wildflower show at Anza-Borrego is usually amazing. So amazing, in fact, that the park has set up a wildflower hotline and a post card notification system to keep you abreast of the peak blooming times.

To be notified by mail of the status of the wildflower season, send a self-addressed stamped postcard to: Anza-Borrego Desert State Park, 200 Palm Canyon Drive, Borrego Springs, CA 92004. The post card will be sent back to you about two weeks prior to the predicted peak of the blooming season…usually sometime in March.

For current wildflower information, call the hotline at: 760.767.4684.

Town of Julian

Located just outside the park, beautiful little Julian sits at 4,000ft, high above the worst of the desert heat. This former mining town is graced with historic storefronts and boardwalks, and is surrounded by oaks, pines, and apple trees. That's right, apple trees. This environment seems to be perfect for growing apples, and the people of Julian do it famously. In fact, during the month of October more then 10,000 apple pies a week are baked here.

Get to Julian, from Borrego Springs, by heading south on Borrego Springs Road to Highway S-3. Turn right (south) on Highway S-3 (Yaqui Pass Road) and stay on it for about 7-miles to Highway 78. Head west on highway 78, climbing the Banner Grade, for about 18-miles to the town of Julian.

For more information about Julian, its sweet apple pies, or its variety of lodging options, contact: Julian Chamber of Commerce, P.O. Box 1866, Julian, CA, 92036, or by phone at 760.765.1857.

The Adventures

In an attempt to make sense of the many, many cool things to do in this huge park, I've organized them as follows:

The adventures under the heading, *Journey #1* are grouped, more or less, around the Borrego Palm Canyon Campground. *Journey #2* generally follows Highway S-22 east from the town of Borrego Springs to the Salton Sea.

Journey #3 follows Borrego Springs Road south, from the town of Borrego Springs, and then southeast on Highway 78

towards the Salton Sea. *Journey #4* heads generally south out of Borrego Springs, and then southeast on Highway S-2 to the town of Ocotillo, Interstate 8, and beyond.

Make sense? Here we go…

JOURNEY #1

The Culp Valley Overlook, Morteros & Spring

To get to Culp Valley, from Borrego Springs, head west on Highway S-22 (Montezuma Valley Road) for about 8-miles, and then turn right onto the dirt road to the Culp Valley Primitive Campground. This dirt road forks just past the entrance station; the left fork heads to Pena Spring, the right fork enters the campground. To get to Pena Spring, take the left fork of the dirt road for about 0.5-mile and park in the lot.

On foot now, head east on the access road for another 0.5-mile, crossing the California Riding & Hiking Trail, and then descending slightly to an area of obvious ground water; the spring is on the left, at the end of a short path that winds through thick brush. The water flowing from this raised pipe is clear, cold, and life giving to the area animals and the flowers that thrive in the soggy soil. It also once gave life to the Native Americans that called this place home; look for morteros in the bedrock around the spring.

After you've explored the area around the spring, hop back in your car, and head over to the overlook by bearing right at the fork of the entrance road, towards the primitive camping area. On foot, take the short 0.5-mile long trail heading north to the junction with the California Riding and Hiking Trail and then, from this junction, make your way out to the rock outcrop about 100 feet to the north—the views of Hellhole Canyon, Borrego Valley, and the Santa Rosa Mountains are fantastic.

Note: The Culp Valley Primitive Campground (3,400ft) is the highest in the park, with temperatures that are consistently 10 to 15 degrees cooler then on the valley floor; this makes it a great place to stay during the warmer months.

Maidenhair Falls Hike

This is a great 4.6-mile round trip hike across an alluvial fan, and through a narrow canyon, to a wonderful 25-foot high desert waterfall.

Catch this trail, from Borrego Springs, by traveling south on Montezuma Highway, from Palm Canyon Drive, for about 0.7-mile. The parking area/trailhead is on the right (west) side of Montezuma Highway.

Heading west-southwest, on foot now, the first 1.2 miles of the trail crosses Hellhole Canyon's large alluvial fan before entering the canyon itself. Thread your way over and around boulders, fallen trees, and dense vegetation while passing Cottonwoods, Sycamores, and a few palms. About 200 yards or so beyond an especially heavy grove of palms, where the canyon walls close in tight, look for the 25-foot high Maidenhair Falls tucked into a small grotto.

When you find it, take a cooling soak, wonder at the amazingly diverse plant life (including the falls namesake plant, the Maidenhair Fern), enjoy your lunch, and thank our God for such beautiful places.

When you're finished retrace your route to the trailhead.

Borrego Palm Canyon Hike

This, the most popular walk in the park, is a fairly easy 3.5-mile loop hike to a wonderful spring-fed stream, hundreds of California Fan Palms and, perhaps, Peninsula Bighorn Sheep and other wildlife. Catch this trail in the Borrego Palm Canyon Campground, at the pupfish pond located at the northwest end of the picnic area.

The trail heads out through a beautiful desert garden and then, at about 1.3-miles, enters the narrow canyon and the shade of more then 800 Fan Palms (Borrego Canyon is one of the largest palm oases in the United States). Continuing up the canyon for another short 0.2-mile will bring you to the grotto and a 15-foot waterfall.

Soak your feet in the clear pool at the base of the waterfall, listen to the desert wind rustle the palm fronds, look for beautifully colored hummingbirds and, if you feel up to it, take the short, steep path above the falls to a great overlook. There is also great adventure in journeying above this waterfall, but it requires route finding skills, a lot of boulder hopping, and the ability to identify & dodge poison oak and various types of thorny plant life.

After you've enjoyed the shade, scenery and the falls, backtrack to the second bridge that you crossed on the way in. Here you have the option of either continuing to retrace your route to the trailhead or taking the trail that climbs slightly to the west. This higher route back to the parking area is 0.5-mile longer, but it comes with great views.

Be sure to grab an interpretive brochure before setting off—you'll want to be able to identify the fascinating plant-life along the way.

Panorama Overlook Hike

The trail for this 1.4-mile (round trip) hike begins at the Borrego-Palm Canyon Campground, near campsite #71. The route traverses the hillside for about 0.4-mile to a sign marked, "Overlook Trail", and then switchbacks steeply up the slope for about 0.3-mile to an open ridge and the overlook itself.

Use your map to identify San Ysidro Peak, Borrego Valley, Borrego Palm Canyon, the Borrego Badlands, and the Vallecito & Santa Rosa Mountain ranges.

For an even greater view, head west on the ridge for another 0.6-miles where, after some scrambling and route finding, you'll come to a rocky ledge with several flat spots; rest here and take in the amazing panorama.

Don't forget to bring your binoculars on this one; you'll want to use them to pick out landmarks and to scan the mountains for Bighorn Sheep.

San Ysidro Mountain Hike

This extremely challenging hike has more then 4,400ft of elevation gain in a short 3.5-miles (one-way). That would be difficult enough if the elevation gain were spread out evenly over the length of the hike, but it's not. In fact, one section of this route has a gradient of more than 3,000 feet for one rugged, trail-less, boulder strewn mile. This is definitely a hike for the *strong and prepared.*

The first 0.7-mile of this hike follows the same route as the Panorama Overlook Trail; catch the trail at campsite #71 of the Borrego-Palm Canyon Campground, and follow it as it first traverses the hillside for about 0.4-mile to an, "Overlook Trail" sign, and then switchbacks steeply up the slope for about 0.3-mile to an open ridge and the overlook itself.

From this point, continue up the ridge on a narrow trail that gets less and less defined until it eventually disappears altogether. When this happens continue slugging up the ridge, eventually passing a relatively flat area beyond which the ridge really gets steep, the brush gets thick and large boulders hinder forward progress; the summit is about 2,000 feet above that flat, high in the Pinyon Pines at 6,147ft.

Enjoy the awesome views and your conquest of this mountain, find and sign the register, take photos, and share lunch together. When you're ready, retrace your route back down the mountain, while taking extra care in navigating your descent. You have got to be sure and stay on the main ridge as you descend; if you lose the "trail" (easy to do) and get off route you may hit the desert far from where you wanted to come out. Be sure to take your time, too, and control your descent—this steep, rocky, heavily vegetated slope is the perfect environment in which to twist an ankle or knee.

This hike is about 7-miles round trip, but plan on taking most of a day to do it. Plan, also, to carry more water then you think you'll need and to stay hydrated. This is a dry route—there is absolutely no water at all—and you'll be working really, really, really hard to earn this peak.

Finally, this can be a great overnight backpack—there are several potential campsites on the summit—just be sure to carry the extra water that you'll need.

Cougar Canyon Hike

This fun hike follows a year-round creek to a wonderful pool at the base of a 20-foot waterfall.

Get to the trailhead for this hike, from the intersection of Palm Canyon Road and Borrego Springs Road (Christmas Circle, in Borrego Springs) by heading east on Palm Canyon Road for about 0.5-mile to DiGiorgio Road. Turn left (north) onto DiGiorgio Road for about 4.8-miles to the end of the pavement.

Continue on the unpaved road, crossing the usually dry Coyote Creek wash, and head northwest along the foot of Coyote Mountain. At about 3.8-miles from the end of the pavement you'll re-cross the now wet Coyote Creek; you can park in this area if you'd like, or continue on to the next crossing about 1-mile further on—about the limit of two-wheel drive vehicles. The mileage for our hike will be figured from this point, the third crossing.

Park your vehicle, grab your gear & maps, and cross the creek heading southwest on the Lower Willows bypass trail. Over the next 1-mile you will climb a divide, descend into Colins Valley, and eventually (1.8-miles) arrive at a short spur trail coming in from the right (northeast), which leads to Santa Catarina Spring about 0.5-mile away.

Santa Catarina, at several acres in size, is the largest single natural spring in San Diego County, a primary source for perennial Coyote Creek, and home to the largest Cahuilla Indian archaeological site in the park. Take some time to explore it, if you can.

Back on the main trail, continue for about 0.2-mile (2-miles from the start) to a junction at the mouth of Sheep Canyon.

From here, head south on the trail that follows the west side of Indian Canyon for about 0.8-miles, and a couple of creek crossings, to a point just a bit south of the mouth of Cougar Canyon (At this junction look for a cave, presumed to have been an ancient Cahuilla Indian sweathouse, to the north, on a bench overlooking the creek).

From this point, catch the dim path that heads west into Cougar Canyon, crossing and re-crossing the creek, and passing another cave, a palm grove, and a small cascade. As you progress through Cougar Canyon, the path will become less defined and the canyon walls will continue to close in until, about 3.5-miles from the trailhead, you'll come to a rock wall that impedes further progress up the canyon.

At this point you may have to use the limbs of a nearby cottonwood tree to climb up and over the rock wall and into a grotto concealing a beautiful deep pool at the base of a wonderful 20-foot waterfall.

Enjoy this spot; soak your feet, eat your lunch, share some good fellowship, read a few pages of a good book, and reflect on the Lords goodness. When you're finished, retrace your steps to the trailhead.

This hike is about 7-miles round-trip, with a total accumulated elevation gain of somewhere around 1400ft.

Journey #2

Fonts Point

Get to Fonts Point, from Borrego Springs, by heading east on Palm Canyon Road (Hwy S-22) for a little over 8-miles. Turn right (south) at mile-marker 29 and follow the signs to Font Point, about 4-miles beyond. Note: Check on road conditions before heading out; in poor weather this can be a rough route for 2 wheel-drive vehicles.

The views are best—even magnificent—along the 0.5-mile stretch east of the parking area, but use care as the cliff can be unstable near the edge.

Truckhaven Rocks

The Truckhaven Rocks are huge, beautiful, orangish-reddish-brownish boulders tilted at a 45-degree angle.

Get to the Truckhaven Rocks by parking on the shoulder of Highway S-22, about 0.5-miles east of mile-marker 35, and walking up the wash on the north side of the road. This wash, bordered by a high wall of rock on the west side, appears to aim for a spot a little east of the Truckhaven Rocks.

As you head north the wash becomes a canyon and, in about 0.75-mile, these monstrous boulders will suddenly appear, jutting out above you; from this point just climb up and over the canyon walls to explore the rocks.

Bring your camera and catch these beauties in the low-angle light of sunrise or sunset.

Calcite Mine Hike

From where you parked for Truckhaven Rocks, it's only a short hop to the turnout at mile-marker 38. Park here, and then walk east about 0.1-mile to where the old Calcite jeep trail intersects Hwy S-22 from the north. Follow the jeep trail northwest, heading generally towards a light-colored block of sandstone called Locomotive Rock; the mines are in front of that rock.

At about 1.4-miles from the highway, the jeep trail takes a dip to cross a ravine—the north end has a fantastic slot canyon—and then ends in the mine area about 0.5-mile beyond.

Calcite was mined here—and only here in this country—during World War II for use as gun-sights. Explore the area's mining relics, fantastic sandstone formations, and the calcite crystals everywhere glinting in the sun. When you're finished adventuring in the calcite mine area you'll have at least two options to get back to the highway: The first is to simply retrace your steps back to your vehicle.

The second option is more fun. From the mine area backtrack 0.5-mile down the jeep trail to the slot canyon that you passed on the way in, drop down into it, and then descend through the canyon as it becomes deeper and deeper and narrower and narrower until it towers above you and is only wide enough for one person to pass through at a time. When you reach the chaotic slabs of sandstone in Palm Wash, at the bottom of the ravine, turn right and walk 0.3-mile downstream. Exit the canyon by way of a short stretch of jeep trail that leads back to the Calcite road.

This hike is about 4-miles roundtrip, with about 800ft of elevation gain.

Ancient Fish Traps

To get to these fascinating archaeological relics, from the Calcite Mine turnout on Highway S-22, travel east for about 9-miles to Highway 86. Turn left (north) on Highway 86 and continue for about 3.7-miles to the bridge over 'Grave Wash'. At the bridge, turn left (west) onto the 0.5-mile long dirt road that ends at the shoreline of ancient Lake Cahuilla. (This lake became extinct about 500 years ago. The Salton Sea, a fraction of the size of its predecessor but still the largest lake in California, was formed only a century ago when the Colorado River overran its banks).

The horseshoe-shaped rock arrangements that you see in the area—the fish traps—are more then 500 year-old. It is believed that the natives operated them by either (1) driving the fish into the enclosures or (2) allowing the fish to congregate in the enclosure, and then sealing the open end.

Enjoy these treasures, but please don't disturb them. They are delicate and priceless.

Note: As you leave here and head north on Highway 86 for the next adventure you'll cross Brawley Avenue, about 3.8-miles to the north. Turning right (east) here will bring you, in just over 1-mile, to a marina on the Salton Sea. For more information about the recreational possibilities at the Salton Sea contact: Salton Sea State Recreation Area, 100-225 State Park Road, North Shore, CA 92254, or by phone at 619.393.3052, or on the web at www.saltonsea.ca.gov.

Travertine Palms Hike

From the fish traps, backtrack to Highway 86 and turn left (north) for about 8-miles (11.7-miles from the junction with Highway S-22) to a dirt road heading west (left); follow this dirt road (it parallels a power line) for about 1-mile to the trailhead.

From the parking area the trail heads southwest along Travertine Palms Wash. When you reach the third canyon coming in from the left (south), about 2.5-miles from the trailhead, take the short 0.5-mile spur up this canyon to the oasis.

The oasis has a trickle of water, about 70 palms, and a sweet rock shelter at the base of a high red and gray cliff, just to the west of the palms, on the far side of the saddle. The campfire-blackened roof and nearby bedrock mortars attest to its use as a shelter for ancient peoples.

This hike is about 6-miles, round trip, with about 320ft of elevation gain.

JOURNEY #3

The Slot/Wind Caves

This moderate 2-mile (round-trip) walk will lead you to both the most accessible slot canyon in Anza-Borrego AND some really cool caves.

Get there, from the junction of Borrego Springs Road & Highway 78, by heading east on Highway 78 for 1.5-miles to Butte Pass Road. Head north on Butte Pass Road for about 1-mile, to a junction with Borrego Mountain Wash, and then bear left for about 0.7-mile; park where the road bears sharply to the left.

The rock here is a deep red and angled upward; look for a fracture in it just below where you parked—this is The Slot. Descend steeply into this chasm and hike downstream as it twists and turns and narrows until, at its narrowest point, it is a mere 16 inches wide with walls that tower overhead. The canyon opens up again after about 0.5-mile and the caves are another 0.5-mile down the canyon.

After you've explored these wonders, retrace your route back to your vehicle(s). Note: Save this trip for another day if rain threatens; a slot canyon is a bad place to be in a flash flood.

Elephant Trees Discovery Trail

To get to this fun trail, from Borrego Springs, head southeast on Borrego Springs Road to Highway 78. Turn left (east) onto Highway 78, for about 6.5-miles to Ocotillo Wells. Turn right (south) onto Split Mountain Road and follow it for about 5.8-miles to a turnoff to the right, signed for the Elephant Trees Trail. Turn right here, for about 0.8-mile, to the trailhead. (Note: Be prepared to walk the last 0.8-mile stretch if it is too sandy for your vehicle.)

This easy 1.5-mile loop hike meanders in and out of a dry wash and past all kinds of beautiful desert flora, including the featured Elephant Tree.

Although fairly common south of the border, these trees weren't discovered here until 1937 and even then this grove was thought to be the northernmost until another, in the Santa Rosa Mountains, was stumbled upon in 1987.

This area contains about 100 of these wonderful trees, which are named not for their size but for their wrinkled trunks. Be sure to grab a brochure to assist in identifying them and the other wonderful plant life.

Wind Caves

These sandstone caves are wind carved, expansive, multi-tiered, and awesome! Get to them, from the Elephant Trees Discovery Trail parking area (as described above), by backtracking about 0.8-mile to Split Mountain Road, and then turning right (south) and following Split Mountain Road for about 5-miles. At this point, (about 10.8-miles from Ocotillo Wells) Split Mountain Road makes a sharp turn to the right (west) and heads up Fish Creek Wash. Drive up this wash for about 5.1-miles to the parking area.

From the parking area, climb a short but rather steep 0.2-mile to the plateau where the trail then splits into several branches— thought to be remnants of trails first used by the prehistoric peoples who utilized these caves as shelters. Continuing on any one of these trails (they'll all get you to the caves), at about 0.5-mile from the parking area you'll spot the caves, and arrive at them in about 0.7-miles.

This hike is about 1.4-miles roundtrip, plus exploration.

San Sebastian Marsh

From the Wind Caves trailhead, backtrack to Ocotillo Wells and turn right (east) onto Highway 78 for about 12.5-miles. Look for a four-wheel drive road (now closed to motorized traffic) heading south between mile-marker 8.5 and 9. Park in the area and walk down this road to the San Sebastian Marsh—about 2-miles distant.

This fascinating fresh water marsh has been a dependable source of water for centuries. In fact, the Spanish explorer, De Anza, stopped here on his way to the coast, naming this area after his Native American guide, Sebastian Tarabel.

This is a great place to observe wildlife too, such as the endangered pupfish.

JOURNEY # 4

Cactus Trail Loop

This is another short nature trail packed with great information about the park's wonderfully diverse fauna.

Get to the Cactus Trail Loop, from Borrego Springs, by heading south on CR-3 for about 5.6-miles to a Y junction. Bear right (south) at the Y, continuing on CR-3 (now Yaqui Pass Road) for another 7-miles to the Tamarisk Grove Campground. The Cactus Trail Loop hike originates across from the campground entrance.

From the parking area, head up canyon on the winding trail, looking for interpretive signs that identify all of the great fauna represented here; teddy bear cholla, saltbush, beavertail cactus, and much more. Reach the trails' highpoint at about 0.5-mile, enjoy a wonderful view, and then descend to the trailhead, hitting the road just east of where you parked your car.

This hike is only about 1-mile in length with about 230ft of elevation gain.

Morteros Village

This is a very short 0.5-mile round trip stroll to the morteros (grinding holes) that mark the site of an ancient Kumeyaay Indian village.

Get to the trailhead, from Borrego Springs, by heading south on Borrego Springs Road to Highway S-3. Turn right (south) on Highway S-3 (Yaqui Pass Road) and stay on it for about 7-miles to Highway 78. Turn right (west) onto Highway 78 and travel about 7.4-miles to Scissors Crossing. Turn left (south) onto County Road 2 for about 6.3-miles to Blair Valley Road, and then turn left (southeast) on Blair Valley Road (dirt) for about 3.5-miles to the Morteros Village trailhead.

The route heads southeast for a short 0.25-mile to a large split boulder, behind which are the bedrock mortars, or morteros. The Kumeyaay Indians are thought to have used this village site seasonally, for more then 1,000 years, to harvest Pinyon nuts and desert agave. While you're here, take some time to enjoy the magnificent, sweeping views of Little Blair Valley.

As you head back to your car look for a large boulder on your left (northwest); it's about 10 feet high, about 15 yards from the trail and has a smaller boulder (about 4 feet high) next to it, but not touching. The backside of the larger boulder has a small panel—near ground level in a small depression in the rock—of black pictographs (paintings) thought to be associated with puberty rites for Kumeyaay Indian boys. Also, look for a small mortero on a nearby horizontal rock, the byproduct of people grinding, for centuries, the pigment (hematite, charcoal, etc.) from which they made the 'paint' used to create the rock art. The pulverized pigment would have then been mixed with a binding agent, such as animal fat, and then applied to the stone. Wherever there is a pictograph panel, there is also bound to be at least one small mortero.

On the smaller boulder, next to the large one, look for a series of cupules (small depressions), which have been ground into it. This site, and the one described below, is the most accessible of the more then 50 known rock art sites in the park.

Little Blair Valley Pictographs

From the Morteros Village parking area, hop back in your car and continue heading northeast on Blair Valley Road for another 1.4-miles, to the trailhead for the Little Blair Valley Pictographs.

From the parking area, catch the well-marked trail that gradually climbs towards a low saddle to the east. At about 0.7-mile you'll see a large, solitary boulder on your right (south) with two eye-level panels of red, yellow and black pictographs. While the pictographs that you saw at Morteros Village are thought to be associated with boy's puberty rites, these are believed to have been painted at the culmination of young girls puberty ceremonies.

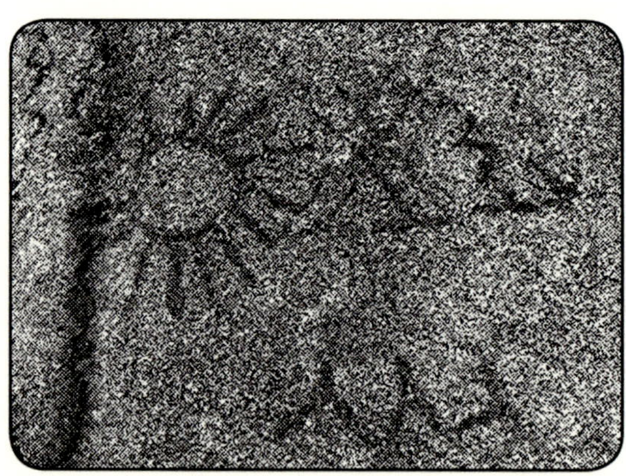

After contemplating the rock art, you have a couple of options; either turn back and retrace the route back to the parking area, or continue heading east on the trail to an amazing viewpoint above a dry 150-foot high waterfall.

The trail to the viewpoint—about 0.4-miles (one-way) from the pictographs through an ever-narrowing canyon—abruptly ends at the magnificent view. The small hill to the east provides an even more dramatic vista.

Agua Caliente Hot Springs Regional Park

Seismic faults running beneath this interesting park have allowed geothermally heated water to rise to the surface in the form of natural springs. These springs have been channeled into two separate pools; one is an outdoor pool with a temperature of about 90 degrees, the other an indoor pool (with Jacuzzi jets) heated to about 102 degrees. This is the perfect place for a good soak after a long day on the trail.

This park, managed by San Diego County, has in addition to its namesake hot springs, a campground with 140 sites, a small store, showers warmed by piped in geothermal water, a picnic area, and several miles of awesome hiking trails.

The park is 910 acres in size, open from Labor Day to Memorial Day, and totally surrounded by Anza-Borrego Desert State Park. For more information, including fees & camping reservations, contact: Agua Caliente County Park, 39555 County Route S-2, or by phone, toll free, at 877.565.3600, or on the web at: www.sdcounty.ca.gov/parks/camping/agua_caliente.

Get to Agua Caliente Springs County Park, from the Little Blair Valley Pictograph site, by backtracking on Blair Valley Road to Highway S-2. Turn left (southwest) on Highway S-2 for approximately 15-miles; the turnoff for the Agua Caliente Springs County Park is on the right (south).

The following two hikes—*Moonlight Canyon* and *Squaw Peak & Pond*—originate at Agua Caliente Springs County Park.

Moonlight Canyon Loop Hike

This well-worn trail originates near campsites 39 & 40, climbs a low ridge, and then drops into a creek bottom leading into Moonlight Canyon, with its amazingly colorful rock formations, and hidden seeps and springs where the observant may spot wildlife.

At about 1.1-miles into the hike you'll reach a trail junction; take the short spur trail to an interesting box canyon, or continue on through an ever-widening canyon with a really cool Ocotillo forest.

This loop ends back at campsite # 63, a short 1.5-miles from the start.

Squaw Peak & Pond

From the ranger station at Agua Caliente Springs County Park, cross the parking lot to the campfire circle and catch the trail signed for the park's amphitheater, Squaw Peak, and Squaw Pond.

This trail climbs a short 0.1-mile to a junction; take the left (south) fork and switchback up 150 feet, in 0.3-mile, to the summit of Squaw Peak (1,450ft) and panoramic views of the Carrizo Valley and Badlands.

Enjoy the views, then retrace your route to the junction and turn left (west), following a sandy wash for about 0.5-mile to Squaw Pond, a really cool desert spring.

Relax in the shade of willows, watch for unique birds, and simply enjoy this wonderful place. When you're finished, retrace your steps to the parking area.

The overall length of this walk is about 1.9-miles.

Carrizo Badlands Overlook/Canyon Sin Nombre & Slot Canyon Hike

From Agua Caliente Springs County Park, head southeast on Highway S-2 for about 13-miles to Sweeney Pass. As you climb Sweeney Pass, look for the turnout on the left (just beyond mile-marker 51), which leads to a magnificent panorama of the

Carrizo Badlands—more then 10 square miles of grotesquely tilted rock formations, mud hills & caves, cliffs, deep cut ravines, small arches, and slot canyons. If at all possible, hike down the four-wheel drive track into this canyon (Canyon Sin Nombre) and experience firsthand these fantastic geological features, as well as a really cool slot canyon.

From the parking area it's about 1.3 miles down canyon to a narrow wash coming in from the left (west); this is the slot canyon. When you locate this canyon wander through it (squeezing at times) as it narrows and the walls rise up as high as 150ft.

Depending upon how much extra exploring you do this is, at a minimum, a 2.6-mile round-trip hike with 550ft of elevation gain.

Bring plenty of water for the walk out.

SITES OUTSIDE THE PARK

The following adventures are located on land administered by the Bureau of Land Management. For more information, and to request access guides to these sites, contact: BLM El

Centro Resource Area, 1661 South 4th Street, El Centro, CA 92243, or by phone at 760.337.4400.

Fossil Canyon

The fossils embedded in the walls of this canyon are believed to be remnants of the life that once thrived in ancient Lake Cahuilla.

From the Carrizo Badlands overlook, continue southeast on Hwy S-2 for about 12-miles, and then turn left (north) on Shell Canyon Road for another 2.4-miles and the end of the pavement. Stay north at the intersection here (there is a cement operation to the south), and in another 1.5-miles park your car and explore the canyon.

Painted Gorge

The walls of this narrow canyon are dyed bright reds and mustards by the occurrence of copper, iron, and sulfur deposits within the weathered rock. While you're here, check the upper canyon for fossilized coral reefs and marine life, including muscles and worms.

Get to the Painted Gorge, from Fossil Canyon, by backtracking to Hwy S-2 and turning left (southeast) for about 1.5-miles. Turn left (east) on Hwy S-80 (Evans Hewes Highway) for about 4.2-miles, and then turn left (north) again onto Painted Gorge Road, which eventually becomes BLM Route Y181. In about 4.5-miles you'll come to a hilly, wash area; bear west up the wash and into the gorge.

The Yuha Basin Geoglyphs

The area known as the Yuha Desert sits in the bed of what was, at one time, 115-mile long, 34-mile wide and 300 feet deep Lake Cahuilla. It is a fascinating area of fossilized oyster shells and bizarre geoglyphs.

The Yuha Basin straddles Interstate 8, just east of the town of Ocotillo. Get there from Painted Gorge by backtracking on Hwy S-80 to Hwy S-2 in the town of Ocotillo. Turn left (south) on Hwy S-2 for about 1-mile, where it T's. Turn left (east) on Hwy 98 (the Yuha Cutoff) for about 5.9-miles to the BLM Route Y1928 (Anza Trail Road, or Hocker Drive). Turn left (northeast) on BLM Route Y1928 for 0.9-mile to an intersection; turn left at this intersection, continuing on BLM Route Y1928 for 1.1-miles to yet another intersection.

Three BLM routes fork here; bear right (northeast), remaining on BLM Route Y1928 for another 0.5-mile to the geoglyph, a giant form of rock art created by Native Americans who cleared the dark top layer of rocks ('desert pavement'), while leaving the lighter soil underneath as a contrast.

The Yuha Basin's many dirt roads branch off in every conceivable direction, making it a very complicated area to navigate. Because of this, and because there are a lot of other cool things to see out here—fossilized oyster beds, historical wells, etc.—I recommend that you contact the El Centro BLM office before visiting and request maps, the *Access Guide* for the area, and local conditions. Note: A four-wheel drive vehicle may be required at certain times of the year.

CHAPTER FIFTEEN

The Santa Catalina Island Area

Watch for whales, dolphins and seals on your journey to this fantastic island; Explore a picturesque waterfront town; Swim, snorkel, and kayak in the Pacific Ocean; Hike to the island's high points and remote coves; Take in beautiful views from seaside cliffs; Fish for your dinner; Dodge wandering bison; Relax by a campfire; Fall asleep to the sound of crashing waves…and more!

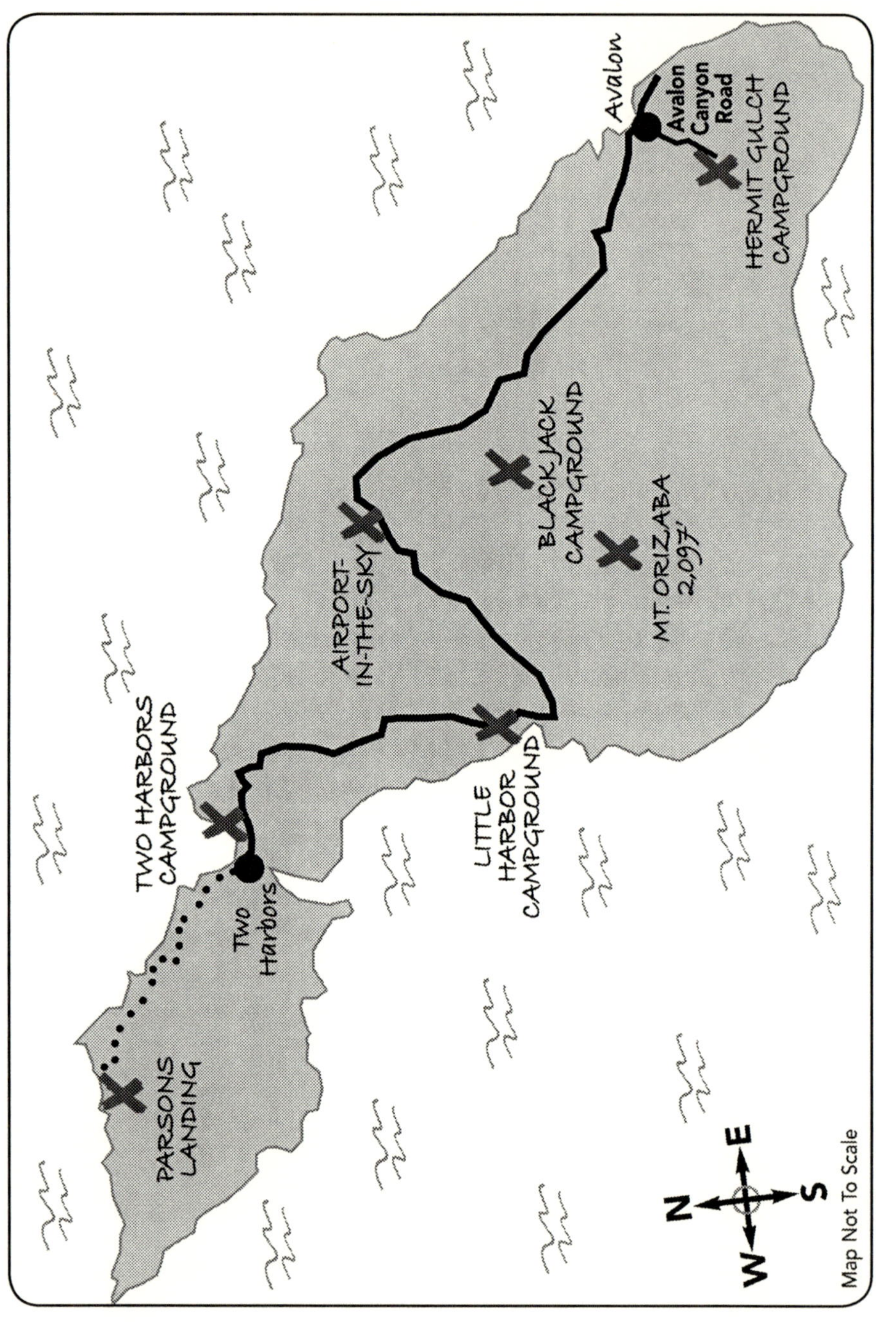
Avalon
Avalon Canyon Road
HERMIT GULCH CAMPGROUND
BLACK JACK CAMPGROUND
MT. ORIZABA 2,097'
AIRPORT-IN-THE-SKY
TWO HARBORS CAMPGROUND
Two Harbors
LITTLE HARBOR CAMPGROUND
PARSONS LANDING
N
E
S
W
Map Not To Scale

About the Santa Catalina Island Area

Santa Catalina Island, one of eight islands located just off the Southern California coast, is about twenty-one miles long and eight-miles wide at its widest spot. A one-half mile wide isthmus, called Two Harbors, is the narrowest point on the island and separates the six-mile long northwestern end from the longer southeastern end. This island—inhabited through the ages by no fewer than five separate cultures—has a quaint little beach town named Avalon, the smaller village of Two Harbors, and many beautiful broad valleys, isolated coves, pristine beaches, huge cliffs, and high mountains.

There are at least 396 native plant species on the island and wildlife that includes the Catalina Fox, Mule Deer, Bald Eagle, and several hundred wild bison—the descendents of animals used in a 1920's film. The sea life here is amazing too, and includes seals, sea lions, dolphins, whales, and California's state fish, the bright orange Garibaldi.

Since 1975, The Catalina Island Conservancy has overseen the islands management with its primary mission being that of the preservation of the island in its natural state. They've done a great job; you're going to love this place!

Getting There.

Catalina Island is 26-miles across the Pacific Ocean from the City of San Pedro, necessitating a trip by sea or air. Be sure to make your travel reservations early, especially in the summer.

Travel By Boat

One of the highlights of a trip by sea is the opportunity to witness the breathtaking sight of hundreds of common dolphins racing the ship and frolicking in its wake. Whales of all kinds can be spotted as well.

There are two primary companies that ferry passengers from the mainland to the island of Catalina:

Catalina Express—Provides year-round service with as many as thirty daily departures from Long Beach, San Pedro and Dana Point to Avalon, or from San Pedro to Two Harbors. For more information, contact Catalina Express at 800.481.3470, or on the web at: www.catalinaexpress.com.

Catalina Passenger Service—Serves passengers traveling from Newport Beach to Avalon. Contact them at 949.673.5245, or on the web at www.catalinainfo.com.

Travel By Helicopter

Island Express Helicopter Service—You can also make a fifteen-minute jaunt across the San Pedro Channel by helicopter on flights that depart from San Pedro and Long Beach. Contact them by phone at 800.2AVALON, or on the web at: www. islandexpress.com.

Travel By Private Plane

Catalina Island's 'Airport-in-the-Sky' is located in the center of the island, at an elevation of about 1,602ft. Its 3,250ft runway is able to accommodate most small planes, as well as the occasional bison herd. For more information about the airport or the airport shuttle that runs to Avalon, call 310.510.0143. For current weather conditions—the airport is often impacted by fog and/or heavy cloud cover—call toll free from anywhere in Southern California: 800.255.8700.

Lodging, Supplies, Maps & Information

Catalina Island, and particularly the town of Avalon, has a wide variety of lodging options ranging from semi-remote campgrounds to luxury hotels, quaint inns, bed & breakfasts, and waterfront homes.

For more information regarding lodging, or any other aspect of your trip to Catalina Island, contact: Santa Catalina Island Conservancy, Post Office Box 2739, Avalon, CA 90704, or by phone at 310.510.2595, or online at www.catalinaconservancy.org.

Avalon

Avalon, the islands only "city", is two square miles of hotels, restaurants, shops, boardwalks, and beaches. Most of the supplies that you may need can be found in Avalon, including groceries, stove fuel, and firewood.

Two Harbors

More of a rustic village than a town, Two Harbors has a hotel—the Banning House Lodge—a general store, restaurant, snack bar, laundry, warm showers, and a dive & kayak center.

The Catalina Safari Shuttle Bus

The Safari Bus, the primary mode of transportation across the island, runs the 26-miles between Avalon and Two Harbors with stops at Black Jack Mountain trailhead, the airport, and Little Harbor Campground. It runs daily through the summer, but after September 1st you must make advanced reservations to guarantee that there will be a bus available to transport your party. In fact, to be on the safe side, I recommend that you always make your Safari Bus & camping reservation simultaneously.

For rates, times, reservations, and other information, contact the Catalina Safari Shuttle Bus at: 310.510.8368.

Maps

Franko puts out a relief map of Catalina, which includes the mileage between points as well as island highpoints, highlights, and features. For more information, contact: www.frankosmaps. com.

Camping & Hiking On Catalina Island

There are five primary campgrounds on the island: *Hermit Gulch, Black Jack, Little Harbor, Two Harbors,* and *Parsons Landing*. To make reservations at any one of them, contact: Catalina Island Camping Reservations, Box 737, Avalon, CA 90704, or by phone at 310.510.2800, or on the web: www.scico. com (click on the camping link).

The Catalina Conservancy also maintains eleven very primitive boat-in campgrounds, which are accessible only by private boat or kayak. To camp at one of the sites you must provide everything you'll need, including your own porta-potty. Get more information on boat-in camping on the web at: www. campingcatalinaisland.com.

As far as hiking on the island goes, the Catalina Island Conservancy requires all hikers to have a permit. These are free, but can only be obtained in person at one of three locations: (1) the Catalina Island Conservancy located at 125 Claressa Street in Avalon, (2) the Two Harbors Visitors Information Center (at the foot of the pier), and (3) the Catalina Airport.

The following are the campgrounds, and a couple of hikes, arranged geographically from east to west:

Hermit Gulch Campground

This campground is located in Avalon Canyon, a short 1.5-miles inland from the boat landing in Avalon. It has 43 general campsites (plus 1 group site), restrooms, hot showers, BBQ's, picnic tables, vending machines, and lockers. Wood fires are not permitted here.

To reach this campground, from Avalon, head up Summer Avenue to the sign that says, "Avalon Canyon Road." The campground is 1-mile inland from that point, across from the picnic grounds.

Check in with the rangers when you arrive at Hermit Gulch.

Hike To Lone Tree Point

The trail to Lone Tree Point starts out from the Hermit Gulch Campground and heads up Hermit Gulch, the ravine to the west of the campground, on a narrow but quite steep trail that gains nearly 1,200ft of elevation in the first 1.5-miles. At this point the trail reaches a fire road called, 'Divide Road.' Turn right on Divide Road, for just a few steps, and then head up the embankment on the left and catch the fire road heading to the southwest. This fire road undulates over several rounded hilltops for about 0.9-mile to Lone Tree Point at 1,634ft.

The view from this point is amazing; on a clear winter day you can see from the snow-capped San Gabriel Mountains all the way to the San Diego area.

After you've taken in the views, had your lunch and, per-haps, taken a nap in the sun, retrace your steps to the trailhead. The total mileage of this hike is about 5-miles, round-trip, with somewhere around 1,500ft of elevation gain.

Bring your binoculars on this one if you have them, and don't forget your sunscreen & hat as the route has very little shade.

Black Jack Campground

Black Jack Campground is located about 10-miles from Avalon and 15 miles from Two Harbors, so you'll need to arrange transportation on the Safari Bus. Even with the bus, though, you'll still need to be prepared for the moderate 1.5-mile walk from the bus drop off point to the campground.

This inland campground—nestled in a beautiful pine forest at an elevation near 1,500ft—has 10 large sites, pit toilets, drinking water, BBQ's, fire pits, picnic tables, and rinse off (i.e. cold!) showers.

When you make reservations for your campsites, be sure to also make them for the Safari Bus and, if you prepay, for firewood; they'll have it waiting for you when you arrive.

Several cool trails head out from the Black Jack campground area, including routes to Mount Orizaba and Black Jack Mountains (the island's high points, both more then 2,000 feet above the sea), the airport, Little Harbor, Middle Ranch, Eagles Nest Lodge, and more. These trails are clearly marked on both your Franko's Map and the hiking map the conservancy provides when you pick up your camping/hiking permit.

Little Harbor Campground

Once the site of a large Gabrielino Indian village, this sandy, ocean front campground has drinking water, rinse off showers, fire pits, BBQ's, picnic tables, pit toilets, and a ranger who can sell you propane, charcoal, and firewood. This excellent waterside campground has 16 sites (including 8 group areas), two coves, nice beaches, dramatic high cliffs, and lots of buffalo—at least when we were there. Because it's located about 16-miles from Avalon, and 6.8-miles from Two Harbors, you'll want to book your Safari Bus reservations at the same time that you make your camping reservations.

Be sure to catch a sunrise or set from Indian Head Point (as you're facing the ocean, the high point on the left)…it's breathtaking.

Hike To Two Harbors

My good friend, Jeff Guldalian, organized a trip to Catalina Island and arranged for us to stay at Little Harbor Campground. It was early season, and a bit cool, but it was beautiful and we had the whole place to ourselves…well, aside from the buffalo.

We had taken the Catalina Express from San Pedro to Avalon, purchased groceries and firewood, grabbed a couple of fish tacos from "Eric's on the Pier" and hopped on the Safari Bus to our campground. The next couple of days were spent snorkeling, fishing, hiking and laughing around the campfire. We climbed up to Indian Head Point, soaked up the sunshine (when the sun was out) and just enjoyed God's goodness.

When it came time to leave this jewel, we packed up our gear and walked through the rain and mud to Two Harbors, about 7-miles away. There we had lunch, sipped hot chocolate and waited for the ferry that would take us back to San Pedro. It was a wonderful adventure with a wonderful group of friends.

If you plan a trip like this, be sure to make advanced arrangements with Catalina Express—to be dropped off in Avalon and picked up in Two Harbors—as well as with the Safari Bus.

The route for the hike to Two Harbors is the primary dirt road that passes by the campground.

Two Harbors Campground

This campground is just a short 0.25-mile uphill from the village of Two Harbors, on a bluff overlooking the azure sea. There are 45 sites, some with shade canopies, all with pit toilets, picnic tables, BBQ's, fire rings, drinking water, showers, and lockers. There are three group areas and a limited number of cabin tents for rent as well.

An on-site ranger will sell you propane, charcoal, and firewood, and nearby are a general store, a restaurant, recreational rentals, and various other amenities.

For a great area hike, see Parsons Landing, below.

Parson's Landing Campground

Located west of Two Harbors, this campground is the most remote and primitive of the five established campgrounds. The only way to get here is by hiking from Two Harbors (7-miles one way) or by taking a shoreboat (available summer only) from Two Harbors to Emerald Cove and then walking 2.5-miles (one way) from Emerald Cove to Parsons Landing.

This campground has 8 sites, pit toilets, fire rings, BBQ's, and picnic tables. There is no running water or showers, however one bundle of firewood and about 2.5 gallons of bottled water are included in the campground fee. Additional wood and water are available for a fee, which must be pre-paid at the time of your reservation.

All other supplies must be carried with you. Please remember the 'Leave No Trace' principles here: Pack it in, pack it out!

The Trail To Parsons Landing

The trail to Parsons Landing Campground starts at the village of Two Harbors, just west of Isthmus Cove, on the fire road (West End Road) gouged out of the mountainside. At about 1.5-miles into the hike the West End Road dips southwest into Cherry Valley (named for the indigenous Catalina Cherry Tree that grows here) before turning back towards the coast. At a little over 6-miles, you'll pass an intersection with an old fire road, the Boushay Trail. Continue on the main trail to another junction, about 0.5-mile or so further west, and then take the right fork that leads through a beautiful grassland to the campground.

Return to Two Harbors by retracing your route, for a total of about 14 round trip miles and 1,000ft of elevation gain.

For an alternate way back to Two Harbors, or for a loop hike, backtrack from Parsons Landing Campground to the Boushay Trail and turn right (south), heading uphill. Stay on the Boushay Trail for about 2.1-miles, to a junction with the Silver Peak Trail (also an old fire road), and then turn left (east) to Two Harbors, about 4.6-miles away.

Turning right (west) at the intersection of the Boushay & Silver Peak Trails will, in just a bit over 1-mile, put you about 100 feet below the summit of Silver Peak (1,804ft), the highest point at this end of the island; simply scramble up the slope to bag it.

This loop hike, beginning and ending at Two Harbors, is about 14.2-miles in length or 16.2-miles with the optional side trip to Silver Peak.

Backpacking Santa Catalina Island

I've never done it, but I think it would be a blast to backpack across the island. One could start at Hermit Gulch Campground, near Avalon, and hike to Black Jack Campground which, depending on your route, is about 10-miles away.

There are several route options for the second leg of this trip, from Black Jack Campground to Little Harbor Campground, but the most direct route is about 7-miles in length.

From Little Harbor it's another 7-miles to Two Harbors, and then 7-miles out to Parsons Landing. Of course, depending on your fitness level and level of motivation, you could also finish the hike sooner by extending your mileage and skipping a couple of the campgrounds.

When finished you could grab the ferry from Two Harbors to Avalon, or grab a lift on the Safari Bus.

If you do such an adventure, be sure to carry a good map (your Franko's Map would probably work for a hike like this), have the conservancy folks mark the water sources on it and, when you're done, drop me a line—at <u>www.godgrowthand-greatadventure.com</u>—and let me know how it went. I would love to hear about it.

Trans Catalina Trail

In the near future, begin looking for the Trans Catalina Trail which, when completed, will allow hikers to traverse the length of the island without stepping foot on a road.

OTHER ACTIVITIES ON SANTA CATALINA ISLAND

There are boat rentals & charters, SCUBA lessons and equipment, kayak rentals and guided trips, snorkeling, glass bottom boat tours, jeep tours, educational hikes, and fishing opportunities galore. Contact the Catalina Island Conservancy for a list of businesses offering these services.

CHAPTER SIXTEEN

The Leo Carrillo State Beach Area

Explore rich tide pools; Hike to a pond, a waterfall, and a wonderful overlook; Sunbathe, swim, snorkel, surf, and play on sandy beaches; Worship around a campfire; Hike up (and slide down) a huge sand dune; Discover wintering Monarch Butterflies and migrating Grey Whales; Walk an ancient trail; Enjoy a latte (only minutes away!)…and more!

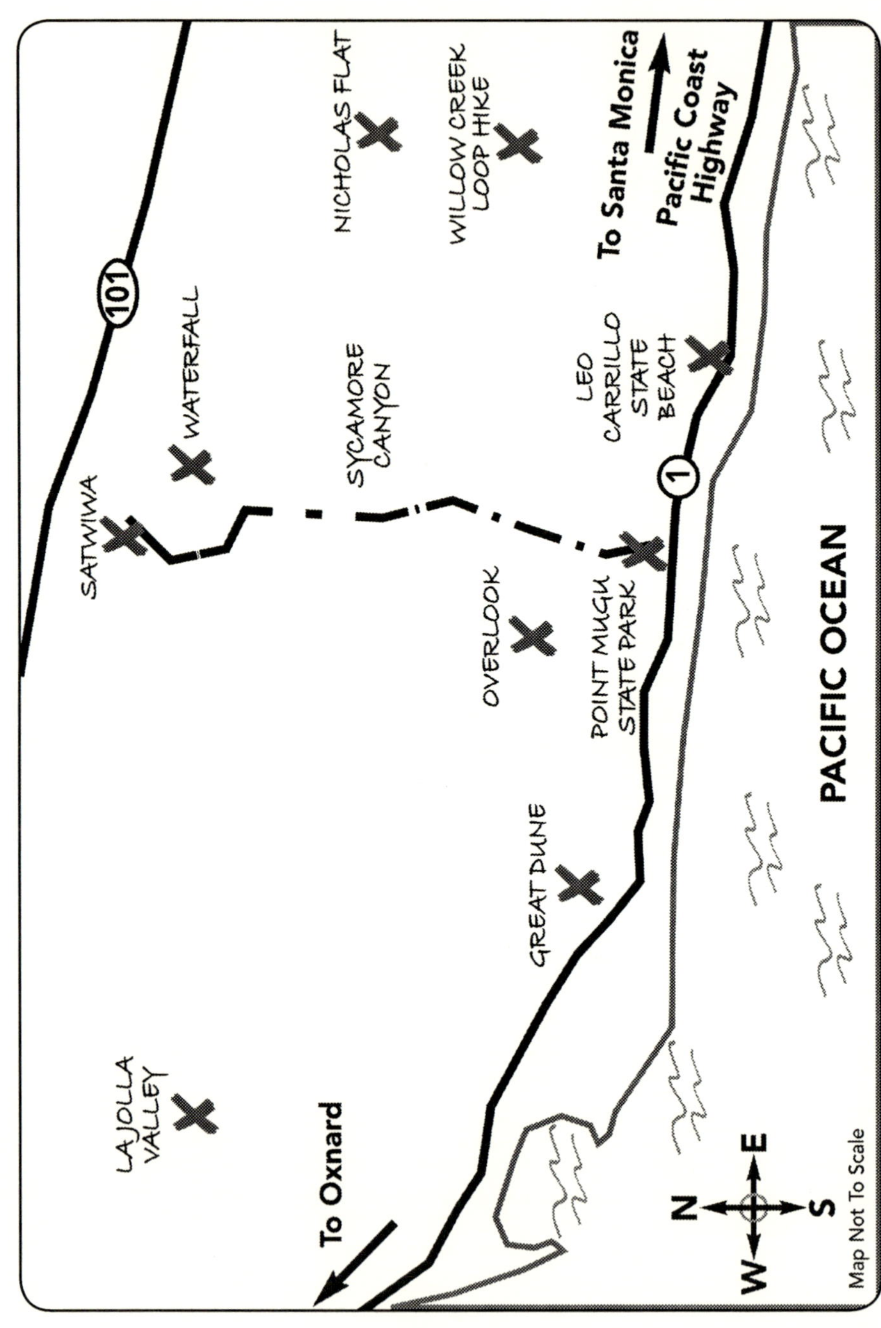
NICHOLAS FLAT
WILLOW CREEK LOOP HIKE
To Santa Monica
Pacific Coast Highway
101
WATERFALL
SYCAMORE CANYON
LEO CARRILLO STATE BEACH
1
SATWIWA
OVERLOOK
POINT MUGU STATE PARK
GREAT DUNE
PACIFIC OCEAN
LA JOLLA VALLEY
To Oxnard
N
E
S
W
Map Not To Scale

About the Leo Carrillo Area

Just a few miles from the masses of Los Angeles, this wonderful coastal region offers more than 20,000-acres of rocky cliffs, sandy beaches, chaparral covered hills, lush inland grasslands, a giant sand dune, and long, sycamore-shaded valleys.

Hills as high as 1,000-feet above the sea provide beautiful views of the Channel Islands and, nearer to shore, the spouts of migrating Grey Whales. There are beautiful, well-formed waves that attract surfers, rich kelp forests that lure divers & snorklers (and dolphins & seals), and tide pools & sea caves that draw the beachcomber. Inland, a beautiful wilderness area, wintering monarch butterflies, and centuries old Native American archaeological sites fascinate the explorer.

Two of the area's most popular campgrounds—both shaded by huge sycamore trees and enlivened by resident flocks of parrots—are easily accessed from Pacific Coast Highway, while a third more primitive campground is reserved for backpackers hiking in on foot.

Come to Leo Carrillo, catch a sunrise, listen to the surf, and watch your cares, as John Muir once said, "…drop away from you like the leaves of autumn."

Getting There

Leo Carrillo State Beach is located on California Highway 1 (the Pacific Coast Highway/PCH) in Los Angeles County, roughly 28-miles northwest of Santa Monica, and 19-miles south of the City of Oxnard.

Lodging, Supplies, Maps & Information

South of Leo Carrillo, on Hwy 1, lodging, supplies and gas are available in Malibu and Santa Monica. To the north these amenities can be found in the city of Oxnard. Contact the chambers of commerce or tourism bureaus of these cities for more information regarding lodging:

- Malibu Chamber of Commerce: 310.456.9025, or online at www.malibu.org.
- Santa Monica Convention and Visitors Bureau: 800.544.5319, or online at www.santamonica.com.
- Oxnard Convention and Visitors Bureau: 800.269.6273, or online at www.visitoxnard.com.

The campground at Leo Carrillo, just across the highway from the beach, has 138 family campsites, a few hike/bike sites, and a group site that can accommodate up to 50 people. An additional 32 beachfront sites exist for those with self-contained vehicles under 8ft in height. All of the sites have picnic tables and fire rings, but only the inland sites have restrooms and showers. There is a small, seasonal (summer only), general store that carries staples such as soda, sandwich stuff, charcoal, firewood, film, sunscreen, ice, etc.

Aside from DeLorme's, "Southern & Central California Atlas & Gazetteer", or its equivalent, I suggest that you pick up Tom Harrison's (www.tomharrisonmaps.com) maps titled, "*Santa Monica Mountains West*" & "*Santa Monica Mountains East*", as well as the American Automobile Association's '*Los Angeles County*' & '*Ventura County*' maps.

As far as area hiking guides go, you'll want to grab the most current version of, "*Hiking Trails of the Santa Monica Mountains*" (Milt McAuley).

For more information, or to reserve a campsite (recommended from May through October and on holiday weekends), contact: Leo Carrillo State Park, 3500 W. Pacific Coast Highway, Malibu, CA 90265 or by phone at: 805.488.1827 or online at www.parks.ca.gov

For more information regarding the hiking and camping potential within the Santa Monica National Recreation Area, which surrounds both Leo Carrillo State Beach and Point Mugu State Park, contact: Santa Monica Mountains National Recreation Area, 401 West Hillcrest Drive, Thousand Oaks, CA 91360, or by phone at 805.370.2300, or online at: www.nps.gov/samo/.

Finally, if you are one of the billions of people on the planet who can no longer function without at least one stop per day for designer coffee, then do I have good news for you—there is a Starbucks located just five minutes south of Leo Carrillo State Beach, on the corner of Hwy 1 and Trancas Canyon Road!

Leo Carrillo State Beach

Leo Carrillo State Beach has about 1.5-miles of rocky coastline with bluffs, cove-like sandy beaches, and a really cool sea cave. Inland, the hills within the park rise high above the sea, affording the hiker and explorer outstanding views of the ocean and surrounding mountains.

Activities along the shore include surfing, wind surfing, snorkeling, scuba diving, skim boarding, body surfing, surf fishing, tide pool exploration, beachcombing, sunbathing, reading, relaxing, etc.

Sequit Point

Sequit Point juts out into the ocean and separates the parks eastern stretch of beach from the western one (Leo Carrillo is a south facing beach). This is a great place to watch for spouting Grey Whales, particularly during the months of February and March, and an even better place to propose marriage; my wife, Lesley, said, "yes" here one foggy evening.

Just below the point, across a narrow land bridge, are some nice tide pools. Stop in here twice a day, during low tide, to check out sea life that includes sea stars, anemones, sea urchins, sea slugs, turban snails, mussels, tubeworms, and more. (While enjoying these creatures, please go easy on them; don't harass or remove them or any of the rocks or empty shells that you come across in the tidepools—they provide essential shelter and protection.)

There is also a sea cave—actually more of a tunnel—running under a portion of the point; it can be found by heading down the stairs into the cove just east of the point.

I've come to this place many, many times to photograph the sunrise, and have been blessed to witness sea lions and dolphins fishing in the surrounding kelp forest.

One morning, if you can, wake up early and come out here too, while it's still dark, and take in the changing light and moods—you'll appreciate the beauty, the peace, and the time alone with the Lord.

Nicholas Flat-Willow Creek Loop Hike

Although both of these hikes, the Nicholas Flat and the Willow Creek Loop, can be done anytime of year, springtime, when the hills are green and flower covered, is definitely best.

Find the trailhead for this hike, marked by a small sign, near the kiosk at the Leo Carrillo Campground entrance station. As you head up, keep left at the first junction, only yards from the trailhead, and climb for about 0.8-mile to a saddle. From this saddle, head uphill about 100 feet to the Willow Creek Overlook (612ft) and its awesome views of the campground, shore, kelp beds, and the Channel Islands; you can clearly hear the crashing waves from here.

After taking in the views from the overlook, return to the saddle and either continue down the Willow Creek Trail, or up to Nicholas Flat. If you choose the Willow Creek Loop Trail, continue traveling downhill, clockwise, for about 0.7-miles to the trailhead. The total length of the loop trail is somewhere around 1.5-miles. If you decide to continue on to Nicholas Flat, head uphill from the saddle for another 1.4-miles to a pair of even grander overlooks.

Just beyond these vistas the chaparral along the trail closes in for a short time before opening up again into Nicholas Flat and its fields of grass & wildflowers, a small, cattail-lined pond, a rocky bluff, and a grove of oaks.

Explore the area, take some photographs, enjoy your lunch and a short nap and then, when you're ready, retrace your route back to the campground.

This steep trail—about 6-miles round trip in length with about 1,800 feet of accumulated elevation gain—is very exposed and best done during the cooler parts of the day.

Be sure to bring your Ten Essentials, a sunhat, and your route finding skills; many side trails intersect the Nicholas Flat Trail along its higher reaches. Also, watch for poison oak in the canyon bottoms and in small patches around Nicholas Flat—remember, "leaves of three, let it be."

Point Mugu State Park

Point Mugu State Park is located on Hwy 1, about 4.5-miles north of Leo Carrillo State Beach, or 15-miles south of the city of Oxnard. It has about 5-miles of coastline, 15,000 acres of coastal hills & canyons, more then 70-miles of hiking trails, a great sand dune called, appropriately, 'The Great Dune', and a wilderness area. One of the parks major canyons, Sycamore Canyon, has a campground, hiking trails, and a popular mountain bike route.

Sycamore Canyon Campground

Sycamore Canyon, part of Point Mugu State Park, spills out into the Pacific Ocean about 4.5-miles north of Leo Carrillo State Beach. There's a campground here with about 50 family sites, 80 undeveloped beachfront sites, restrooms, and showers. It is smaller, and less popular, then the campground at Leo Carrillo, but it is usually much quieter too—or would be but for a resident flock of parrots.

For more information contact the park at: Point Mugu State Park, 9000 West Pacific Coast Highway, Malibu, CA 90265, or by phone at 805.488.1827, or for camping reservations 800.444.7275 or www.parks.ca.gov

Sycamore Canyon To Satwiwa Hike/Bike

This roughly 16-mile round-trip route—a nice mountain bike journey or a good long hike—follows the dirt road along the bottom of Sycamore Canyon, a major drainage that once served as a trade route for area Native Americans.

Begin this adventure by heading north through Sycamore Canyon Campground into this deep, pleasant gorge shaded by oaks & sycamores, and graced by a shallow creek and, especially in the mornings and evenings, deer.

At about 7.5-miles, from the campground, the route switchbacks steeply upward for about 0.5-miles, and then levels out again. A short distance beyond this point, watch for a wooden footbridge on your right that leads to a reconstructed *ap* (the Chumash Indian word for their domed houses), and the nearby Satwiwa Cultural Center.

Satwiwa was at one time a major Chumash village located on this important trade route, which connected the inland valleys and deserts with the sea. Today there is a self-guided interpretive loop-trail through the reconstructed village, as well as weekly (Sunday only) historical presentations and cultural interpretive displays. For more information regarding Satwiwa, or the surrounding area, including maps & books, contact the Santa Monica Mountains National Recreation Area at the above address.

Waterfall Option: This is a great little side trip to make during wet periods, when the waterfall is flowing well. Here's how you get to it: Head up-canyon from the campground—as described above—for about 7.5-miles, where the route climbs steeply upward. When the trail levels out, look for a dirt road (Old Boney Trail) on the right, across from a white water tank. Take Old Boney Trail to the bottom of the valley and then, when it makes a sharp switchback uphill, take the left spur to Sycamore Canyon Falls, just a few hundred feet away.

This waterfall, more than 100-feet from top to bottom, is made up of a half-dozen cascades carved into the soft sandstone cliff. This tree-shaded setting is also a great refuge from the hot sun.

You can also make this an 8-mile (one-way) shuttle by either having someone drop you off at the top of the canyon, near Satwiwa, and traveling down-canyon to the campground, or by leaving a car at the top of the canyon and traveling up to it.

Satwiwa can be accessed, by vehicle, by exiting Highway 101 (The Ventura Freeway) at Wendy Drive in Newbury Park. Travel about 2.5-miles south on Wendy Drive to Potrero Road, and then turn right on Potrero Road for about 1.8-miles to the park entrance, across from Pinehill Road. Park here and head south along the paved fire road, passing two residences and then, on the left, Satwiwa. Continue south into Sycamore Canyon and, in about 8-miles, the campground itself.

Sycamore Canyon Overlook Hike

Catch this scenic trail at the north end of the Sycamore Canyon Campground, just beyond and to the left of the gate. From here the trail climbs to a small saddle overlooking the sea. For better views, either walk downhill a bit to the small flat or make your way across the narrow ridge to the southeast.

Below you, against the mountain, is the Great Sand Dune heaped up and kept in place by prevailing winds from the south and west. Beyond is the ocean with its sublime patterns created by the light on the swells. Grey Whales can be spotted as they migrate past this point during the months of February/March and later around October/November.

When you've finished taking in the wonderful views, hop back on the Overlook Trail— the fire road heading down from the high ridge to the north— and follow it as it winds downhill to Sycamore Canyon. At the bottom, turn right to get back to the campground.

This is an easy trail; about 2.6-miles in length and only about 350ft of total elevation gain. For a more difficult hike, extend its length by piecing together intersecting trails.

As always, watch for poison oak in the canyon bottoms and deer on the hillsides.

The Great Dune Of Point Mugu

Get to the Great Dune, from the entrance to the Sycamore Canyon Campground, by heading north on Hwy 1 for just a few minutes. You'll see the dune on your right. Park someplace safe and have a blast sliding, surfing, or racing to the top.

A few individuals will use a cardboard box to slide down the dune, and then discard it at the bottom. If you come across any of this trash, please pack it out with you.

Chumash Trail/La Jolla Valley Loop Hike

Some say that for as many as seventy centuries the Chumash Indians, and the people who lived in the land before them, trod what is now known as the Chumash Trail in their travels between the Mugu Lagoon and the La Jolla Valley. There are other, easier, routes that we could take into the awesome La Jolla Valley, but this first 0.5-mile is the coolest, the most interesting—at least from a historical perspective—and one of the least used.

Catch this trail from the Sycamore Canyon campground entrance by heading north on Hwy 1 for about 6.5-miles, to a parking area on the right (inland) side of the highway directly across from a military rifle range.

From the parking area, head straight up the steep hill to the east. This is the ancient Indian path and it is straight up and no-nonsense; there are no switchbacks whatsoever. As you climb, look for the broken seashells (primarily abalone, a food source) along the trail that were dropped by the perhaps tens of thousands of people who walked this route before you—remember, it's thought to be about 7,000 years old!

In about 0.5-mile you'll reach a saddle, at an elevation of about 886ft, where you can rest and take in views that include the lagoon that was once the site of a substantial Chumash village and beyond, out to sea, the Channel Islands.

From the saddle, head northeast (downhill) into La Jolla Valley. The Chumash once had several permanent settlements in this valley, and centuries-old shell middens (piles of shell fish thrown away by Native Americans) can still be found here. La Jolla Valley also contains one of the finest remaining native California grasslands anywhere. Overgrazing and introduced, non-native grasses have impacted most areas of the state but, unbelievably, not here; several pristine areas have managed to hold out. Finally, La Jolla Valley is the seasonal home of a small number of Monarch Butterflies that spend the winter here; look for them between December and February.

About 1-mile from the saddle (having ignored the several trails that came in from the right and then left) the trail crosses two tributaries of the West Fork, and then turns east for another 1-mile to the La Jolla Valley Walk-In Campground, on the left. The campground, in a nice grove of oaks, has drinking water, and restrooms and is a great place to spend the night if your group wants to turn this loop into an overnight backpack.

After you've had your lunch and topped off your water bottles, continue your walk by backtracking just a bit (perhaps 150-yards) and then taking the south branch of the trail, along the pond, beyond which you'll intersect the main La Jolla Trail and turn right onto it for about 0.75-mile to another well-marked trail on the right.

Take this trail, heading northwest, and soon cross the creek and climb the hillside to an overlook. About 0.5-mile beyond the overlook you'll come to a grove of oaks and, continuing upstream from here, a junction. At this junction take the left fork for about 1-mile to the intersection with the Chumash Indian trail; turn left here and descend to the parking area.

This hike is about 6-miles round trip with somewhere around 1,200ft of elevation gain; most of it in the first 0.5-mile.

Be sure to bring your Ten Essentials, a map (a simple one is available at the Sycamore Canyon Campground entrance station) and your route finding skills—lots of trails bisect the route described here and you'll need to stay on the correct one. Watch for poison oak, and remember that all archaeological artifacts and material are protected by law.

For more information regarding area maps, information or required permits for camping at the La Jolla Valley Walk-In Campground, contact: Point Mugu State Park, 9000 West Pacific Coast Highway, Malibu, CA 90265, or by phone at either 818.880.0350 or 805.488.5223, or on the web at <u>www.parks.ca.gov.</u>

CHAPTER SEVENTEEN

The Channel Islands National Park Area

Sail to, camp on, and explore any one of five extremely unique islands; Watch for four species of whales, two species of dolphins, six species of pinnipeds (seals & sea lions), and many, many thousands of sea birds; Explore hidden coves, historic buildings, and pristine tidepools; Hike to a remote beach where between 50,000 and 100,000 pinnipeds 'haul out'; Kayak into a giant sea cave; Snorkel, SCUBA dive, relax in the sun…and more!

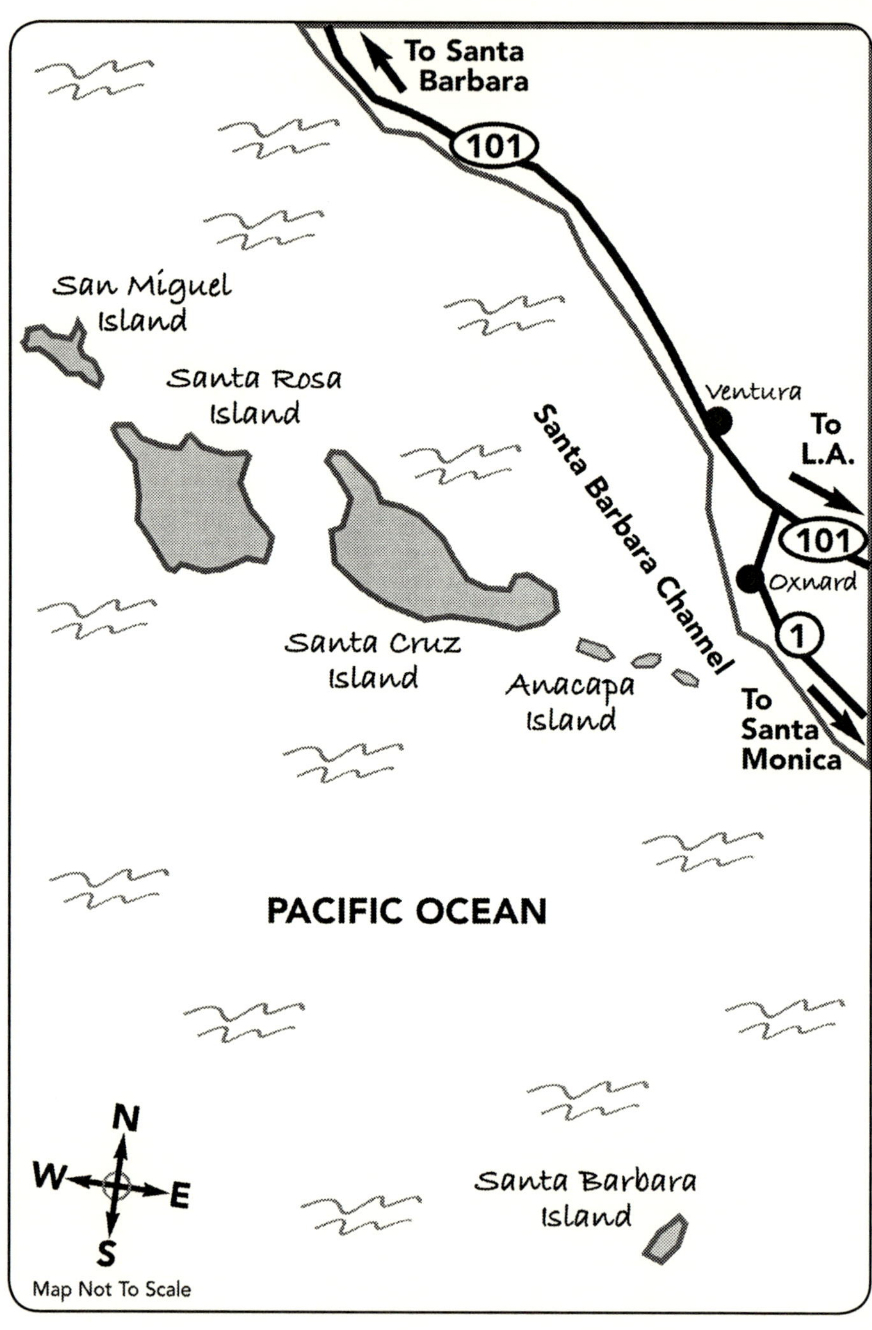

To Santa Barbara
101
San Miguel Island
Santa Rosa Island
Santa Barbara Channel
Ventura
To L.A.
101
Oxnard
1
Santa Cruz Island
Anacapa Island
To Santa Monica
PACIFIC OCEAN
N
W
E
S
Santa Barbara Island
Map Not To Scale

ABOUT THE CHANNEL ISLANDS NATIONAL PARK AREA

The Channel Islands National Park encompasses five—Anacapa, Santa Cruz, Santa Rosa, San Miguel and Santa Barbara—of California's eight islands, their surrounding ocean environment, and a beautiful Visitors Center in the mainland city of Ventura.

The islands, each one extremely distinct from the next, are home to more then 2,000 plants and animals—145 of which are found nowhere else in the world—and cultural & archaeological resources dating back many thousands of years.

The waters of the park are fantastic too; colder northern water and warmer southern water collide here, forming a wonderful transition zone habitat for amazing sea life that includes at least 27 species of whales, dolphins, and porpoises, and six species of seals & sea lions.

Because travel to the islands is by boat or plane only, the islands are lightly visited, relatively pristine, and a great place to seek solitude, to observe wildlife, and to dream away the day seaside.

You're going to have a great time here!

Getting There

To the Visitors Center:
Get to the Channel Islands National Park Visitors Center, from the north, by traveling south on Hwy 101 to the city of Ventura. Exit at Seaward, then turn left onto Harbor Blvd. Continue on Harbor Blvd to Spinnaker Drive. Turn right onto Spinnaker Drive. The Visitors Center is at the end of Spinnaker drive, on the right. The total distance, from Santa Barbara to the Visitors Center, is about 27-miles.

Get to the Channel Islands National Park Visitors Center, from the south, by traveling north on Hwy 101 to the city of Ventura. Exit at Victoria Avenue and turn left, then turn right onto Olivas Park Drive and continue to Harbor Blvd where Olivas

Park Drive becomes Spinnaker Drive. The Visitors Center is at the end of Spinnaker drive, on the right. The total distance, from Los Angeles to the Visitors Center, is about 65-miles.

To the Islands:

Aside from making your way by private vessel (contact the National Park Service for more information regarding this alternative), there are three year-round options for travel to the islands themselves:

1) *Island Packers*, departing from Channel Islands Harbor, is licensed by the park service to transport visitors by boat to any one of the islands. They offer a variety of half-day to multi-day trips. For more information (prices, schedules, and reservations), contact: Island Packers, 1691 Spinnaker Drive, Ventura, CA 93001, or by phone at 805.642.1393, or via the web at: www.islandpackers.com.

2) *Truth Aquatics*, departing from Santa Barbara Harbor, is also licensed to transport visitors by boat to all five of the islands. They, too, offer trips from one to several days long. For prices, schedules, and reservation information, contact: Truth Aquatics, 301 West Cabrillo Blvd, Santa Barbara, CA 93101-3886, or by phone at 805.962.1127, or via the web at: www.truthaquatics.com.

3) *Channel Islands Aviation*, departing from the Camarillo Airport, is licensed by the park service to fly visitors to Santa Rosa Island. For more information, contact: Channel Islands Aviation, 305 Durley Avenue, Camarillo, CA 93010, or by phone at 805.987.1301, or via the web at: www.flycia.com.

Photo credit: National Park Service

As you cross the Santa Barbara Channel on your way to the islands, keep an eye out for whales, dolphins, and porpoises. At least 27 species—one third of the planets' total—have been spotted here. Among the most common are:

Gray Whales, which reach lengths of up to 50 feet, weigh from 20 to 40 tons and make a yearly 10,000-mile round-trip migration from Alaska to Mexico. Look for them in the Santa Barbara Channel between December and April.

Humpback Whales, which are also known as singing whales for their beautiful songs that change from year to year, reach up to 51 feet in length and weigh up to 37 tons. They can be seen in the western part of the Santa Barbara Channel, typically from June through October.

Blue Whales, which are larger even than any dinosaur yet discovered. They reach lengths of 100 feet, weigh up to 160 tons, possess a heart the size of a Volkswagen, and a tongue that weighs as much as an adult African Elephant. In the summer months Blue Whales can be seen near San Miguel and Santa Rosa Islands.

The *Orca Whale* (Killer Whale), which travels in groups (or, *pods*) of from 6 to 30 animals. They are easily recognizable by their black and white pattern and dominant dorsal fin, which can be as much as six feet tall in adult males. Orca pods can be seen migrating through the Santa Barbara Channel anytime of year.

Bottlenose Dolphins, like Flipper from the TV show of the same name, reach lengths of 10 feet. These year-round residents of the Santa Barbara Channel are very acrobatic and can often be seen surfing the bows of sea craft.

Common Dolphins, which have a black back, yellow or tan sides, a white belly, reach lengths of about 6 feet, and travel in groups of hundreds. With as many as 60,000 Common Dolphins in the Santa Barbara Channel, it's very likely that you'll get to experience the thrill of watching them ride the bow of your boat.

Lodging, Supplies, Maps & Information

There is absolutely no lodging or supplies of any kind on any of the Channel Islands; you'll have to pack enough gear, supplies, and (on most islands) water for your stay.

The National Park Service has an awesome Visitors Center, The Robert J. Lagomarsino Visitors Center, in the city of Ventura. It's packed with interpretive programs, three dimensional models of the islands, a 25-minute movie titled, "Treasure in the Sea", a living tide pool display, interactive exhibits featuring the unique characteristics of each island, a tower with telescopes for viewing the islands, a bookstore, and knowledgeable staff to answer all of your questions. The Visitors Center is open daily from 8:30am to 5:00pm, closing only on Thanksgiving and Christmas.

As far as maps go, I recommend the Trails Illustrated map for Channel Islands National Park. You can purchase this map directly from the park, or contact Trails Illustrated by phone at 800.962.1643 or on the web at: www.trailsillustrated.com.

I recommend, too, that you contact the park for brochures, a copy of their very informative visitors guide (*Island Views: A Visitor's Guide to Channel Islands National Park*), and any other information you may need regarding camping, special regulations, required permits or closures: Channel Islands National Park, 1901 Spinnaker Drive, Ventura, CA 93001, or by phone at 805.658.5730, or via the web at: www.nps.gov/chis/.

Camping On The Islands

Here are a few basic issues to consider while traveling and camping within the Channel Islands National Park:

- Camping is available year-round, on all five of the Channel Islands, at a cost of $10.00 per night. Reservations are required and can be made, no more than 3 months in advance, by calling 800.365.CAMP (2267) or online at: www.reservations.nps.gov.
- Boats usually fill up before the campgrounds do. Generally, when planning a trip, a party makes camping reservations and then considers their travel arrangements. Here, in this park, that formula is reversed; the travel arrangements need to be made first, and then the campsites reserved.
- Each of the islands has a single, primitive, campground (except Santa Cruz which has two) with picnic tables, and pit toilets.
- Santa Cruz and Santa Rosa Islands have drinking water, but you'll have to bring your own to the other islands. How much will you need for drinking and cooking? A good estimate is one-gallon per person, per day, but only you will know if that's enough for your particular group.

- There are no supplies of any kind on any of the islands; no way to run to the market to pick up matches, or guacamole, or whatever. No stores, no taco stands, no ice machines, nothing. Be sure and bring absolutely everything that you'll need and pack it in such a way that you'll be able to transport it to your campsite once you arrive on the island.
- Camp stoves are allowed on all of the islands, all of the time, but campfires are only allowed on Santa Cruz, and then only between December 1st and May 15th.
- There are no trash containers for visitors use anywhere on the islands, so please pack out what you pack in— and then some.
- Backcountry beach camping is allowed, between June 1st and December 31st, only on Santa Rosa Island. To protect wildlife, various restrictions apply at various times to various beaches. Coordinate your plans with the park service.
- Some of the islands have piers with ladders as much as 20 feet high, which you'll need to be able to climb while carrying your gear. On other islands the landing is made directly onto the beach in a rubber boat, virtually guaranteeing a wet arrival. You may also have to transport your gear, on foot, at least 0.5 mile from the landing to the campground. Check with the concessionaire for

details about the landing on the island you plan to visit, and how you can best prepare for it.

- Prepare for weather changes and temperatures fluctuations, even on summer days, by dressing in layers with a wind/water-proof top layer; fast moving fog can cause the temperature to plummet in a very short while, intense sun (there is little shade on some islands) will make a hat & sunscreen critical, and the sea breeze will always be blowing.
- Be prepared for a good sea-spray dousing while traveling by boat, and then a potential soaking while disembarking.
- Be prepared for stout winds, especially on the wild outer islands, by having a solid, low-profile tent, including stakes and parachute-type chord to adequately secure it.
- Watch for poison oak on the islands; remember, "Leaves of three, let it be"
- While not at all likely, it is possible that weather events or sea conditions could prevent a timely pick up for your return home; you'll want to carry a days worth of extra food & water just in case.

Sea Kayaking The Islands

Sea Kayaking is a wildly popular way to experience elements of the Channel Islands unavailable to the land-bound visitor, including sea caves, wildlife, amazing solitude, and a unique perspective on this awesome place; it's just a great way to see the islands.

If you're an experienced sea kayaker, and are interested in exploring the islands from your boat, give the park's concessionaires (Island Packers & Truth Aquatics) a call and arrange to have one of them transport your kayak for you. If you're headed to Santa Rosa Island, and you don't want to take the ferry, call Channel Islands Aviation; they'll fly you and your folding boat to that islands airstrip.

If you are very experienced—and are conditioned and equipped—you can ditch the concessionaire plan altogether and simply paddle from the mainland to Anacapa Island, 14 miles away. There are some hazards to this trip, though; you'll be paddling across one of the busiest shipping lanes in the state, currents around the islands are strong, and poor weather—including very dense fog and high winds—can sweep in very quickly and require you to navigate by compass and chart.

For more information regarding kayaking the waters of Channel Islands National Park, including *extremely* important safety considerations, contact the park rangers or go to www.nps.gov/chis/kayaking.

A guided trip through one of the concessionaires is the greatest way for the less-experienced kayaker to safely explore the islands. The concessionaire will handle the logistics; they'll transport your group to the chosen island, supply them with kayaks and safety gear, and assign them an experienced, safety-conscious, guide who is familiar with the local waters.

As a bonus this guide will probably be a trained naturalist, know the best areas to see wildlife, tour the best sea caves, and feed you lunch.

Contact Island Packers or Truth Aquatics regarding their island kayak trips. If these aren't satisfactory, contact the parks' Visitors Center and request a listing of area outfitters offering kayak trips to the Channel Islands.

THE ISLANDS

Anacapa Island

Anacapa Island (700-acres), a short 14-miles from the mainland, is really made up of three small islets that stretch about 5-miles in length and are accessible to each other only by boat. These islets boast high cliffs, lava tubes, at least 130 sea caves, and a fantastic 40-foot high natural bridge called, "Arch Rock." Anacapa also has a huge sea bird population—including the largest breeding colonies of California Brown Pelicans & Western Gulls in the world—and rocky coves where California sea lions and harbor seals haul out to rest and breed.

Sea kayaking, snorkeling, SCUBA diving, and wildlife viewing are among the most popular activities on Anacapa. Not SCUBA certified? No worries. Every Tuesday and Thursday, during the summer months, park rangers dive into Landing Cove with video cameras hooked up to onshore monitors, allowing you to check out the beauty without ever getting your feet wet!

Though this is a cliff island, with no beach access, the wildlife, scenery, and amazing spring wildflowers more than make up for it.

Hiking On Anacapa

There are only a couple of miles of trails on this island, but the scenery is unparalleled. The trails to Pinniped Point and Cathedral Cove, for example, overlook seal and sea lion haul-outs. The Inspiration Point Trail has magnificent views, and the Lighthouse Hike will take you to the last lighthouse built on the West Coast.

Check with the Visitors Center or, once on the island, the resident ranger for wildlife viewing tips, and detailed hiking information.

Camping On Anacapa

The island's primitive campground, with 7 sites and a capacity of about 30 people, is located on the plateau, about 154 steep steps from the landing dock. Be sure to pack your gear in such a way that you can carry it to the top.

Remember, there is no drinking water available on Anacapa Island.

Santa Cruz Island

Located just 19-miles from the mainland, Santa Cruz is—at about 24-miles long, 6-miles wide and with 77-miles of rugged coastline—the largest island in the park. Jointly managed by The Nature Conservancy and the National Park Service, Santa Cruz is home to Picacho Diablo (2,434ft), the highest peak in the Channel Islands, a large central valley, several springs and year-round streams, beautiful beaches, pristine tidepools, and many miles of coastal cliffs.

Santa Cruz is also home to one of the largest sea caves in the world. Painted Cave, named after the colorful rock, lichens, and algae found within it, is about 100-feet wide, 160-feet high, nearly 0.25-mile long and, in the springtime, has a beautiful waterfall that flows over its entrance.

More then 650 species of plants and 140 species of birds inhabit the island, as well as seals and sea lions, which can often be seen warming themselves along the waters edge, and dolphins and whales that feed just off shore.

The Chumash Indians are believed to have inhabited Santa Cruz for more then 80 centuries. They lived in 12 separate villages, traveled between the mainland and the islands on large plank canoes, called Tomols, and left behind thousands of shell middens that still dot the island today.

The adobe ranch houses, barns, a chapel, blacksmith and saddle shops are relics of the other history on the island, the ranching days of the 19th & 20th centuries.

Sea kayaking, snorkeling, beach combing, SCUBA diving, tide-pooling, hiking, sunbathing, wildlife watching, and landscape photography are popular on Santa Cruz.

Oh, and don't miss the exceptional springtime wildflower show.

Hiking On Santa Cruz

The trails and roads that traverse the island provide stunning views of pristine beaches, coves, mountains, and canyons. One of these trails is The Nature Conservancy's 4.2-mile (round trip) coastal trail between Prisoner's Harbor and Pelican Bay; contact The Nature Conservancy for a required permit.

The eastern end of the island (the 14,500 acres managed by the National Park Service) also has several trails and roads that lead to fantastic places with names like Cavern Point, Potato Harbor, and Smugglers Cove. Some of these hikes are up to 18-miles (round trip) in length and quite strenuous. For more information, contact the Visitors Center and request the brochure, *"Hiking Eastern Santa Cruz Island"* and inquire about any required permits, closures, etc. Also, study your map before heading out and then, once on the island, grill the resident ranger for current route information.

Camping On Santa Cruz

The National Park Service operates two year-round campgrounds on Santa Cruz Island. The first campground is at Scorpion Ranch—once the site of the largest Chumash Indian village on the island—with 25 sites, tables, drinking water, pit toilets, and a capacity of about 200-persons. Camp stoves are permitted year-round here but, because of the danger of wildfire, campfires are only permitted between December 1st and May 15th. As with the other islands, there are no supplies of any kind on Santa Cruz, so bring everything with you that you'll need and be prepared to carry it at least 0.5-mile from the boat landing to the lower campground.

There is also an oak-shaded backcountry/backpacking campground at Del Norte on, well, the north side of the island. The 3.5-mile (one way) route to this site follows the historic Ranch Road Trail, from Prisoners Landing, as it climbs through oak woodland and coastal sage to a great overlook about 700ft above sea level.

Get to the Del Norte backcountry camp, from Prisoners Landing, by following the Navy Road (maintained gravel) out of the harbor as it climbs about 600 feet in the first 1-mile. Turn left (east) onto the signed Del Norte Trail and follow it for about 2-miles to a signed junction with Del Norte Road. Follow the short 0.5-mile trail to the campground.

This campground, set in an oak grove, has four sites, picnic tables, a pit toilet, and great views of Santa Cruz's unspoiled coastline. Please note that fires are not permitted here anytime of year and that you will have to carry everything that you need on your back, including lots of water.

Another option, from Del Norte, is to continue on to Scorpion Ranch, about 11.5-miles east by unmaintained trail. If this sounds interesting to you, coordinate a strategy with your concessionaire; they'll drop you off at one end (Prisoner's Landing) and pick you up at the other (the Scorpion Campground). Don't forget (1) that you'll need extra water, and (2) no camping is allowed between Del Norte and Scorpion Ranch.

Contact the park service for detailed route information, including the brochure, *"Backcountry Camping on Santa Cruz Island."*

There is no camping of any kind allowed on The Nature Conservancy's western majority of the island, but those wishing to hike—and kayakers wishing to land there—may do so with a permit. This permit takes at least a couple of weeks to process and there is a fee involved. Contact The Nature Conservancy by phone at 805.642.0345 (ext.510), or online at: www.nature.org.

Santa Rosa Island

Santa Rosa Island is, at about 15-miles long and 10-miles wide, the second largest of the islands. It's about 40-miles from the mainland and is endowed with high mountains, steep canyons, grass-covered hills, sandy beaches & coastal marshes, and is home to at least 195 species of birds, and several plants and animals found nowhere else in the world. Thousands of fascinating paleontological/archaeological sites have been mapped here too, including a complete pygmy mammoth skeleton excavated in 1994.

This island is a great place to hike, fish, SCUBA dive, snorkel, kayak, beach comb, and photograph. With a ranger-guide there are also opportunities to explore some of the protected resources on the island, including fantastic midden sites and tide pools.

Hiking On Santa Rosa

Several sections of trail, road, and beach have been patched together to create some great island hikes of varying degrees of difficulty.

Contact the National Park Service to inquire about hiking opportunities to such places as midden sites, tide pools, wildlife viewing areas, sculpted cliffs, white sand beaches, awesome canyons, and panoramic overlooks. Also, be sure to request the brochure, *"Backcountry Beach Camping on Santa Rosa Island"* for additional hiking information.

Camping On Santa Rosa

The campground at Water Canyon, on Santa Rosa Island, is about 1.5 level miles from the boat landing, or 0.25-mile from the airstrip. It has 15 sites with windbreaks, a capacity of 50 people, and drinking water.

Backcountry beach camping is also available for kayakers and hikers but, to protect breeding wildlife, various stretches of beach are closed at various times of the year. For more information about permits, closures, and restrictions, contact the park managers and ask for a copy of the brochure, *"Backcountry Beach Camping on Santa Rosa Island"*,.

San Miguel Island

San Miguel Island is, at about 55-miles west of Ventura, the furthest island from the mainland. It is 8 miles long, 4-miles wide and has about 27-miles of rugged coastline, sandy white beaches, lush grasses, and beautiful wildflowers. Because of its location and exposure to the elements, it is subject to frequent heavy fog and high winds.

During the winter months the westernmost beach on San Miguel, Point Bennett, is packed with between 50,000 and 100,000 seals, sea lions, and their pups. In fact, this is the only place in the world where as many as six species of seals and sea lions (pinnipeds) can be found at the same time.

There are more than 600 documented archaeological sites here that represent, it is believed, up to eleven centuries of human habitation, and paleontological discoveries that include fossilized pygmy mammoths. Another of this islands wonder's, a geological one called the 'Caliche Forest', was created when plant stumps and roots were cast in caliche sand, leaving behind, after the plants decayed, a stone ghost forest.

As on the other islands, SCUBA diving, snorkeling, hiking, photography, wildlife, and wildflower viewing are the activities most enjoyed here.

Hiking On San Miguel

Because of the fragility of this island's cultural and environmental resources, there are only a couple of hikes that visitors can do unescorted: Cuyler Harbor Beach (2-miles round-trip) and the Lester Ranch Site (also about 2-miles, round-trip). The balance of your wanderings must be done in the company of a ranger.

One of those ranger-led treks must be the 16-mile round-trip walk to the Point Bennet overlook, an area that the park service calls one of the largest concentrations of wildlife in the world; the male Elephant Seals are audible from nearly 3-miles out!

Contact the Visitors Center ahead of your trip for details regarding ranger led walks on San Miguel Island.

Camping On San Miguel

The campground on San Miguel Island is a steep 1-mile uphill from the landing, has 9 sites with a capacity of 30 people, windbreaks, picnic tables, and pit toilets, but no drinking water.

If it's a wilderness experience that you're looking for, San Miguel may be it; fewer than 200 people per year experience the extremes of camping on this remote, ruggedly beautiful, and often very windy island.

Santa Barbara Island

Among the five islands in Channel Islands National Park, Santa Barbara Island is the smallest (only 638 acres) and the furthest south. Located about 38-miles west of San Pedro, it boasts a few narrow & rocky beaches, canyons, a badlands region, and Signal Peak, at 635 ft the islands highest point. Like Anacapa, Santa Barbara Island is a breeding ground for a tremendous number of sea birds, with some even nesting alongside the trails.

Snorkeling & SCUBA diving are big here, as are hiking, fishing, kayaking, and wildlife watching. The island also has a small Visitors Center with a few exhibits.

Hiking On Santa Barbara Island

The island's trails include Arch Point Loop Trail, the Elephant Seal Cove Trail, and the Signal Peak Loop Trail, and offer about 6.5 miles of fantastic coastal, wildflower and wildlife viewing.

The Canyon View Nature Trail is a self-guided trail located near the ranger station and campground; grab a brochure before heading out on this one.

Camping On Santa Barbara Island

The campground on Santa Barbara Island is a steep 0.5-mile uphill from the landing, has 10 sites, a capacity of about 30 people and is, of course, without water.

CHAPTER EIGHTEEN

The Carrizo Plain National Monument Area

Explore one of the last and largest tracts of California grass-lands, a fascinating mineralized lake, and several historic farms; Wonder at amazing Native American rock art & village sites; Watch for Pronghorn Antelope, Tule Elk, Sandhill Cranes, and the rare California Condor; 'Bag' the highest point in the monument; Be amazed by one of the most incredible wildflower displays in the state; See, firsthand, a shifting fault; Visit an elk preserve; Fall asleep to singing coyotes…and more!

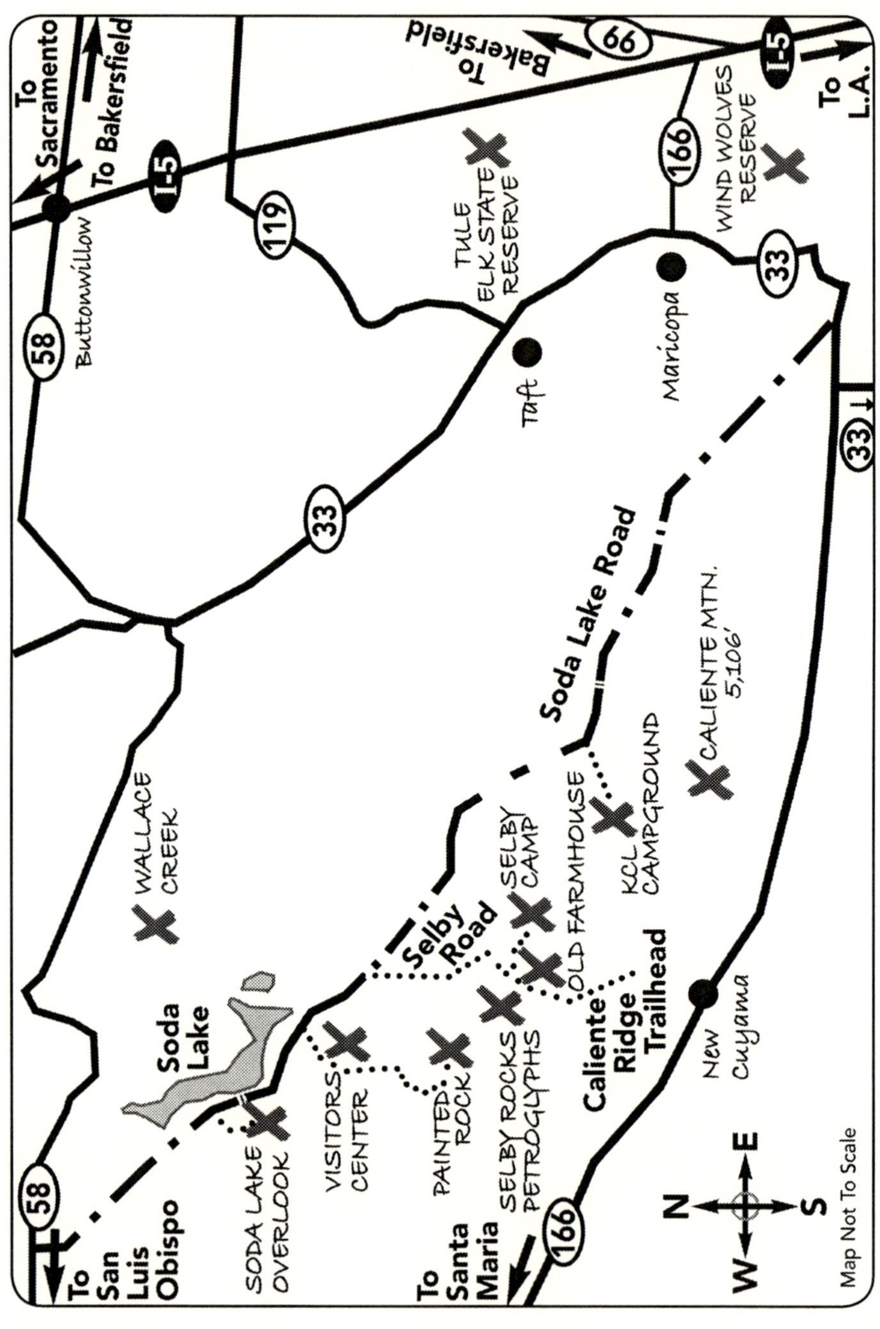

To Sacramento
To Bakersfield
Buttonwillow
58
I-5
119
To Bakersfield
99
66
I-5
To L.A.
166
WIND WOLVES RESERVE
33
TULE ELK STATE RESERVE
Maricopa
Taft
33
33
Soda Lake Road
CALIENTE MTN. 5,106'
WALLACE CREEK
Soda Lake
SELBY CAMP
Selby Road
OLD FARMHOUSE
KCL CAMPGROUND
VISITORS CENTER
PAINTED ROCK
SELBY ROCKS PETROGLYPHS
Caliente Ridge Trailhead
New Cuyama
SODA LAKE OVERLOOK
To San Luis Obispo
To Santa Maria
166
N
E
S
W
Map Not To Scale

ABOUT THE CARRIZO PLAIN AREA

The 250,000-acre Carrizo Plain is a vast grassland pierced by the San Andreas Fault, bordered by beautiful mountains, and home to re-introduced populations of Pronghorn Antelope and Tule Elk. This place is adorned by Soda Lake, a bright bed of white salt for most of the year, but seasonally a beautiful lake and winter home for hundreds of Sandhill Cranes.

In addition there are fascinating rock formations containing ancient Native American rock art, remnants of historic homesteads, many rare and endangered animals, including the California Condor with its 9 foot wingspan and, when conditions are right, phenomenal wildflowers displays.

This is truly one of my favorite places.

Getting There

From the Los Angeles area, travel north on Interstate 5, climbing over the Grapevine to the Central Valley. Exit at Hwy 166, about 3.75-miles north of the Interstate 5/Hwy 99 split, and then head west for about 23-miles to the very small town of Maricopa.

Gas up in Maricopa and continue on Hwy 166 (now signed 166/33) heading southwest, for about 8.5-miles. Near the top of the grade, on the right, look for a very old Union 76 filling station (now closed); this is the intersection of Hwy 166/33 & Soda Lake Road. Turn right (northwest) here, onto Soda Lake Road, for approximately 30-miles, and then turn left (west) onto Painted Rock Road. The Goodwin Education Center (the Visitors Center) is located 0.5-mile west of the intersection of Soda Lake Road and Painted Rock Road, on the left.

Get to the monument from the north, on Hwy 58 between Santa Margarita and McKittrick, by heading south on Soda Lake Road for about 10-miles into the monument.

Note: Soda Lake Road, the primary road through the monument, is a good dirt lane for most of its length, but can be muddy and slippery after heavy rains. Be sure to watch for livestock and wildlife as well, particularly when traveling at night.

Supplies, Lodging, Maps & Information

Supplies, gas, and very limited lodging are available in the nearby towns of New Cuyama, Taft and Maricopa.

The monument's Visitors Center, the Guy L. Goodwin Educational Center, has several exhibits, books & brochures, a very knowledgeable staff, and handicapped accessible restrooms.

The educational center is open from 9am to 5pm, Thursday through Sunday, from December to May. At other times, informational maps and brochures are available at the front door of the center. Also, check the kiosks located at the monuments north and south entrances for up to date information regarding road conditions/closures, camping regulations, etc.

Contact the Carrizo Plain National Monument, between the months of December and May, at: Guy L. Goodwin Education Center, PO Box 3087, California Valley, CA 93453 or by phone at 661.475.2131.

Other months, contact: Bureau of Land Management, Bakersfield Field Office, 3801 Pegasus Drive, Bakersfield, CA 93308, or by phone at 661.391.6000, or on the web at: www.ca.blm.gov/bakersfield/carrizoplain.html.

As far as maps go, be sure that you have DeLorme's, "Southern & Central California Atlas & Gazetteer", or its equivalent, and AAA's *"Kern County"* & *"San Luis Obispo County"* maps. Also, pick up the simple (but free) 8 ½" x 11" map available at the Guy L. Goodwin Visitors Center; it's marked with all of the sites described in this chapter, including their mileage.

Traveling And Camping On The Carrizo Plain

There are a few things to consider when traveling and camping on the beautiful, and fairly remote, Carrizo Plain:

- Most of the roads that crisscross the Carrizo Plain are unimproved dirt and may become impassable during periods of heavy rain. Even the main road through the monument, Soda Lake Road, can be muddy and slippery. Check with the Visitors Center or the BLM for information about current road conditions & temporary closures.
- The monument is without water or trash pick-up; carry at *least* one gallon of water per person, per day, and please, please pack out more trash than you packed in.
- A campfire permit is required for any open fire. They're free; pick one up from the BLM, the employees at the Visitors Center, or any patrolling ranger.
- Camping at either of the campgrounds discussed below is on a first come, first served basis only.
- You'll need to have a permit if you have a group of 20 or more participants, or if you intend to charge them anything. Contact the Bakersfield BLM office at 661.391.6120.

There are basically three options for camping within the monument—(1) the KCL Ranch Campground, (2) the Selby Rocks Campground, and (3) primitive camping:

The KCL Ranch Campground, on land formerly owned by the Kern County Land Company, has 8 sites with picnic tables, fire rings, pit toilets, shade trees, a few of the original barns & outbuildings to explore, and a corral for your horses, if you have them. Camping here is first come, first served and, again, you'll need (1) a free fire permit, (2) to bring all of the water that you require, and (3) to pack out all of your trash.

Get to the KCL Ranch Campground, from the south, by traveling north on Soda Lake Road, from its junction with Hwy 166/33, for about 20-miles. The campground is on the left, just before Soda Lake Road angles sharply to the right (east).

The Selby Rocks Campground, with five picnic tables and four fire pits (but no shade), is in an awesome setting at the base of the Caliente Mountains and boasts fascinating rock formations, an old farmhouse & barn, and many acres of wilderness to explore.

Get to the Selby Rocks Campground, from Hwy 166/33 to the south, by heading north on Soda Lake Road for about 29.2-miles and intersect with Selby Road coming in from the left. Follow Selby Road up the hill for about 4.5-miles, to an abandoned farmhouse and a fork in the road; the left fork takes you, in about 1 more mile, to Selby Rocks Campground.

Primitive Camping-Primitive camping is allowed on the Carrizo Plain within certain areas. Contact the BLM, or swing by the Visitors Center, for rules, regulations and permits.

Tours

On Saturdays and Sundays, during the months of April and May, docents lead two separate tours out of the Visitors Center—*The Painted Rock/Wildflower Tour* & *The Wallace Creek/Wildflower Tour.*

The Painted Rock/Wildflower Tour, offered on Saturdays from 10am to 3pm, begins at the Soda Lake overlook, goes on to explore the area's plant communities, and ends at Painted Rock.

The Wallace Creek/Wildflower Tour, offered on Sundays from 10am to 2pm, begins at the Soda Lake Overlook, goes on to explore the Carrizo's plant communities, and ends on the San Andreas Fault line at Wallace Creek.

There is also a guided tour to Painted Rock during the months of March through May, which is nesting season for sensitive Prairie Falcons. This is the only way to visit this site during this period.

These tours are by reservation only and limited to 25 participants per leader. For more details, and to reserve your space (they fill up early), contact the Visitors Center staff ASAP at 661.475.2131. While you're on the phone with them, inquire about arranging a special midweek tour just for your group.

Soda Lake Overlook

Soda Lake is a fascinating 3,000-acre alkali lake where hundreds of Sandhill Cranes winter and, in the spring, thousands of shoreline wildflowers explode in brilliant colors. In the other seasons, the summer and fall, it is a dry, salt-encrusted, lakebed speckled with twisting, heat-driven dust devils.

Photo credit: Bureau of Land Management

Catch all this action, as well as some wonderful sunrises and sets, by heading north on Soda Lake Road from the Visitors Center, for approximately 5-miles, and then taking the dirt road coming in from the left. This road winds around the back of the hill to a parking area (with restrooms) and the overlook.

Soda Lake Trail

Catch this short 0.75-mile trail—a portion of which negotiates a shoreline boardwalk—by parking at the Soda Lake Overlook parking area and walking across Soda Lake Road.

In the cooler, wetter, months search the lakeshore for Sandhill Cranes (November to February), fairy shrimp, and wildflowers. In the warmer, dry season check out one of the last remaining alkali wetlands in the state, and the unique salt loving plant community that thrives there.

Painted Rock

Painted Rock is an isolated 55ft high, horseshoe-shaped rock just to the southwest of the Guy L. Goodwin Visitors Center. Within the inner walls of this outcrop are some beautiful paintings, the remnant of what was at one time possibly the most elaborate pictograph panel on the continent.

Get there, from the Visitors Center, by traveling southwest on Painted Rock Road to the trailhead, and then walking just over 0.5-mile down a gently sloped dirt road.

Souvenir hunters descended upon this site at the turn of the last century—breaking off pieces to take home and leaving behind their own graffiti—but enough of the panel remains to get a sense of its former greatness. Look beyond the vandalism to appreciate the small but intact paintings, and the setting as a whole. There is a Chumash Tomol, or plank canoe, carrying dancing humans, and a red snake that runs the entire length of the southern panel, seemingly slithering into and out of a crack in the rock. There are turtles, and rattlesnakes, and grid patterns, and chevrons, and several other panels along the outside of the rock as well.

Bring your sunhat & water—it can be extremely hot here in the summer—and watch where you step and where you put your hands; I've seen several rattlesnakes in the area, and both black widow spiders and bees make their homes in the cracks and potholes of the rock. As with all rock art sites, please do not climb on the rock, or touch the paintings themselves.

Please note: From March 1st through June 15th, access is restricted to protect the Prairie Falcons that nest within the alcoves and on the ledges of this and other area rock formations. During the months of March through May, though, access may be made through participation in a guided tour.

Between June 16th and February 28th visitation is unrestricted; you can visit on your own, without a tour guide.

For more information regarding restrictions or tours, call the BLM's Bakersfield office at 661.391.6000 or, during the months of December through May, the Goodwin Educational Center at 661.475.2131.

Selby Rocks: Pictographs and Bedrock Mortars

Get to the Selby Rocks pictographs, from the junction of Hwy 166/33, by heading north on Soda Lake Road for about 29.2-miles, where it intersects Selby Road coming in from the left. Follow Selby Road up the hill for about 4.5-miles, to an abandoned farmhouse and a fork in the road. Park along here somewhere and walk up the right fork of the road for between 50 and 100 yards where, on your right (east), you'll see two large rock formations in the field. The one closest to the road has pictographs (paintings) on the east (opposite) side, halfway up the rock. The pictographs are somewhat faded and best viewed in shadow.

As you walk through the field, and around the rock formations, keep an eye out for the flat, nearly ground level rock slabs scattered about; many of them have bedrock mortars that were used, for centuries, by the native Chumash & Yokuts Indians to process their food.

As always, please don't climb the rocks or touch the rock art in any way, and take only photographs.

Caliente Mountain Hike

Caliente Mountain (5,106ft), in the range of the same name, is the highest point in San Luis Obispo County.

Get to the Caliente Ridge Trail, from the south, by heading north on Soda Lake Road for about 29.2-miles from its junction with Hwy 166/33. At this point you'll intersect Selby Road coming in from the left. Follow Selby Road up the hill for about 4.5-miles to an abandoned farmhouse and a fork in the road; take the right fork for about 3-miles (passing a wonderful overlook) to the trailhead area.

The route for this roughly 16-mile round-trip hike follows the dirt access road along the ridge, gaining and losing moderate amounts of elevation along the way.

This distance is sort of relative, but about 1.5-hours into your walk you'll come across an old cow camp, if it still exists, complete with an old trailer, a corral, and a dilapidated picnic table shaded by a juniper.

Over the next couple of hours or so you'll pass a wildlife guzzler (a watering station; look for Black-tailed Deer and other wildlife through here), and wonderful views of both the Carrizo Plain and the Cuyama Valley. As you near the summit, watch for fossils in the rocks along the road.

There is a very, very run down shack on the summit that was used as an early warning system during the Second World War, when it was feared that the Japanese might attack the oil fields around Maricopa. Inside this shack, if it is still standing, in the corner, on a rickety table, is the register for this peak. Be sure to sign it, enjoy your lunch, take plenty of photographs and, when you are ready, retrace your steps to the trailhead.

Spring or Fall—or under a full moon—are the optimum times to climb this peak. Winters on the ridgeline can be very cold and snowy, while summer temperatures can exceed 100 degrees.

The Caliente Ridge Road to the trailhead—twisty and rutted but passable by two-wheel drive vehicles—may be closed during periods of heavy rain or snow. Contact the BLM for information and current conditions.

Wallace Creek Trail/San Andreas Fault Tour

This very short (0.20-mile) trail leads to an overlook of the San Andreas Fault, which runs along the eastern length of the Carrizo Plain.

Get to the Wallace Creek Trail, from the Goodwin Education Center, by driving north on Soda Lake Road for about 1-mile and then turning right (northeast) onto Simmler Road. Stay on Simmler Road for about 6.2-miles, and then turn right (southeast) onto Elkhorn Road. The parking area is about 1.4-miles down Elkhorn Road.

Before heading out, be sure to swing by the Visitors Center to grab an interpretive brochure and check on road conditions; Simmler Road may be inaccessible during the wet season.

Check, too, '*The Resources*' section of this book for creation science organizations that offer other views on geological ages and such.

ADVENTURES OUTSIDE THE MONUMENT

Below are a couple of interesting sites to visit just outside the monument:

Tule Elk State Preserve

If you missed seeing the reintroduced and very reclusive Tule Elk while visiting the Carrizo Plain, it's not too late—a nearby preserve contains dozens of them and they're absolutely beautiful. Look for them during the late summer and early fall when the bull elk, driven by the rut, spend their days bugling, clashing, and tearing up the sod with their antlers. Winter can be a beautiful time too, especially on very cold mornings when the elk's breath vaporizes in clouds around them.

Get to the Tule Elk State Preserve, from the south, by heading north on Interstate 5, from the Interstate 5/Highway 99 split, for about 35-miles. Exit at Stockdale Road and head west (left) over the interstate for 1.2-miles to Morris Road. Turn left (south) on Morris Road for about 1.5-miles; the preserve is 0.2-mile ahead, on the left, just at the bend in the road.

The preserve has a small observation deck, restrooms, and a nice picnic area under the trees. Be sure and bring binoculars if you have them. Questions? Contact: Tule Elk State Preserve, 8653 Station Road, Buttonwillow, CA 93206, or by phone at 661.764.6881, or online at: www.parks.ca.gov.

Wind Wolves Preserve

This fantastic place—"Wind Wolves" are the waves that roll through tall grass on windy days—is, at more than 97,000-acres, the largest privately owned nature preserve on the West Coast. Located in the San Emigdio Mountains, its elevations range from 640ft to 6,000ft and its landscape embraces rolling grasslands, oak savannah and, higher up, pinion-juniper, and ponderosa pines. The preserve is home to Black Bears, Mountain Lions, Bobcats, Black-tailed Deer, re-introduced Tule Elk, the occasional itinerant California Condor, and several world-class pictograph panels painted by Chumash Indians.

The conservancy has opened this jewel to the public on weekends for hiking, camping, picnicking, and wildlife observation. For more information, contact: Wind Wolves Preserve, 16033 Maricopa Highway (mailing address: PO Box 189), Maricopa, CA 93252, or by phone at 661.858.1115, or on the web at: www.wildlandsconservancy.org.

Get to the preserve, from the junction of Interstate 5/Hwy 99, by heading north on Interstate 5 for about 3.75-miles and exiting at Hwy 166 (Maricopa Highway). Head west on Hwy 166 for about 7.5-miles to Old River Road, and turn left (south) to the preserve entrance.

CHAPTER NINETEEN

The Havasupai Reservation Area

Venture by foot, horseback, or helicopter into a deep canyon, with high red walls and a turquoise, spring-fed river; Camp just outside an Indian Village, along the cottonwood-lined river; Stand in awe of amazing waterfalls as much as 200ft high; Walk to the Colorado River, or into the village for fry bread; Send a letter out by pack mule; Swim, sunbathe, explore the days away…and more!

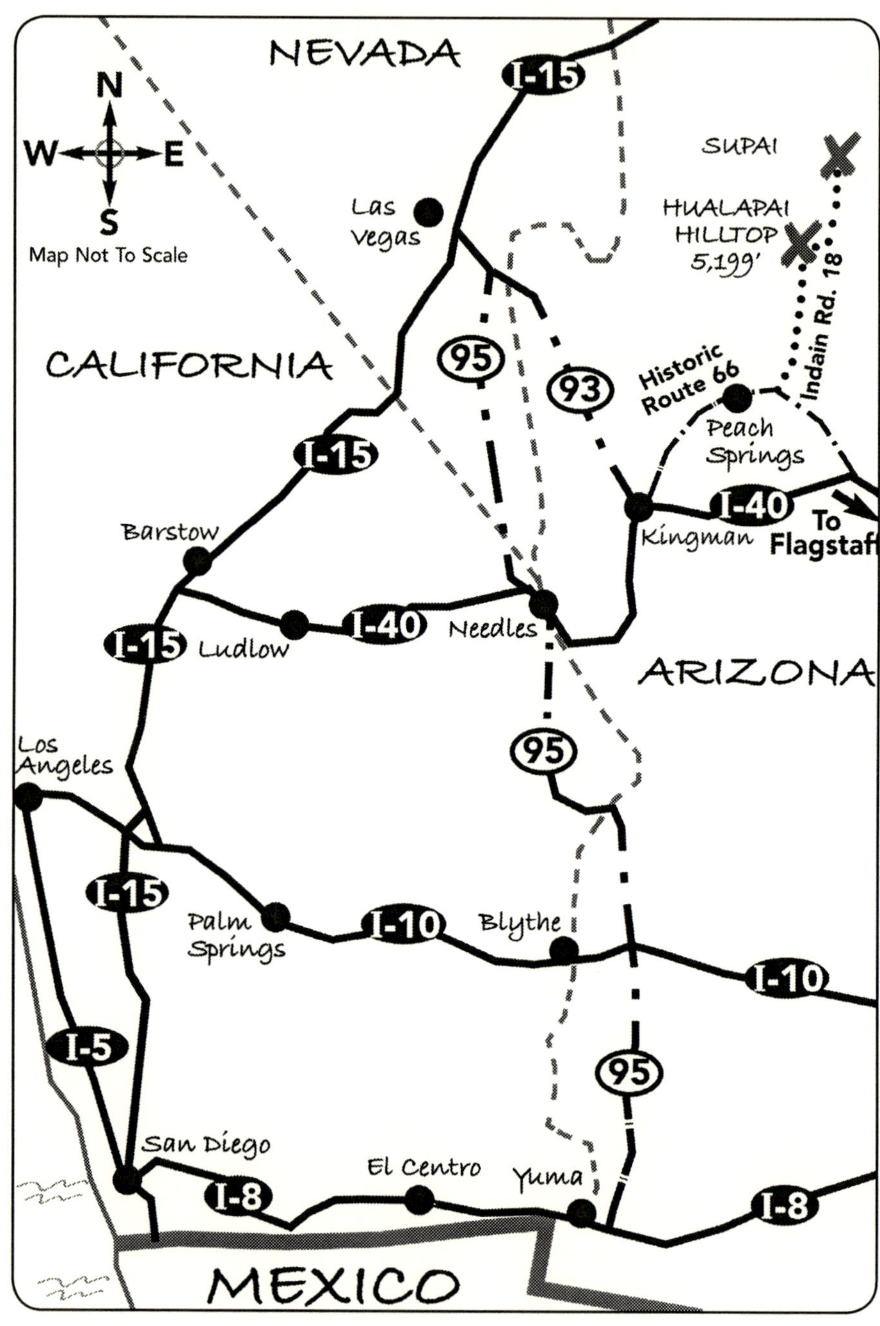

NEVADA
I-15
N
W   E
S
Map Not To Scale
SUPAI
HUALAPAI
HILLTOP
5,199'
Indain Rd. 18
Las
Vegas
CALIFORNIA
95
93
Historic
Route 66
Peach
Springs
I-15
I-40
To
Flagstaff
Kingman
Barstow
I-15   Ludlow   I-40   Needles
ARIZONA
Los
Angeles
95
I-15
Palm
Springs   I-10   Blythe
I-10
I-5
95
San Diego
El Centro   Yuma
I-8   I-8
MEXICO

ABOUT THE HAVASUPAI RESERVATION AREA

The Havasupai (meaning, "people of the blue-green water") Indian Reservation, in the northwest corner of Arizona, is a land of broken plateaus and deep canyons adjoining the south rim of the Grand Canyon. The jewel canyon, Havasu Canyon, has soaring 3,000-foot red walls and a turquoise, spring-fed river that spills over waterfalls as much as 200 feet high.

Within this canyon is a small village, Supai, surrounded by horse pastures and fields of corn. Its main street is a dirt lane bordered by huge cottonwood trees, and it boasts the only post office in the lower 48 states that still sends and receives all of its mail by mule train. There are no roads to Supai, access is only by foot, horseback, or helicopter.

There is a campground downstream from the village, between the second and third waterfalls, where the canyon is narrow, the walls high, and the river slow & deep.

This is an enchanting place and you're going to love it!

Getting There

Get to the Havasupai Reservation, from the Los Angeles area, by taking Interstate 10 east to Interstate 15 north, to the city of Barstow. From Barstow take Interstate 40 east for about 200-miles to the town of Kingman, Arizona, and take Exit #53 (Andy Devine Highway/Historic Route 66).

After gassing up and purchasing any last minute supplies in Kingman, head northeast on Route 66 for approximately 53-miles, through the small town of Peach Springs, to Indian Road 18 coming in from the left (north).

Head north on Indian Road 18 and pass through three distinct ecological zones (grasslands, juniper-pinion, and tall pines) that are home to large numbers of Elk and other wildlife. The trailhead, at Hualapai Hilltop, is at the end of Indian Road 18, about 65-miles from Route 66.

The Hualapai Hilltop Trailhead at the end of Indian Road 18 is home to primitive restrooms, a small trailer (where the horse wrangler/coordinator conducts his business), and the trail that leads down to the canyon, village, and falls. There are no other amenities of any kind here, including water.

Supplies, Lodging, Maps & Information

Kingman is your best chance for gas, supplies, lodging, and water until you reach the village of Supai, which has a lodge, a small café, and a general store (at the time of publication the café and general store operate on a cash-basis only). There is no gas at all between Kingman and Hualapai Hilltop, so be sure to have enough for a round-trip.

The lodge in Supai has 24 rooms, each with two double beds, private baths, and air conditioning. They do not have telephones, TV's, or rollaway beds, but they are smoke-free. For more information, or reservations, contact the Havasupai Lodge: PO Box 159, Supai, AZ 86435, or by phone at either 928.448.2111 or 928.448.2201, or online at: lodge@havasupaitribe.com.

To make camping reservations, to reserve a saddle/pack-horse, or to inquire about helicopter transportation, contact the tourist office at: PO Box 160, Supai, AZ 86435, or by phone at either 928.448.2121 or 928.448.2141, or by email at touristoffice@havasupaitribe.com. For general information and photographs, check out the tribes website at: www.havasupaitribe.com.

The phone lines can often be busy for long periods of time, but be of good cheer and don't give up—it's all part of the experience. When they do answer, you'll want to have the following information ready: (1) the desired dates, (2) the number of nights you will be staying, and (3) the number of people in your party.

You'll want good California and Arizona state travel maps, such as the ones AAA puts out and, if you decide to check out any of the side-trips, you'll also want to have a copy of DeLorme's, "Southern & Central California Atlas & Gazetteer", or its equivalent. The walk into Supai itself is very straightforward (as described below) and you shouldn't need a map to do it, but if in doubt, ask for one when you make your reservations.

The Journey Into The Canyon

The trail to the village and the falls begins at the parking area at Hualapai Hilltop and switchbacks steeply downward for the first 1.5-miles or so, before leveling out at the bottom of the canyon where it remains for the rest of the journey; simply stay in the canyon bottom, heading downhill, for the remainder of the walk to the village.

As you descend towards the village the canyon bottom narrows—in some places to 30 feet or less—and the walls rise, dramatically, many thousands of feet above you.

At about 6-miles from the trailhead, the trail intersects Havasu Creek coming In from the right; continue downstream, following the creek now, for perhaps 0.5-mile, and then cross a bridge to the right side of the stream and remain there until you arrive at the village, about 1.5-miles further on.

It's about 8-miles from Hualapai Hilltop to the village, and about 2-miles from the village to the campground. If you decide to explore further, it's about 3-miles from the campground to Beaver Falls, and another 5-miles from Beaver Falls to the

Colorado River, where its brown waters swirl and mix with the blue waters of Havasu Creek.

Be sure to carry lots of water and hit the trail early if your visit is in the summer; by mid-morning canyon temperatures can easily climb above 100-degrees and increase the risk of dehydration, heat stroke, and heat exhaustion. My favorite way to beat the heat—you should be familiar with the trail before attempting this, though—is to do this walk during the overnight hours.

The Village

The village of Supai—surrounded by acres of farmland and red cliffs several thousands of feet high—has been home to the Havasupai people since about AD 1300. There are no paved roads into this place, only dirt lanes lined by huge cottonwood trees, a small café, general store, lodge, post office, school, church, clinic, police station, and tourist office. The population of this town is about 500, though you'll have a hard time figuring out where they might be.

The post office is advertised as being the last one in the country that regularly delivers its mail via mule train—check out the special postmark by mailing yourself a postcard.

Be sure to check in at the tourist office when you arrive in the village; they'll collect the balance of your entry fees at that time and issue your permits. Lodge employees will collect these fees if that's your destination.

The Campground

After you've checked in with the tourist office, and had a lemonade and burger at the café, sling your pack and head out for the campground 2-miles further down the canyon, just beyond Navajo and Havasu Falls.

The campground stretches for a bit over 1-mile along the banks of Havasu Creek, between Havasu and Mooney Falls. The drinking water comes from a cliffside spring, beautiful cottonwoods & high rock walls provide the shade, and wild grapevines are everywhere. Spaces here are first come, first served and are marked by picnic tables. Fortunately, fires are not allowed or this entire canyon would have long since been desertfied.

Sometime after you get settled, the ranger will swing by to check your permits and document your campsite, and the number in your party.

The Falls

The turquoise waters of spring-fed Havasu Creek feed four primary waterfalls, maintain a fairly constant 70-degrees year round, and are perfect for swimming.

The closest (about 1.5-miles) waterfall to the village is *Navajo Falls*, which cascades 75ft into a beautiful pool. Next is *Havasu Falls* (about 2-miles), which drops nearly 100ft into a great blue-green swimming pool, and then *Mooney Falls* (3-miles), the highest, plunging nearly 200 feet into a roaring, frothy, pool. The access trail to the bottom of Mooney Falls is particularly adventurous; it's a narrow path cut into the travertine, winding through caves, and utilizing iron chains and bars set into the cliff.

Beaver Falls, about 3-miles downstream from Mooney Falls, is a fantastic series of cascades that range from 5 to 40 feet in height.

The Colorado River

The 9-mile (one-way) trail to the Colorado River begins at the campground, and then climbs down to the base of Mooney Falls, crosses hillsides full of wild grape vines, climbs a log ladder to a beautiful cactus garden on a high plateau, scrambles through a streamside rock tunnel, and passes by Beaver Falls before arriving at the mighty Colorado.

Once there, enjoy the beauty of the blue water of Havasu Creek mixing with the chocolate water of the Colorado, catch a nap in the sun and, if they're around, mooch a soda from the rafters that often put in along here.

Get an early start for this daylong hike; bring water, snacks & sunscreen, and wear your bathing suit because there are many, many water crossings along the way. You'll need your navigational skills as well; though you can't get lost in the canyon, some routes are better than others.

ADVENTURES OUTSIDE THE RESERVATION

If you have extra time, you might review Trip Number 6 of this book, *The Mojave National Preserve*, for sites to visit along Interstate 40.

Part Three

The Spiritual Component

"My heart says of you, "Seek his face!"
Your face, Lord, I will seek.

—Psalm 27:8 (NIV)

"My heart has heard you say, "Come and talk with me."
And my heart responds, "Lord, I am coming."

Psalm 27:8 (NLT)

"My soul thirsts for God, for the living God.
When can I go and meet with God?"

—Psalm 42:2 (NIV)

This part of the book, *The Spiritual Component*, is broken down into four primary sections: *Lessons in Learning, Growing as a Group, Worshipping in the Wild*, and *Trailside Talks.*

The four sections are broken down as follows:

- *Lessons In Learning* explores several concepts that will help to create the best environment for processing, and learning from, your adventures.
- *Growing As A Group* will help you get to know each other more deeply through icebreaker and team building/encouragement-types of activities.
- *Worshipping In The Wild* contains a few thoughts on creatively organizing a structured worship service in the outdoors.
- *Trailside Talks* are discussion starters and spiritual lessons based on some of the situations and natural features that you're likely to encounter in your adventures.

Take from each the elements that best meet your needs, and then mix and match them to create your own powerful, worship-filled, experience.

CHAPTER TWENTY

Lessons In Learning

"…be transformed by the renewing of your mind"
—Romans 12:2 (NIV)

Before we jump into the activities, there are a few concepts that will help to create a better learning environment for you and your group. These concepts are *frontloading*, *debriefing,* and *journaling.*

Frontloading

Frontloading is the act of highlighting the learning prior to—*or in front of*—the actual activity or experience. For example, say you had it in mind to teach a lesson on the need to follow God in all areas of life, and say you were going on a whitewater-rafting trip. In this case you might discuss with your group, *beforehand*, the fact of your guide's familiarity with the river—with the rocks, holes, eddies, rapids, strainers, and other features & hazards—and your reliance on him or her to get you through it safely. You might then tell your group that, like the river, our own lives are full of features and hazards (i.e. job, school, relationships, relocations, financial struggles, illnesses, heartbreaks, and losses) that only God can anticipate and guide us through.

Setting up the learning experience like this, beforehand, will allow your group to anticipate and more easily absorb the lesson that you have planned.

Here are some other thoughts regarding frontloading your adventure and/or lessons:

- Frontloading, again, is pointing participants in the direction of the learning objective before it occurs.
- Decide what you want the group to learn and then plan & create the entire experience with that objective in mind.
- Giving your trip a name, a theme, or an objective can be a great help in (1) clarifying expectations, (2) establishing a sense of anticipation, and (3) preparing the participants to learn & grow in a particular area.

Debriefing

Debriefing (Processing) is *formalized, directed reflection*. It is the intentional consideration, discussion, and evaluation of the thoughts and emotions that we have about a particular experience resulting, it is hoped, in a greater understanding of these experiences and the life lessons that come from them.

There are two kinds of debriefings: *informal* and *formal*. Informal processing can take place anywhere at anytime—around a campfire, in your car, on the trail, or during mealtime—and may consist of simple questions about how the participant felt, or what he or she learned as a result of a particular activity or experience.

Formal processing, on the other hand, is structured and pre-planned. Here are some thoughts regarding the establishment of a formalized debriefing time:

- Schedule the debriefing session at the same time every-day—say, every morning at breakfast or every evening around the campfire—to reflect on the previous days experiences.
- Aid the debriefing by taking a few minutes to rehash the experiences that you want to process, such as a particular spiritual exercise, or a hike, etc. As the activities are recounted, ask your group to fill in the blanks of the story—there will certainly be sub plots and interpersonal stories that some might have missed.
- After the activity itself has been discussed ask your people open-ended questions (see below) that lead them to:
    1 Think about and discuss what they have learned.
    2 Think about and discuss the ways that they will apply those lessons in their lives.
- Next, have them find a quiet place to reflect upon and journal these lessons.
- Finally, consider wrapping up your debriefing time by having your people come back together to discuss their findings and commitments.

Below are a few questions to help you process your experiences; pick the ones that best suit your needs:

What made this difficult?
What had to happen to make this work?
How did you feel about the group?
How did you feel about yourself?
Who were the leaders?
Who were the followers?
Did everyone feel that his or her ideas were considered?
What made you uncomfortable?
What kind of problems did you have to overcome?
Did you work together?
What helped you to work together?
What hindered you from accomplishing your goals?
How does this apply to our Christian lives?
How does this apply to our relationships?
What do you feel that God was trying to teach you through this experience?
What new thing did you learn about God today?
What did you learn about each other?
What did you learn about yourself?
How can you relate this experience to God's love for you?
What were some of the gifts that you noticed in other people in the group?
What gifts did you discover that you weren't aware that you had?
What do you think that your gifts are?
What do you think that your strengths are?
What do you think that your weaknesses are?
How did you feel about being alone?
How could you have better encouraged or helped somebody today?
What do you want to achieve with God tomorrow?
What was your attitude at the beginning?
Did your attitude change? At what point? Why?
What did you find difficult?

What part was especially fulfilling?
How have you been aware of God's presence today?
During this experience?
What question(s) would you ask God regarding this____?
How will you now better love God and love others?

Journaling

Journaling can take many forms; it can be free-flowing writing (simply pouring your heart out without regard for form or grammar), poetry, watercolor, sketching, doodling, collage…whatever method best allows you to slow down, express your heart, and:

- Really explore your feelings, thoughts, and experiences.
- Document your memories, life goals, and areas in your life that you want to grow and develop.
- Chart your spiritual journey, track answered prayers & lessons learned, and otherwise observe God's working in your life.
- Record the things that you are grateful for and the kindness of friends.

Some final thoughts on preparing your people to learn

- Leaders should always be ready to point their people beyond the creation to the Creator. However, don't *force* a spiritual connection if your group isn't ready. Instead, enjoy the activity and later, perhaps back at camp, discuss the experience and attempt to tie it in to a spiritual truth.
- Allow participants to engage at their own level of involvement and risk. This sense of control will reduce anxiety and later, when they feel safe, they'll be more likely to open up and share.

- Be sure that your people have ample time to explore their surroundings on their own. Simply being in a beautiful natural setting causes most people to be reflective and contemplative.

In the remainder of this part of the book, '*The Spiritual Component*', you'll find dozens of awesome spiritual exercises that can be done in the car, around the fire, on the trail, or in solitude. Choose the ones that best suit your group, its personality, and its goals.

Growing as a Group

"God is big, really big"
Whitney Atkinson
Student, Columbia Bible College

Below are a few ideas for connecting more deeply with your group, including icebreaker-type questions and various encouragement and group building exercises.

Icebreaker Questions

The following questions will help your group learn more about each other. Ask a few of them in the car, on the trail, or around the campfire:

1. What are your favorite hobbies? Books? Movies?
2. Where in the world would you like to visit?
3. What would be your dream job?
4. What was the happiest day of your life and why?
5. What do you think that your purpose in life is?
6. What is something that you want badly, but cannot afford?
7. What is your idea of a happy family?

8. If you had one year to live, what would you do?
9. What is your most prized possession?
10. What do you like about yourself?
11. What do you do when you are depressed or down?
12. What is an important goal that you would like to accomplish in the next year? The next five years? In your lifetime?
13. Who is the person that has most impacted your life and faith? Why?
14. What was the hardest decision that you have ever made?
15. Name two things that you do very well.
16. What is one thing that you would like to do better?
17. If you could have any four people who have ever lived over to your house for dinner, who would they be? What would be the dinner topic?
18. How would you describe peace?
19. What is success?
20. What is real joy?
21. What talents do you wish that you had?
22. What does courage mean to you?
23. If you wrote a book about yourself, what would it be titled?
24. What is your favorite room in your house and why?
25. If you could have 20 minutes with the President of the United States, what would you say?

Another Icebreaker

Here's another series of icebreaker-type questions. Have each person complete the following sentence(s):

- I think that Jesus can…
- I feel that God is…
- I believe that Jesus will…
- I hope that I will be able to…
- I wish that Jesus would…

- I assume that in the future…
- I am sure that God…
- I understand that Jesus has…
- I know that God does…
- I don't understand why God…

And Yet Another Icebreaker

Have your group members create (write, draw, paint, etc.) a spiritual timeline of their lives and then share it with each other. You could also have them create a spiritual timeline for the future and show how they would like for their walk with Christ to progress.

Games

If you use a game as an icebreaker, keep everybody on an equal footing by using one that is unfamiliar to your group.

The Pinecone Pass Around

This is a great activity for a group whose members are quite familiar with each other; if your group is not, you may want to think about doing this after everyone has had the opportunity to spend some time together.

In this simple but powerful exercise, simply hand a pinecone (or sandal, or hiking boot, or water bottle, or anything else) to a member of your group, and then have everybody else shower that person with blessings, encouragement, his or her strengths & gifts, and how they have affected others with Christ's love. When you have finished, pass the pinecone to the next person and repeat until everyone in the group has been encouraged. Afterward, discuss how each member felt being showered with blessings and how they felt showering the others.

Close with a group prayer, acknowledging that we are who we are because of Jesus.

Prayer Circle

With your group standing in a circle, place one member in the middle and have them give the group a few prayer requests. Have everyone in the group lay their hands on that person while three or four people pray those requests. Repeat this process with everyone in the group.

If necessary, manage the time by limiting both the number of prayer requests that an individual can make, and the number of people praying for each person.

Growing Together

Have each person in the group (1) talk about one or two areas in their lives where they feel they have really been growing on this trip, and (2) share an area that they would like to see more improvement in. Have the group pray for that individual; praising God for the growth in the one area, while asking for growth in the other.

Notes Of Encouragement

With a group that is familiar with one another, do this: Write each persons name on a separate piece of paper, then hand them around and have the other members of the group write notes of encouragement, affirming words, and praise to God for their lives. When finished, be sure that everybody gets their own sheets of paper to take home as a memento of their time together.

Wrap up this time with group prayer and praise to God for allowing friendships to be forged that will last into eternity.

Feet Washing

This exercise—with its roots in our Lord's example of servant leadership—can be a great way to serve one another, and a fantastic addition to your worship. What you'll need is a Bible, a basin, a couple of towels, and a group that is comfortable with this exercise; not everybody is, and it's important that you survey your people prior to springing this on them.

One way to practice this exercise is to have each person in the group wash the feet of the person to their right, or you can make it gender specific (male to male, female to female), or even husband to wife & vice versa. I've also seen this done very effectively with the leader washing the feet of the entire group.

Begin by reading the story of Jesus washing the feet of His disciples (see John 13:1-17), and then with the 'washee' sitting in a chair or on a rock, kneel in front of him or her, have them place their feet in the basin of water, and then bathe and dry them.

After everyone has finished, discuss the following questions as a group:

1. How did you feel as your feet were being washed?
2. How did you feel washing the others feet?
3. Which was more comfortable for you? Why?

Re-read John 13:1-17 and discuss the following:

1. Would you have reacted similarly to Peter if Jesus had wanted to physically wash your feet? Why?
2. What was Jesus' purpose in washing his disciples feet?
   - To love on His disciples
   - To set an example for them (and us) to follow

3. Finally, read Philippians 2:1-11 and discuss the following:
   - How can we regard one another as better than ourselves?
   - In what practical ways can we "wash each other's feet?"

The Web Of Connectedness

This is a great exercise for a group that has shared at least one interesting experience together.

Here's what you do: Grab a ball of string, have everybody get into a circle, and then share one element about the experience that really made an impact on you. When you have shared, hold on to the end of the string and toss the ball to another person, who will then relate his or her own memory of the experience. When that person is finished speaking, have him or her—still holding the string that came to them—toss the ball to someone else, and so on.

When it has gone all the way around—and everybody has shared a memory from the experience—the string in your circle will appear web-like.

Now, discuss how, and in what ways, the experiences of our lives are interconnected.

CHAPTER TWENTY TWO

Worshipping In The Wild

"But as for me, I will always have hope; I will praise you more and more."

—Psalm 71:14 (NIV)

"The essence of praising Christ is prizing Christ"

—John Piper

Worship is a time to love our God, to praise & adore Him, to open our hearts to Him, and to express our gratitude and dependence on the Him. The most elementary way to worship God, of course, is to live a life of obedience to Him, but there are other ways, too, which we'll discuss on the pages ahead. Before we do that, though, lets discuss two types of worship—*spontaneous worship* and *structured worship.*

Spontaneous worship is just that—spontaneous. It is random and unplanned and can be brought on by an event such as an awesome sunset, a fresh understanding of God's love, or an especially emotional connection within the group.

Structured worship, on the other hand, is an organized, pre-planned time that your group sets aside to intentionally adore God. This might be done, for example, on a Saturday evening around a campfire, or on the beach at sunrise or, perhaps, every morning at breakfast. It might be extravagant—with a sermon, worship music, drama, and communion—or as simple as a passage of scripture and a prayer read aloud.

Order Of Worship

The following guidelines and tips may be helpful if you decide to organize such a structured worship service for your trip. Use the elements—presented here in their usual sequence—that best meet your goals and needs:

- *Praise and Adoration*—This can be in the form of praise music, praise psalms, poems, or stories of adoration.
- *Confession*—Choose an exercise of corporate confession such as a group reading, prayer, etc. (see Psalm 51:1-4, for example).

- *Intercession & Communion*—Intercession is about lifting up prayers for each other and those at home. Communion is about sharing in the Lord's Supper and, together, remembering what He has done for us.
- *Proclamation*—This is the sermon, a dramatic reading or the reading of a spiritual story, a testimony, a skit, etc.
- *Commitment*—The commitment is our faith response to what we heard God say to us; we might promise to give up a particular sin, or to repair a wounded relationship, etc. It is an answer to the question, "How am I going to live my life differently now that I've experienced/learned this?"
- *Thanksgiving*—This, the expression of a grateful heart towards God, can be done in prayer or story form.

Creativity In Worship

When it comes to a worship service, most of us get stuck in 'the box' of believing it must look and feel a certain way. The reality, however, is that any expression of adoration towards God can be considered worship. For example, you can write a poem, a love song, or a short story to God or about Him. You can draw, watercolor, sculpt or incorporate drama, dance & group storytelling. You can read psalms aloud, corporately pray, have long moments of contemplative silence, share communion on a mountaintop, hold a lakeside Baptism service, or sing praise songs at sunrise.

Your music can be provided through traditional means—a guitar, congas or harmonica—or you can create non-traditional instruments out of available resources, such as log drums and water bottle shakers (simply put rocks in your water bottle). Spiritual stories read around a campfire are powerful, as are testimonials about what the Lord's been doing in each other's lives. You might even want to create simple, hand-written programs outlining the order of worship, the lyrics of any praise songs, important scripture verses, etc.

The outdoor setting—enhanced with incense & candles—will itself add tremendously to the spirit of worship, as you adore God under the stars, or on a beach, or at the base of a Giant Sequoia.

Don't limit yourself when it comes to worship. God has wired creative expression into us and there is no better way to use that creativity than by returning it to Him in adoration.

Communion

Communion is a powerful element of worship that helps us to recall and memorialize all that our Jesus did to win our freedom. Some ideas for creating a communion service, include:

- Holding it at an especially inspirational vantage point, such as on the beach at sunrise, or from a high mountaintop.
- Reading Matthew 26:17-30 aloud.
- Singing praise songs.
- Baking your own communion bread at the campsite.
- Holding the entire service in absolute quiet & stillness, perhaps as the sun is rising.
- Using candles & incense (if it's safe and legal).
- Having someone give his or her testimony to highlight, in a powerful way, what God has saved us from.

Baptism

You could have a baptism service—either pre-planned or spontaneous—built around a trip to the ocean, lake, or river.

A Monument Of Stones

This is an awesome exercise to memorialize God's faithfulness: You'll need a Bible and enough decent size (not huge) rocks so that everyone in your group will have one.

Here's what you do: Read the story found in Joshua 4, then have each person in your group heft a rock, tell a story of God's faithfulness in their own life, and place it in a pile.

Conclude your time by praising God for His faithfulness.

Responsive Reading

Responsive reading is a powerful way to worship the Lord & connect with one another, and Psalm 136:1-26 is a great passage of scripture to do it with. What you'll do is choose one member of your group to read the primary lines, and then have the group respond aloud. For example:

(Primary Reader) Give thanks to the Lord for He is good
(Group) His love endure forever
(Primary Reader) Give thanks to the God of gods
(Group) His love endures forever

Finish reading through this Psalm in this same manner, and then process your experience by discussing what each person felt and learned while participating in this exercise.

Another way to experience responsive reading is to allow a bit of silence between verses or chapters for reflection.

Commitment Offering

This is a wonderful, and very simple, exercise to incorporate into your worship service. Here's what you do: Have each participant write down his or her faith commitment on paper, and then burn it in the campfire as an offering to God.

Commitments

When the risk of fire is very low, have your group form a large circle and give each person a candle. Light one candle and have that person share a spiritual experience or a commitment that they have made as a result of their time together. When that person is finished, have him or her light the candle of the person next to them and so on, until everybody has a lit candle and has had a time to share.

Close with a group prayer.

PRAYER

"After he had dismissed them,
he went up on a mountainside by himself to pray.
When evening came, he was there alone"
—Matthew 14:23 (NIV)

Prayer, whether personal or shared in community, is simply a conversation between children and their loving Father. There are many kinds of prayers; there are prayers of confession, and prayerful requests for assistance and/or blessing on our own lives or someone else's. Songs or poems or love letters, spoken aloud or in ones heart, are prayers too.

Below are a few ideas for individual and corporate prayer:

Praying Scripture

Have one person read a verse of scripture, and then be silent to allow the members of the group to respond silently or aloud. After some time has passed, have the next person in the circle pray the next verse.

Prayers Of Praise

Use each line of the Lord's Prayer—found in Matthew 6:9-13—as a guide for a few minutes of group prayer.

Another way to praise the Lord is to simply be still and thank him over and over for who He is and what He does. It might look like this: "Thank you, Lord, for being so compassionate…Thank you for being so merciful… Lord, I love you so much for your grace", etc.

Directed Prayer

Have the members of your group break into smaller groups of two or three and then give them specific subjects to pray for and about, such as: "Thank God for each other; pray for each others families; pray for each others ministry & spiritual growth, etc."

Almost any topic will do, but be sure to allow adequate time between directions for everyone to pray.

Meditative Prayer

Instead of focusing on our gratitude and our various requests, this prayer moves us towards the silence necessary to hear what the Lord *has to say to us*. To achieve this silence, and to help you maintain your focus on God, find a place to be alone and repeat, very quietly and very slowly, a sacred or loving phrase, such as, "Lord, have mercy" or, "My Lord, My Lord" or, "I love you, Lord."

Repeat this phrase for at least 20 minutes, and then journal your thoughts.

Intercessory Prayer

Here's what you do: While reading Psalm 23, insert the name of a person that you want to pray for in place of the personal pronouns, "I" and "me". An example of this would be, "The Lord is Joe's shepherd, he shall not be in want" If you do this as a group exercise, you can pray in a circle with each person repeating the psalm with the name of the person that he or she wants to pray for.

Another way to intercede for somebody is to close your eyes and imagine that person surrounded by the light of Christ while you pray for him or her by name.

A Worthy Goal

Try to make it a goal for everybody in the group to be prayed for everyday.

SACRED READING

"Our goal is not to get through the scriptures,
the goal is for the scriptures to get through us."
—John Ortberg, *The Life You've Always Wanted*

The ancient practice of Lectio Divina, or sacred reading, is a deep, meditative reading of the scriptures that allows one to really dig deep into the text and to hear God speaking in a very personal and intimate way.

M. Robert Mulholland, in his book *Shaped by the Word: The Power of Scripture in Spiritual Formation*, describes the foundational roots of sacred reading:

"Formational reading is in depth. You are seeking to allow the passage to open out to you its deeper dynamics, its multiple layers of meaning. Instead of rushing on to the next sentence, paragraph, or chapter, you seek to move deeper and deeper and deeper into the text. In reading the Bible, for example, you seek to allow the text to begin to become that intrusion of the Word of God into your life, to address you, to encounter you."

The following steps will guide you through the process of Lectio Divina:

- First, choose the passage of scripture that you wish to contemplate, keeping in mind that the goal is not to cover a large amount of text, but rather to go deeply in the text that you do cover.

- Then, find a quiet, inspiring place, such as a beautiful overlook, or under a shady tree, or next to a crackling fire—make sure that it is someplace where you will be undisturbed—and then relax, breathe deeply, and clear your mind.
- Next, pray for the Father to open your heart, to teach you and transform you through the reading.
- Next, read your chosen text slowly with, as John Ortberg writes in his book, *The Life You've Always Wanted*, " a readiness to surrender everything." Read it slowly, over and over, silently and aloud. Immerse yourself in it, visualize yourself in the various roles, reflect deeply on it and allow it to really sink into the depths of your heart.
- Go through it again, and this time underline or circle words or phrases that speak to you; note any ideas, thoughts or key ideas that come to you.
- Then, ask yourself, "Where is God speaking to me through this passage? Talk to Him about what you are thinking, feeling, wrestling with, and learning. You may feel His great love, or you may feel convicted in areas of your life or be prompted to take action on some matter.
- Next, journal your deepest response to God's Word, free-style, without concern for grammar or spelling. This is where, if necessary, you will commit to paper your plan for change, to repent, to restore a relationship, or to make right anything that God might have brought to your attention.
- Finally, when you've finished, take time to be still with God, to thank Him for His Word and for what He has taught you. Review the story or passage of scripture that you just read and praise Him for what it has revealed to you about His character or His attributes.

- As you go, if possible, process your reading, revelations, and questions by discussing them with your group and/or other Christians.

Another way to practice lectio divina with your group might be to assign participants a passage of scripture, or the text of a devotional classic, and have them go to a solitary place for a set amount of time to chew on the passage. Perhaps have them journal their thoughts and then return to process what they learned.

Other Spiritual Reading

Bring along a Christian book of some sort, particularly a classic or a biography, for your downtime in camp. Here are a few suggestions to help get you started:

- *The Ragamuffin Gospel* by Brennan Manning
- *Celebration of Discipline* by Richard Foster
- *The Imitation of Christ* by Thomas a' Kempis
- *True Spirituality* by Francis Schaeffer
- *The Practice of the Presence of God* by Brother Lawrence
- *Mere Christianity* by C.S. Lewis
- *The Cost of Discipleship* by Dietrich Bon'hoffer
- Any Christian biography (I'm huge on biographical accounts of Christian heroes)
- Anything by John Eldridge, Donald Miller, John Ortberg, John Piper, A.W. Tozer, or Philip Yancey

SOLITUDE & REFLECTION

"At daybreak Jesus went out to a solitary place."
—Luke 4:42a (NIV)

"The seeking out of solitary places was a regular
practice for Jesus. So it should be for us"
—Richard Foster

Solitude is the discipline of temporarily withdrawing to a private place for the purposes of (1) being alone with God and (2) growing spiritually. *Reflection* is the act of zeroing in on one thing, or one topic, and contemplating it deeply.

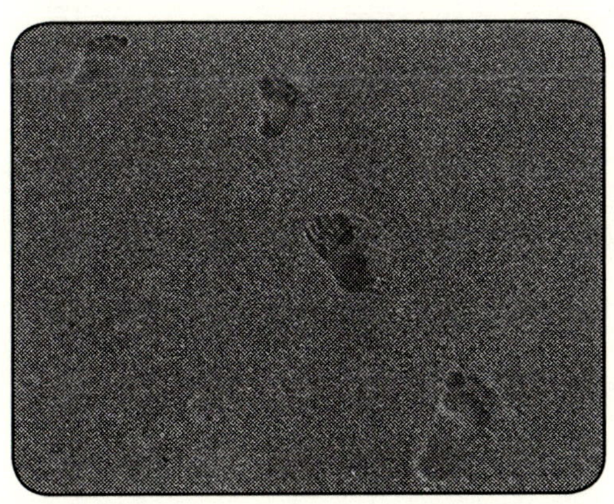

Solitude allows us to connect with God and to quietly rest in Him, to listen for His voice, and to allow His Spirit to do His work in our lives. In solitude we can reflect, self-evaluate, and recalibrate our lives.

A solitude experience can be any length of time, from an hour to an entire weekend, but should be done at least once a day, if possible, during your trip. This will allow participants' time to process their experiences, to journal, and to raise questions that can later be discussed with the entire group.

Below are a few exercises in solitude and reflection; you may want to have participants return between exercises to share their thoughts and feelings with the group.

He Knows You

Grab your Bible, journal, pen & water bottle, and head out to a quiet place. Get comfortable, and then read Psalm 139, reflect on the following, and journal your thoughts:

"As a child, if I considered that I knew something thoroughly (such as my phone number), I would say 'I know it by heart.' What would it mean to you if you heard God say, 'I know you by heart?'"

He is with you

Grab your Bible, journal, pen & water bottle, and head out to a quiet, comfortable place; be still, breath deep, listen to the sounds around you, and relax. Read the following verses and *find a common theme*:

- Psalm 103:8-13
- Jeremiah 29:11
- Matthew 18:12-14
- John 1:12
- Romans 8:37-39
- Galatians 2:20
- Colossians 3:12
- 1 John 3:1-2; 4:10
- Revelation 21:3-4

Now, imagine that God is sitting just a few feet away, watching over you. He has always been there, every moment, only now you can clearly see him. Based on the verses that you read, what do you think He wants to say to you right now about your past? Your future? Who does He say that you are today? What do you think that he knows about your pain & fear? What about your failures? What specific words does He use?

Listen closely, and then journal those words *exactly* as He says them to you.

Created By God

Grab your Bible, journal, pen & water bottle, and head out to a quiet place where you can focus on the natural world. Find a comfortable spot to sit; be still…breathe deep… clear your mind…and relax. Let all that is around you into your being, and you into it as you become more aware of your part in God's creation.

After a period of at least 30 minutes, open your Bible and read Psalm 24 and Genesis 1. Meditate on these scriptures and journal your thoughts. Look deep for your true feelings about your Creator.

Object Reflection/God Focus

Grab your Bible, journal, pen & water bottle, and head out to a quiet place where you can focus on the natural world. Find a comfortable spot to sit; be still…breathe deep… clear your mind…and relax. Pick a single object—a pinecone, a leaf, a mountain, a body of water, etc.—and meditate on it for a set amount of time, perhaps a few minutes to an hour. The object of this exercise is to discover metaphors about the one true God.

Jot these down in your journal, along with any scriptures, poems, songs, etc. that you might think of, and discuss your conclusions with the group.

The Earth Beneath

The object of this lesson is a deeper understanding and appreciation for God's creative majesty: Grab your Bible, journal, pen & water bottle, and head out to a quiet place where you can get comfortable and focus on the natural world. Draw a circle in the soil, perhaps eighteen inches across, and focus on everything in it. Observe as many of the details—living objects & things, colors, patterns, textures, etc.—as you possibly can, and note them in your journal along with any relevant scriptures, psalms, poems and songs that come to mind.

Thank the Lord for each item you observe.

Silent, Reflective Prayer

Only the leader speaks aloud in this exercise, while the rest of the group silently follows his or her directions. For example, the leader might say, "Think about what God has done for you in the past 24 hours (weekend, week, month, etc.) and thank Him for it; think about what God has revealed about Himself during this time and thank Him for that too; confess any sins that you have committed which have separated you from Him; pray for your families; pray for your neighbors; pray for your co-workers; pray for the person to your right..." Etc.

Reflective Reading

In this exercise, have everybody get comfortable, and then have one person read a devotion or spiritual story slowly, while the group quietly digests what is being read. Afterward, allow some time (a few minutes to an hour) for the participants to journal their thoughts, and then have a time of discussion and processing.

Gratitude

This extremely simple exercise will transform your life, particularly during times of depression or sadness, or those times when you feel dissatisfied with your life (job, possessions, appearance, etc.).

Here's what you do: Create and maintain a list of all the things that God has given you—which is everything, really—and then thank Him for it.

Meditate On A Psalm

Psalm 8, 139, and 145 are three of my favorite passages of scripture to meditate on. Find one that really speaks to you and carve out time in your day to reflect on it.

Freestyle Adoration

For this exercise you'll need a Bible, a worshipful state of mind, and your favorite form of expression; pen & paper, watercolors, a camera, clay, your dancing ability, etc.

Read and meditate on John 15:13-16. Read it over and over, reflect deeply on the text, and then consider the following question: How do you feel knowing that Jesus—the Lord of all creation, your Maker, your Savior—has called you His friend, even laying down His life for you to prove it?

Using your chosen form of expression, create a poem, painting, sculpture, photograph, story, interpretive dance, collage, scrapbook…or anything else…to express your feelings about this awesome truth.

Group Journal

Here's a great idea for a group keepsake: Bring a single journal on your trip and have it passed around every morning and every evening for participants to write in. Don't be too strict with the format; allow your people to make either single line or very lengthy entries about whatever they're feeling, experiencing, etc. Sketching and water coloring are also great mediums of expression. Make sure that the journal is available anytime someone wants to make an entry, but make it voluntary.

After the trip, photocopy the journal and give everyone a copy as a keepsake.

CONFESSION

"Let us examine our ways and test them,
and let us return to the Lord."

—Lamentations 3:40 (NIV)

Self-Reflection & Evaluation

Lamentations 3:40 and II Corinthians 13:5 show us the necessity of occasionally examining our lives, and of confessing and turning away from any sin that we may find there (See also, Psalm 32:5, Proverbs 28:13 & 1 John 1:8-9).

In, *The Life You've Always Wanted*, John Ortberg said that "to confess means to own up to the fact that our behavior wasn't just the result of bad parenting, poor genes, jealous siblings, or a chemical imbalance from too many Twinkies…confession means saying that somewhere in the mix was a choice, and the choice was made by us, and it does not need to be excused, explained or even understood. The choice needs to be forgiven."

The following exercise is designed to help you identify and begin the process of dealing with those areas of your life that may be preventing you from fully enjoying your relationships with God and people.

For this exercise, grab your Bible, journal, pen, and water bottle, find an inspiring place to sit—perhaps under a shade tree, or at an overlook, or fireside—and then take a few moments to ask the Lord to open your eyes to any areas of your life that you may need to either develop or renounce (Psalm 139:23-24).

Next, with that same prayerful mindset, slowly read over each applicable question, answer it honestly and, if necessary, ask God's forgiveness for falling short in that area. If repentance is an issue, commit to, and journal, any changes necessary to get your life back on track. Journal, too, your specific plans *and time frames* for asking forgiveness from, and making restitution to, anyone you may have offended.

Regarding Your Spiritual Development

- What have you done this year (month, week, etc.) that has helped you grow in the grace and knowledge of our Lord, Jesus Christ?
- What can you do to strengthen your relationship with the Lord?
- Do you grieve over your sin?
- Are you becoming more and more sensitive to God's presence?
- Are you governed increasingly by God's word?
- Are you ritually performing your spiritual duties (just going through the motions) or are you passionate about prayer and Bible reading?
- Are you facing hardships with the idea that God will grow you through them?
- What idols (career, relationships, possessions, addictions…anything in place of God being #1) have you set up in your life?
- Are you growing in the gifts of the Spirit (peacefulness, patience, kindness, gentleness, self-control, etc. See Galatians 5:22,23)?
- Are you staying pure sexually? (see Romans 12:1)
- Are you avoiding gossip?
- Do you fear this journey to God in any way? Can you name those fears?
- Are you trusting God with what He has given you—time, money, and talents—by returning them to His service? Do you love possessions and things more than God and people? Do you understand that all the things that you possess are God's and you are entrusted to steward them?
- Can you think of anybody who needs either your forgiveness or an apology from you?
- Do you love people more today than you did a year ago?

- Do you have an attitude of gratefulness towards God for the good things in your life?
- Based upon your words and actions, do the people outside your church (coworkers, friends, extended family, etc.) know that you are a Christian, or would they be surprised to find this out? Do you make a stand for your faith in the difficult places—work, school, non-Christian family, friends & acquaintances?
- Is your conduct in the secret areas of your life God honoring?

Regarding Your Relationships

Your Marriage

- What are you doing to strengthen your marriage?
- What areas of your marriage need work and how can you address them?
- Are you having a regular date night?
- Aside from God, are you holding anything (work, friends, hobby's, church or ministry stuff, other family members, etc.) to be more important than your spouse?
- Are you valuing your spouse's opinions?
- Are you praising your spouse in public?
- Are you listening to your spouse and believing that what they are saying is important?
- Are you 'speaking' your spouses love language (see, *The Five Love Languages* by Gary Chapman)?
- Are you encouraging you spouse to be all that they can be (education, exercise, met goals, etc.)?
- Are you attending church together?
- Are you praying together?
- Are you sharing your dreams, fears, concerns, and feelings with your spouse?
- Do you admit when you are wrong?
- Do you recognize your spouse's uniqueness?
- Do you allow your spouse to fail?
- Are you regularly praying for your spouse?

You As A Parent

- Do you regularly encourage your child to be all that they can be?
- Are there areas in your relationship with your child/children that you wish to change or improve?
- Are there parenting skills that you wish to learn or improve? How will you learn them—classes, books, seminars, etc.—and when, *specifically*, will you do it?
- Do you take an active role in your child's education?
- Do you know their friends names?
- Do you sacrifice your personal time for them?
- Do you pray at times other then meals so that your children will learn how to pray too? (See Deuteronomy 6:6-9)
- Do you regularly read the Bible as a family?
- Does your child witness your love for your spouse? (Next to your love for the Lord, some say that this is the most important value that you can model for your children.)
- Does your child see you living out your faith (living in integrity, looking to the Bible for answers to life's questions, speaking Christ's name publicly)?
- Do you hug your child every single day?
- Do you ask your child's forgiveness, in sincerity, when necessary?

In Your Singleness

- Do you have at least one very trusted friend or mentor with whom you are completely transparent and who will spur you on towards purity, accountability, and spiritual growth?
- Do you have regular "dates" with God?
- For those of you who will someday be married, consider this: Somewhere on this planet, right now, is your future spouse. Are you conducting your life in a manner that would make him or her proud? Are you living in the integrity that he or she is depending on?

With Your Friends & Community

- In what ways are you practicing servanthood within your friendships and community?
- Are you mentoring someone and being mentored by another?
- Do you have a lack of balance in your friendships by either having all Christian or all non-Christian friends?
- What have you done lately that you feel has reflected God's grace towards your friends and community?
- Are there relationships in your life that need restoration, prayer, or some other sort of effort from you?
- Are you fervently, and regularly, praying for your friends, your acquaintances, and your family members who are lost without Christ?

Group Repentance

For this exercise, you'll need a Bible and a little charcoal or ash from your campfire.

Explain to your group that in the Old Testament period the Israelites repented in sackcloth and ashes as a way of conveying regret for their sins. Then read Nehemiah 9:1-3 and Matthew 11:21 aloud.

Tell your group that we, too, need to come regularly before God in repentance, and then invite them to come forward, one at a time. As they do so, give them a few moments to silently ask God for forgiveness, and then put a smudge of ash on their foreheads or on the back of their hands. After the whole group has gone through this process, choose one person to read aloud 1 John 1:8-9 and another to read aloud II Corinthians 5:17.

Be sure to remind your group that the ash is symbolic only; it is Christ's blood that truly cleanses us (Romans 5:9, Colossians 1:20 & 1 John 1:7).

Group Repentance II

Grab a Bible, several index cards, and a few pens, and then gather your group around the campfire to discuss the concepts of repentance & forgiveness found in Psalm 32:1-5, Proverbs 28:13 & 1 John 1:8-9.

Have each member of your group write the sins that they are struggling with on the index card, then have them fold it in half and, one at a time, toss the card into the fire. The burning up of the card represents the letting go of the sin, the surrendering of it to God.

In order to help your people confidently receive the Lord's grace and forgiveness, be sure to follow this event up with a prayer of assurance based on the above scriptures.

Group Repentance III

This fantastic exercise—focused on forgiveness and renewal—is perfect if you are camping on, or near, a beach that allows open fires.

Here's what you do: Grab a Bible, several index cards, and a few pens, and then gather your group around a small campfire built *BELOW* the high tide line to discuss the concepts of repentance & forgiveness found in Psalm 32:1-5, Proverbs 28:13 & 1 John 1:8-9.

Have each member of your group write the sins that they are struggling with on the index card, then have them fold it in half and, one at a time, toss the card into the fire; the burning up of the card represents the letting go of the sin, the surrendering of it to God as an offering.

Read Psalm 51:10 aloud and then head quietly to bed (*before the tide comes in!*).

Very early the next morning, walk back to the beach together, to the spot that the fire had been. It is now gone; no longer a scar, but swept clean with fresh sand that is ready for new life and new patterns. Re-read, aloud, Psalm 51:10 & 1 John 1:8-9 and discuss how God does this very same thing in the life of the Christian.

Letters Of Commitment

If your time together was particularly spiritual and your group especially committed as a result, on your last night together you might have them write a letter to *themselves* expressing their love and devotion towards God, and any commitment that they may have made—such as giving up a particular sin, or bridging a relationship gap, etc.

Collect the letters and mail them back to the individuals a month or more after returning home.

CHAPTER TWENTY THREE

Trailside Talks

"God writes the Gospel not in the Bible alone,
but also on trees, and in the flowers and clouds and stars."
—Martin Luther

"While God's glory is written all over His work,
in wilderness the letters are capitalized"
—John Muir

Trailside Talks are discussion starters and lessons with a spiritual slant, which can be utilized by your group as they adventure in the field. They are categorized alphabetically around natural features, such as deserts, forests, mountains, trails, water, etc; choose the ones that are most appropriate for your specific location and/or experience.

BLISTER

- Got a blister? Read and discuss 1 Corinthians 10:13. The blister is a hot spot caused by friction. How does temptation cause a "hot spot" in our lives? What is the good news of this passage of scripture?

BRIDGE

- Are you crossing a bridge? If at the beginning of the hike, read and discuss Luke 9:62. How does crossing this bridge represent leaving your old life behind?
  If at the end of the hike, read and discuss II Corinthians 5:17. How does crossing this bridge represent a new life in Christ?

BUTTERFLIES

- Read, reflect on, and discuss II Corinthians 5:17. How does the transformation of the caterpillar to a beautiful butterfly compare with the transformation of a child of God?

CAVING

- Are you in a dark cavern where you can turn off the lights? If so, read Matthew 5:14-16, John 8:12 and 1 Peter 2:9, turn off the lights, and then light a single candle and discuss how Christians are to be lights illuminating the dark places of the world. Move around the room with the candle to demonstrate how the light produced by a single source can illuminate a large area and reveal great beauty. Ask the questions: How can we be light to others in our own lives? How can we reveal the beauty of Jesus to a dark world? Specifically, who in our own world (school, work, neighborhood, etc.) can we share that light with? Have your group members' be specific in their answers.

- How is exiting from a dark cave like leaving behind our old lives to follow Christ?
- How is entering a dark cave like going back to work or school on a Monday morning (after church) or returning home to an unbelieving family?

CREATION

- Meditate on, and discuss, this quote from Martin Luther:
  "Now if I believe in God's Son and bear in mind that He became man, all creatures will become a hundred times more beautiful than before. Then I will properly appreciate the sun, the moon, the stars, trees, apples, pears as I reflect that He is Lord over and the center of all things."
- Read and discuss Genesis 1:1-2:2, Psalm 8:3-4, Psalm 104, Isaiah 6:1-4, and Revelation 4:1-11. Discuss the paradox of God being so big and powerful, yet so intimate and caring.

DESERT

- Read Matthew 3:13-4:11, and Luke 3:21-22, 4:1-5. How was Jesus' experience in the desert a time of discovery and of committing to the Father's purpose in His life & ministry?

- Read Psalm 63:1. How does this passage come alive for you now that you've prowled this desert? How is God an oasis in your life? How is the world like a desert?
- Read Psalms 23. Explain that, while tending his flock, David wrote in an arid environment and not the lush one that this psalm might imply. With this knowledge, what do you think of God's faithfulness toward David? How about David's attitude toward God?

DIRTY/NEED A SHOWER

- Are you dirty? Read and discuss 1 John 1:9. How often do you bathe (confess your sins) and allow God to cleanse you? Do you need to do so today?

ENDURANCE

- Does someone need encouragement on the trail? Read and discuss Hebrews 10:24, and then ask your group how, specifically, they can spur someone on today.
- Is your endurance being tested? Read and discuss James 1:2-4. What trials are you facing in your life right now? What are some ways that you can handle those trials? In what ways can you be joyful through them?
- Tired? Read and discuss Isaiah 40:28-31.
- Is someone going slower than you want him or her to? Read and discuss Ephesians 4:2-3.
- Do you have strong legs/weak legs? Read and discuss Psalm 147:10-11.
- Are you carrying a heavy pack? Read and discuss Psalm 38:4 and Hebrews 12:1. What is weighing you down? What extra baggage are you carrying around? How can God help to relieve you of the heavy burdens that life in this world places on you?
- Someone in the group need help carrying their load or pack? Read and discuss Matthew 27:32 and Galatians 6:2.

FLOWERS & BIRDS

- Flowers or birds? Read and discuss, Matthew 6:25-34.

FOREST

- Do you see a branch broken off and separated from the tree? Read and discuss John 15:4 and Hosea 14:8b. How is this branch separated from the tree and a Christian separated from the Father similar? Can they survive for long apart from the "Vine"? How can the Christian (the branch) stay connected to Christ (The Vine)?
- Are you in an area with a mix of healthy & unhealthy trees? If so, read and discuss Psalm 1. In what ways can the Christian be like a healthy tree?
- Do you see a decaying tree? Consider the life that it is providing for the next generation as it adds nourishment to the soil. What will your life (legacy) provide for the generation to come?

MAP & COMPASS

- Read and discuss Psalm 119:9,105, 127-128, 133, 165. How is God's Word like the map & compass that you hold? How can the Christian remain on course while navigating through life?

MEADOW

- Read and discuss Psalm 23. In what ways does the Lord use the pastoral setting in this psalm to achieve his ends with the psalmist?

MOON

- Moonlight is really reflected sunlight. In what specific ways can we reflect the Lord's light to a dark world?

MOUNTAINS

- Read and discuss Psalm 36:6. In what way does this passage describe God? In what other *specific* ways is God's character like a mountain?
- If you find a landslide or other area of pronounced erosion—such as a hillside, wash, gully, or canyon—read and discuss Ephesians 6:10-18. In what ways do Christians without spiritual armor erode just like hillsides without a covering of vegetation.
- As you are *approaching* a peak, read and discuss Psalm 121.
- On the summit of a peak? Read and discuss Psalm 103:11-12. How great is God's love for you? How far away has God cast your sins?

NATIVE CULTURES

- Do this activity when near an ancient cultural site—a rock art panel, village site, morteros, etc. Read and discuss Matthew 6:25-31 and Psalm 104. How do these passages describing God's provision for all things take on new meaning while at this ancient site?
- When near an ancient Native American village site, consider this: The native peoples who once lived here held a holistic view of spirituality. That is, they incorporated spirituality into every aspect of their lives; hunting, farming, war, relationships, etc. How can we better incorporate the Holy Spirit into more areas of our own lives? (See Galatians 5:25)

NIGHT

- This is a great after-dark talking point. Using a flashlight, read Psalm 119:105 and discuss the following questions: Do you really believe that God's Word is a lamp unto your feet? What have you been tripping over lately? Could it be that God wants you to let Him reveal a stumbling block in your life?

- A night hike is a great way to get out and experience new things—beautiful stars, wonderful sounds, and a new perspective. While you're out there, read and discuss one of the following: Psalm 19, Genesis 15:1-6, or Philippians 2:14-15.
- In the dark, use a flashlight to read the following verses and discover a common theme: Psalm 4:6, 27:1, 43:3, 76:4, 104:2, 118:27, 139:12, and Isaiah 2:5.
- Using a flashlight, read and discuss Psalm 90:8.

PINECONE

- Read, reflect on, and discuss Matthew 28:19-20. How are Christians to be like pinecones, which begin dead, but then open up to spread seeds. Is the Word of God a seed? In what way?

ROCKS

- Read and discuss Isaiah 26:4, Psalm 18:2, and Deuteronomy 32:3-4. How is God a Rock? How, specifically, is He a Rock in your life?
- Read, reflect on, and discuss Psalm 40:1-2. How does this passage parallel a time in your own life?
- Read, reflect on, and discuss Matthew 7:24-27. In what ways are you building your own life on the solid rock of Christ?

SEASONS

- Humans experience seasons—cycles of life and death—that are similar to the seasons in the wilderness. What are the seasons in the wilderness and what are the seasons in our lives? How are they similar? What are their purposes? How is God working through these seasons?

SNOW

- Read, meditate on, and discuss 1 Peter 4:8 & Isaiah 1:18. How are these two passages of scripture similar? What are some of the similarities of God's forgiveness of our sins and this snow covered ground?

STORMS

- Read, reflect on, and discuss Matthew 7:24-27. What type of foundation is your life built on—sand or rock? If it's sand, what can you do to shore it up?
- Read and discuss Genesis 7:11-12; 17-20, Psalm 65:9-13, Psalm 147:8; 16-18, and Matthew 8:23-27. How is weather both a blessing and a curse? Who is always in control?

SUNRISE OR SET

- For a sunrise, read, reflect on and discuss Proverbs 4:18. Are you, like this sunrise, shinning ever brighter to the world around you? In what specific ways? If not, then what specific steps can you take to become this person?
- Enjoy a sunrise or set together, reflect on it, and then…
    1. Ask the group if they have ever felt let down by God (i.e. unanswered prayers, or the wrong answer, or silence, etc.); discuss these disappointments.
    2. Next, repeat the following Chinese proverb aloud: "We can never see the sunrise by looking towards the west"
    3. Apply this proverb to our faith by discussing the fact that, too often, we're disappointed in the way God is working because we're looking in the wrong direction for His beauty. In many cases we simply need to turn around and face the right direction to find it.

4. Finally, ask the following questions: Do we spend too much time looking where we want to look instead of where God wants us to? How, specifically, can we turn and face the direction in which God has provided the beauty?

WATER

- If whitewater rafting, compare the image of the guide safely leading you through the river with God safely navigating us through life (John 16:13a).
- Are you at a waterfall? Water, in the Bible, is often seen as a source of renewal and cleansing. If they're willing, have your group members share the thing(s) that they would like for God to cleanse in their lives. Pray for each person, and then have him or her symbolize the cleansing by immersing themselves in the waterfall.
- Near a winding stream? Read Romans 12:1-2. Water takes the path of least resistance; why is this often not such a good idea for Christians?
- Just as, over time, water polishes and shapes rock, so God uses the things (experiences, situations, people, etc.) in our lives to polish and smooth us. What are some things in your life that God is using to polish and smooth you to make you more like Christ?
- Consider this: A powerful current is able to sweep away trees, soil and even large boulders. God's Spirit is able to do likewise in our lives, flowing through us and bringing the debris of our past to the surface and washing it away so that we might enjoy more and more of His freedom (Galatians 5:16-25).

Cutting Switchbacks

Read, reflect on and discuss Proverbs 3:5-7, Proverbs 14:12, Psalm 119:1-9, and Isaiah 30:21.

Contrary to how it may appear, cutting switchbacks is never easier or more efficient than remaining on the trail. In addition to the additional expenditure of energy, cutting switchbacks (for whatever reason—laziness, haste, etc.) can lead to washouts and other trail damage. In what ways do we experience spiritual "washout" when we leave the Lord's path?

What are some of the reasons that people leave the Lord's path? What can you do, *specifically*, to remain on it?

Deceiving Appearances

When near a rock face or a talus slope/scree field, discuss the following points, in sequence:

1. If you just look at the rock face, how would you describe it? (i.e. solid, hard, enduring, impressive, intimidating, etc.)
2. If you included the talus slope beneath it, would that change the way that you described the face? (i.e. it's slowly falling apart.)
3. What is causing it to crumble? (i.e. over a period of many years it weathers, and then a crack forms, then that crack enlarges and, eventually, it crumbles altogether.)

The rock face and talus slope resembles the lives of many Christians who are not careful to deal with the sin in their lives. They may appear solid and impressive on the outside, but because they have not dealt properly with wrong attitudes, inappropriate desires, bad habits, etc., a crack forms that, if not taken care of right away, begins the process of crumbling their lives. Eventually these little sins make Christians, who appear to be "solid rocks", into fragments and pebbles. Like this rock face, these types of Christians do not just crumble and fall, but instead go through a gradual process of weathering that can only be seen over time.

Although there is nothing that the rock can do to avoid becoming talus, there are steps that we as Christians can take to keep from experiencing this in our own lives. Discuss the steps that we can take, individually and corporately, to keep from crumbling. Be very specific.

Inner Renewal

This is a great discussion to have when near a tree whose bark has been split, torn off, or otherwise marred or damaged:

As a tree grows—or is wounded—the bark splits and the inner cambium (the green part of the tree) produces new cells and deposits cork, which then dries out and dies to form new bark. Bark is continually dropped off of trees by animals, natural forces, etc., and so, if it weren't for the healing and renewing of the cambium, the tree would die.

II Corinthians 4:16 states, "Therefore we do not lose heart. Though outwardly we are wasting away, yet inwardly we are being renewed day by day."

Though we are outwardly decaying (aging, etc.), inwardly Christ can renew us day by day. How can He heal our inner wounds and renew us just as the tree is healed from the inside? In what specific ways does He also grow us from the inside (Prayer, Bible study, accountability, fellowship, etc.)?

How does Proverbs 4:23 fit into this?

Part Four

The Resources

"In his hands are the depths of the earth,
and the mountain peaks belong to him"

—Psalm 95:4 (NIV)

The Gear

WHAT TO BRING

The following gear and clothing checklists are intended to aid you in packing for your adventure. Select the items that best meet your trip needs and your desired level of luxury, while taking into account such factors as terrain, elevation, season, weather patterns, activities, the number of people in your party, and whether you'll be car camping or backpacking.

If after reading through this list you're still unsure of what to bring, call your local outdoor store and/or the land manager for the area you'll be traveling to; they'll be happy to help you out.

The following items, known collectively as '*The Ten Essentials*', should always be in your possession when you travel outdoors:

1. Map(s) of the area
2. Compass
3. Headlamp or flashlight w/extra bulbs & batteries
4. Sunglasses (on snow)
5. Extra food & water
6. Extra clothing (layers)
7. Waterproof matches or lighter
8. Candle or fuel tablets
9. Pocketknife
10. First Aid kit
11. Toilet paper (11th essential)
12. Sunscreen—a minimum of 15 SPF (12th essential)
13. Emergency rain clothing or poncho (13th essential)
14. Sun hat (14th essential)
15. A whistle (15th essential)

Hiking Gear

- The Ten Essentials, as listed above
- Daypack
- Hiking boots/shoes appropriate to the terrain

Camping Gear

- The Ten Essentials, as listed above
- Tent, tarp, or bivy sack
- Ground cloth
- Sleeping bag in waterproof stuff sack
- Sleeping pad
- Stove & fuel
- Fire blanket or tub (to contain a campfire)
- Chairs
- Food

- Ice Chests
- Bear-proof canisters (required in some areas)
- Extra nylon stuff sacks
- Cookset, dishes, cups, skillet, utensils, spatula, mixing spoon, pot lifter, & can opener
- Liquid biodegradable soap and pot scrubber
- Garbage bags (Remember, pack it all out!)
- Resealable plastic bags
- Water bottles
- Collapsible water container (2-3 gallon capacity)
- Water filter or purifier w/a backup water treatment, such as purification tablets
- Lantern
- 100-foot accessory cord
- Backpackers/campers trowel
- Binoculars
- Guide books
- Camera and film
- Notebook and pencil
- GPS receiver
- Watch/alarm clock or altimeter watch
- Lip Balm
- Aloe Vera lotion
- Foam ear plugs
- Insect repellant/insect netting
- Eye glasses or contact lenses (w/extras if possible)
- Toothbrush & paste
- Small bath towel
- Brush/comb
- Other personal toiletry items
- All necessary passes and permits
- Money, photo ID
- Map and trip itinerary, including the names of participants and the phone numbers of the nearest land man-

agers and/or law enforcement agency; to be left with a responsible person at home.
- Personal Medications, including sea sickness pills
- Firewood (if permitted)
- Bible, journal, devotional books, etc.
- Fishing tackle
- Salt, pepper, spices
- Powdered milk, sugar, coffee, & tea bags

Personal First Aid Kit

- Aspirin, Tylenol
- (6) 1" Band-aids
- (10) Butterflies
- (6) 4"x 4" sterile pads
- 1 roll of 1/2" adhesive tape
- (2) Rolls of gauze
- 2" elastic wrap
- Moleskin
- (6) Alcohol wipes
- 1 tube of Vaseline
- Eye drops
- Scissors
- Tweezers

Group First Aid Kit

- First aid book
- Aspirin, Tylenol
- Antihistamine
- Decongestant
- Antacid
- Laxative
- Anti-diarrhea
- Anti-nauseate
- Caffeine pills
- Sleeping pills
- Vaseline

- Anti-bacterial cream
- Cortisone cream
- Rubbing alcohol
- Eye drops
- Thermometer
- Scissors
- Tweezers, hemostat
- 3/4" Band-aids
- 1" Band-aids
- Butterflies
- 2"x 2" Sterile pads
- 4"x 4" Sterile pads
- Adhesive tape, 1/2" roll
- Adhesive tape, 1" roll
- 2" roll of gauze
- 4" roll of gauze
- 4" roll of elastic wrap
- Cotton swabs
- Moleskin
- Tincture of iodine
- Alcohol wipes
- Inflatable splints
- Triangular bandages
- Safety pins
- Razor blades
- Calamine lotion

Hiking & Camping Clothing

Unlike other creatures, our skin is insufficient for protection or insulation and so we must wear clothing to create a microclimate of warm air next to our skin. Combinations of wetness, cold, and wind can undo that microclimate and initiate a dangerous reduction in our body temperature that can, potentially, lead to a condition known as hypothermia. This condition, if unresolved, can itself eventually lead to death.

On the flip side, over-exertion or excessive temperatures can cause the improperly clothed person to overheat, a condition that can be just as deadly as hypothermia.

When it comes to appropriate clothing for the outdoors, cotton is at the very bottom of the list. If you have ever worn a wet pair of jeans, then you know what I mean; wet cotton takes forever to dry, is extremely restricting, and draws heat from your body, which in the wilderness can be life threatening. So, when packing, try to keep in mind the adage, "Cotton kills!"

The best fabrics are fleece, wool, polypropylene, and silk. They wick—or draw—moisture away from your body, dry quickly, and help to retain your body heat even when wet. Outdoor stores carry clothing made from these materials, but your local Wal-mart and army surplus stores will have better deals.

Layering your clothes for warmth and dryness is the best bet; you can remove layers as you warm up and add them as you cool down. Depending on the environment that you're traveling through, this might mean having a first layer of thermal underwear made out of a breathable material that will move perspiration away from your body, such as silk or polypropylene. The next layers would be lightweight, yet warm and breathable—wool, fleece, etc.—and the final layer would be a windproof/waterproof outer shell.

For an intensive treatise on clothing and gear, see the most current edition of, "*Mountaineering: The Freedom of the Hills*", published by The Mountaineers. See, also: "*The National Outdoor Leadership School's Wilderness Guide*" by Mark Harvey.

The following items encompass a multitude of seasons and conditions. Adjust them to meet your specific needs:

- Sunhat (with brim)
- Fleece or wool cap
- Moisture-wicking long underwear tops and bottoms
- Moisture-wicking briefs or boxers
- Long-sleeve wicking or fleece shirt

- Fleece or wool vest
- Fleece jacket or wool sweater
- Fleece or wool pants
- Short-sleeve shirt
- Quick-drying pants/shorts
- Quick-drying swim suit
- Sandals (camp shoes)
- Fleece or wool gloves
- Waterproof gloves/over-mitts
- Gaiters
- Heavy or mid-weight wool or synthetic-fiber socks
- Appropriate boots/shoes & socks

Winter Camping Gear

There is nothing in the world like skiing or snowshoeing into a pristine winter setting and spending a few days exploring, glissading down big mountains, drinking hot chocolate, watching the snow banners blowing off the high peaks, and snuggling into your tent or snow cave. Before undertaking such an endeavor, though, you'll want to take, at a minimum, classes on snow camping, snow travel, and avalanche awareness; contact your local outdoor store for information on winter camping courses.

The following is a suggested gear list for your snow camping trip. Choose the items that best meet your needs:

- The Ten Essentials, as previously described
- Metal edged backcountry skis or snowshoes
- Backcountry ski boots or winter hiking boots
- Adjustable ski poles
- Sleeping bag (rated to 0 degrees)
- Full length sleeping pad(s)
- 5,000 to 7,000 cubic inch backpack (internal frame recommended)
- Polypropylene top & bottom
- Wool, fleece, or polypropylene shirt

- Heavy-weight wool, fleece, or polypropylene sweater
- Down jacket
- Wool or fleece pants
- Wool or polypropylene socks (3-4 pair)
- Polypropylene sock liners (3-4 pair)
- Wool or fleece gloves or mitts (with shells)
- Wool or fleece watch cap
- Balaclava
- Gore-Tex jacket and pants or bib
- Knee high gaiters
- Stove and extra fuel
- Food
- Insulated cup and spoon
- Foam ear plugs
- Personal toiletries
- Good quality DARK sunglasses w/side shields
- Sunblock rated 25+
- Sunhat
- Bible, journal, pen, devotional
- Camera & film
- Lots of hot drinks (coffee, tea, chocolate)
- Chemical heat packs

Vehicle Gear

Before heading out on any adventure, be sure that your fluids & gasoline are topped off and that your battery, belts, and spare tire(s) is in good shape. If maintenance work is due or nearly due to be done on your vehicle, take care of it before leaving on your trip.

After making sure that your vehicle is mechanically reliable, be sure that it is stocked with enough gear to get yourself out of a pickle or, barring that, to comfortably spend a night or two outdoors. In addition to *The Ten Essentials,* backcountry travelers may want to carry the following articles of equipment in their vehicles:

- A basic tool kit with a full socket set, pliers, wrenches, screwdrivers, spark plug socket, wire cutters, vice grips, channel locks, Allen wrenches, hammer, knife, fuses, etc.
- A shovel, saw, fire extinguisher, & duct tape.
- A spare tire, jack, air pressure gauge, & tire inflator.
- A tow strap, jumper cables, flares, extra coolant, oil, fan belt, a current Auto Club membership card, and a shop manual for your vehicle.
- A first aid kit, flashlight & batteries, cell phone, extra food, three gallons of water per person—plus five gallons of water per vehicle—and blankets/sleeping bag.
- In the winter, snow chains and the ability to install them.

WHERE TO FIND IT

Each of the following stores—Adventure-16, REI, and Sport Chalet—has several locations throughout Southern California. These are great places to pick up clothing, gear, and maps, as well as to take outdoor skills classes. Check online for locations near you:

- Adventure-16—www.adventure16.com.
- REI (Recreational Equipment, Incorporated)—www. rei.com.
- Sport Chalet—www.sportchalet.com.

The above stores carry some of the best outdoor gear there is (and it's important that you purchase the best that you can afford), however as far as clothing goes you can often find the same technical fabrics for much less at your local army surplus or Wal-Mart stores.

CHAPTER TWENTY FIVE

Trip Planning Helps

READS & WEBSITES

Below are several books and websites to aid you in pulling off a safe, growth-generating trip to the outdoors.

Trip Planning

- *California Road Conditions*—1.800.427.7623 or online at: www.dot.ca.gov.
- *California Department of Tourism* online at: www.visit-california.com.
- *National Weather Service* has real-time weather for any location in the world at: www.nws.noaa.gov.
- Check out www.abovecalifornia.com for additional maps, photos, and information.

Outdoor Locations, Information, & Reservations

- *National Park Service*—The site to visit for information about America's national parks, national preserves, national military parks, etc. is www.nps.gov. Reservations at National Park Service campgrounds can be made at Reservations.nps.gov, or by phone at 800.365.CAMP.

- *United States Forest Service*—America's national forests and grasslands encompass 193 million acres, which is an area about the size of the state of Texas. Discover national forest lands within the state of California at: www.fs.fed.us. Reservations at Forest Service campgrounds can be made at www.reserveusa.com, or by phone at 800.444.7275.
- *Bureau of Land Management*—The BLM administers nearly 261 million acres of public lands in the western states, including California. Research these lands at: www.blm.gov.
- *California State Parks*—Check here regarding information and campground reservations for California's 278 state parks: www.parks.ca.gov.
- www.recreation.gov is loaded with recreational opportunities and locations that are categorized by state & activity; you'll find some great maps here, too.
- www.gorp.com is a clearinghouse for America's wilderness areas and outdoor recreational opportunities.
- www.desertusa.com is packed with fascinating information regarding the deserts of the American Southwest.
- Learn more about the 'Leave No Trace' guidelines by visiting www.lnt.com.
- *Christian Camp and Conference Association*—This is an organization that provides extensive programs, products, and services for the leaders of Christian camps & conference centers nationwide. Discover nearby resources by accessing their online database of Christian camps, conference centers, retreat centers, and adventure programs at: www.cciusa.org or by mail at PO Box 62189, Colorado Springs, Colorado 80962, or by phone at 719.260.9400.

Group Dynamics, Games, Lessons, And Curriculum Development

- *The Role of the Instructor in the Outward Bound Process* (Ken Kalisch).
- *Effective Leadership in Adventure Programming* (Simon Priest & Michael Gass).
- *Adventure Recreation: An Adventure in Group Building* (Sharon Baach, Hal Hill, and Joe Palmer).
- *Quicksilver: Adventure Games, Initiative Problems, Trust Activities and a Guide to Effective Leadership* (Karl Rohnke).
- *Silver Bullets: A Guide to Initiative Problems, Adventure Games, and Trust Activities* (Karl Rohnke).
- *In Touch With God: 52 Interactive Object Lessons From Nature* (Institute of Outdoor Ministry).
- *My Fathers World: 52 Interactive Object Lessons From Nature* (Institute of Outdoor Ministry).
- *Awesome Wonders: 52 Interactive Object Lessons From Nature* (Institute of Outdoor Ministry).
- *Guide for Planning a Learning Expedition* (Expeditionary Learning Outward Bound).
- *How to Use Camping Experiences in Religious Education: Transformation Through Christian Camping* (Steve Venable & Don Joy).

California's Ecology

- *California Forests and Woodlands: A Natural History* (Verna R. Johnston)
- *Nature Guide to the Mountains of Southern California* (Bill Havert & Gary Gray)
- *Mojave Desert Wildflowers* (Jon Mark Stewart)
- *Sierra Nevada: The Naturalist's Companion* (Verna R. Johnston)
- *National Audubon Society Field Guide to Western Forests* (Alfred A. Knopf)

- *National Audubon Society Field Guide to Deserts* (Alfred A. Knopf)
- *National Audubon Society Field Guide to Wildflowers: Western Region* (Alfred A. Knopf)

As you adventure in the wilderness, you'll notice that the land managers (National Park Service, Forest Service, BLM, etc.) interpret many of the geological formations within their domain. What I mean by interpret is they create signage and brochures describing how certain formations and natural features came to be. Most of the time they take an evolutionary approach and tell of these things being formed over periods of millions of years.

Many people, however, believe that when the Bible says God took six days to create the world, they were literally six 24-hour days. The following organizations exist to defend this view and offer—in addition to brilliant scientist-types who can answer your questions—seminars, conferences, books, tapes, videos & DVD's, workshops, tours of various areas of geological interest, and monthly newsletters.

Bring your questions to these folks and/or just check in with them to balance the stuff that you'll read about on your journeys onto public lands.

1. *Answers in Genesis*: PO Box 6330, Florence, KY, 41022-6330, or online at: www.answersingenesis.org
2. *Institute For Creation Research*: 10946 Woodside Avenue North, Santee, CA 92071, or online at: www.icr.org

MAPS, MAPS, AND MORE MAPS

Here are a few sources for the maps you'll need for your journeys. Become proficient in their use by taking advantage of the excellent books, videos and/or classes that are available at your local outdoor store:

The United States Geological Survey—The USGS produces detailed topographic maps of the entire state (and nearly the entire country). For a free California Map Index, contact: USGS Information Services, Box 25286, Denver, Colorado, 80225, or by phone at 800.USA.MAPS, or on the web at: http://mapping.usgs.gov.

National Park Service—Contact the NPS for maps covering the national parks: NPS, Room 1013, Washington, DC 20240, or by phone at 202.208.4747, or on the web at www.nps.gov.

U.S. Forest Service—Contact the USFS for maps covering the national forests & grasslands: USFS, Public Affairs Office, 2nd Floor, Auditors Building, 14th & Independence Avenue S.W., Washington, DC 20250, or by phone at 202.205.1760, or on the web at www.fs.fed.us.

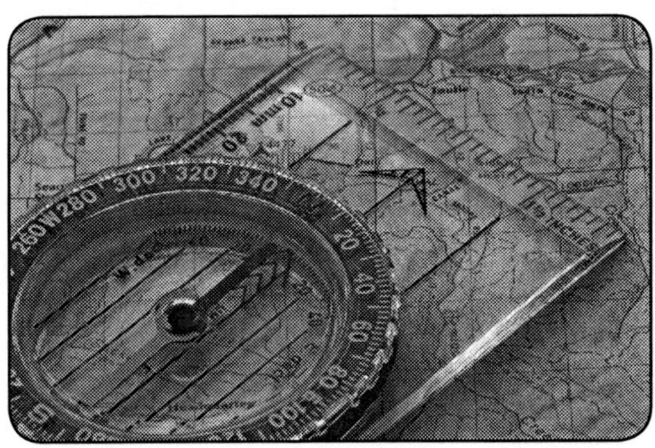

Trails Illustrated—Trails Illustrated produces outstanding maps printed on a waterproof, tearproof plastic-like paper. Though not as detailed as the 7.5 minute USGS maps, these are excellent maps that will meet the needs of most adventurers. Contact: Trails Illustrated, PO Box 4357, Evergreen, CO 80437, or by phone at 800.962.1643, or on the web at www.trailsillustrated.com.

Tom Harrison—These maps are very similar to the ones produced by Trails Illustrated. If one company doesn't cover the area you need, try the other. Contact: Tom Harrison

Maps, 2 Falmouth Cove, San Rafael, CA 94901, by phone at 800.265.9090, or on the web at www.tomharrisonmaps.com.

DeLormes Southern & Central California—This handy topographical map book is perfect for an overview of your trip. One book covers the southern and central portion of the state; there's another for the northern part. Contact your local outdoor store, bookstore, or the manufacturer direct at: Delorme, P.O. Box 298, Freeport, Maine, 04032, or by phone at 207.865.4171, or online: www.delorme.com.

American Automobile Club (AAA)—The AAA has fantastic state and county maps available free to members. Locate the nearest AAA office in your local phone book or online at: www.aaa.com.

Your Local Outdoor Store—Your local outdoor store will carry many of these maps too; call them direct for more information.

Your Local University—Your local university may have a map library where you can research areas of interest. Many of the older topographic maps have historic information (locations of old cabins, mines, rock art sites, etc.) that have been deleted on the newer, revised editions. If you find this info, ask for a copy from their oversized photocopying machines, take it home, and make notations on your contemporary maps.

Maptech! —This is great topographical map software that includes all 2,815 US Geological Survey topographical maps of California. All of the towns, rivers, passes, mountains, etc. are indexed alphabetically and can be quickly located on the maps. You can also trace a route from point to point and the software will compute the distance and elevation gain and loss. One of the benefits of this software is that it can be used, on-site, with your laptop and GPS. Contact Maptech by phone at 800.627.7236, or on the web at: www.maptech.com.

TerraServer-USA (www.terraserver-usa.com) and Google Earth (www.googleearth.com) are two websites containing aerial photos and topographic maps.

CHAPTER TWENTY SIX

Taking It To The Next Level

WILDERNESS SKILLS TRAINING

There are lots and lots of fantastic books out there to help you get started in developing your wilderness skills; I recommend the most current editions of the following:

- *Outdoor Leadership: Technique, Common Sense, and Self-Confidence* (The Mountaineers).
- *Mountaineering: The Freedom of the Hills* (The Mountaineers).
- *NOLS Wilderness First Aid* (National Outdoor Leadership Schools).
- *NOLS Cookery* (Claudia Pearson/National Outdoor Leadership Schools).
- *The Backcountry Classroom* (Jack Drury & Bruce Bonney).
- *The National Outdoor Leadership School's Wilderness Guide* (Mark Harvey).
- *Desert Hiking* (David Ganci).
- *High Altitude Illness and Wellness* (Charles Houston MD).

The primary outdoor retail stores—REI, Adventure-16, and Sport Chalet—offer classes on subjects such as backpacking, rock climbing, canyoneering, map & compass, low impact camping, outdoor photography, winter camping, camp stove cuisine, wilderness first-aid, mountain biking, bicycle maintenance, kayaking, and much more. Contact them for a schedule of classes.

There are many wonderful wilderness skills schools, but two of the best are *National Outdoor Leadership School* and *Outward Bound:*

- *National Outdoor Leadership School (N.O.L.S.),* advertising itself as the "premier teacher of outdoor skills and leadership', offers courses from 10 days to a full semester in length. For a catalog call 1.800.710.NOLS or online at <u>www.nols.edu</u>.
- *Outward Bound* has a mission to "…inspire character development and self-discovery in people of all ages and walks of life through challenge and adventure, and to impel

them to achieve more than they ever thought possible." This is accomplished, in part, through wilderness expeditions and education. Contact them for more information by phone at 866.467.7651, or online at <u>www.outwardbound-wilderness.org.</u>

It is really important that some members of your group have medical training, particularly wilderness medicine. There are two levels of this training—Wilderness First Aid and Wilderness First Responder (or WOFER). This latter option is extensive, about 80 hours in length, and geared totally towards potential emergencies in a wilderness setting. Ask the folks at your local outdoor store for more information regarding this training.

The following Christian Colleges & Universities offer various certificates and degrees in Outdoor Leadership, Outdoor Education, Christian Camping, and/or Wilderness Ministry. Courses include, in addition to core Bible classes, mountaineering & winter camping, white-water rafting, backpacking, first aid, orienteering, administration of outdoor programs, ropes course management, plant & animal identification, survival, curriculum development, crisis counseling, and much more.

- *Appalachian Bible College*, PO Box ABC, Bradley, West Virginia, 25818, or by phone at 800.678.9222, or online at: <u>www.abc.edu.</u>
- *Colorado Christian College*, 8787 W. Alameda Ave, Lakewood, Colorado, 80226, or by phone at 800.44. FAITH, or online at <u>www.ccu.edu.</u>
- *Columbia Bible College*, 2940 Clearbrook Road, Abbotsford B.C., V2T 2Z8, Canada, or by phone at 604.853.3358, or online at <u>www.columbiabc.edu.</u>
- *John Brown University*, 2000 West University Street, Siloam Springs, Arkansas, 72761, or by phone at 479.524.9500, or online at <u>www.jbu.edu.</u>

- *Montreat College*, PO. Box 1267, Montreat, North Carolina, 28757, or by phone at 800.622.6968, or online at www.montreat.edu.
- *North Greenville College*, PO Box 1892, Tigerville, South Carolina, 29688, or by phone at 800.GOTONGC, or online at www.ngc.edu.
- *Prairie Bible College*, Alberta, Canada. Contact this school by phone at 800.661.2425, or online at www.prairie.edu/biblecollege.
- *Wheaton College (Honeyrock Camp).* Contact this school by phone at 630.752.5124, or online at www.honeyrockcamp.org.

Finally, *The Christian Adventure Association* (formerly, Christian Wilderness Leaders Coalition) is a professional association for those who use outdoor adventure activities to impact lives for Christ. Sign up for their monthly Internet newsletter or attend one of their two yearly conferences. Contact them at: 321 Highway 135 South, Plains, Montana 59859, or by phone at 509.747.1735, or online at: www.cwlc.net.

HANDS ON WITH SOME OF YOUR FAVORITE ACTIVITIES

Following are some fantastic outdoor activities, along with the information that you'll need to explore them more deeply on your own:

Archaeology

The United States Forest Service has a great volunteer program, called Passports in Time (PIT), which allows volunteers to work side by side with archaeologists in national forests and grasslands. For more information regarding upcoming projects and opportunities, contact: PIT Clearinghouse, PO Box 31315, Tucson, AZ, 85751-1315, or by phone at 800.281-9176, or on the web at www.passportintime.com.

The Society For California Archaeology has a 'California Archaeological Site Stewardship Program' (CASSP), which trains volunteers to protect archaeological, and historical sites by regularly monitoring assigned sites and reporting any changes or public visitation. For more information, contact www.cassp.org.

Partners In Preservation is a volunteer stewardship program created by the Los Padres National Forest to monitor archaeological sites throughout their jurisdiction. For more info, contact the Santa Barbara Ranger District at 805.967.3481

Below are a few local archaeological societies; check with your county museum, or the Society for California Archaeology (www.scahome.org), for other archaeological societies in your area. These organizations participate in surveys and excavations, hold regular meetings with guest speakers, conduct field trips, publish their own papers, etc. If you have an interest in archaeology, membership in one of these groups would be a great way to learn and to network with others who share your interest.

- Antelope Valley Archaeological Society—www.avarchaeologicalsociety.org.
- Fresno County Archaeological Society—www.historicfresno.org/groups/groups.htm.
- Kern County Archaeological Society—www.kcas.org.
- San Diego County Archaeological Society—www.sandiegoarchaeologicalsociety.com.
- San Luis Obispo County Archaeological Society: www.tcsn.net/sloarchaeology/HOME.
- Ventura County Archaeological Society—www.sunny.moorparkcollege.edu/~rlopez/vcas.htm.

Caving

There are several caving clubs in Southern California, all of which are under the umbrella of the 'Western Region of the National Speleological Society.' These clubs have regular meetings, teach basic to advanced classes, and hold really cool field trips to explore and map caves throughout the state (and the world!). The National Speleological Society, the umbrella organization, can be reached at 2823 Cave Avenue, Huntsville, Alabama, 35810-4431, or on the web at, www.caves.org.

The local clubs can be contacted at the following addresses:

- In the San Diego area, contact The San Diego Grotto online at www.sdgrotto.com.
- In the Huntington Beach/Long Beach area, contact: The Desert Dog Troglodytes, PO Box 30398, Long Beach, CA, 90853, or online at www.desertdogs.org.
- In the Pasadena area, contact: The Southern California Grotto, PO Box 127, La Canada, CA 91012, or by phone at either 626.578.9720 or 818.248.6546.
- In the Fresno/Central Valley area contact: The San Joaquin Grotto, c/o Roger Mortimer, 4845 North Arcade, Fresno, California 93704.

Hiking, Backpacking & Peakbagging

Backpacking is the act of walking into the wilderness for an extended stay (1 night, at least) with the hiker carrying on his or her back all of the supplies necessary to survive. Many of the backpacking books, classes, and trips have been featured under the heading 'Wilderness Skills Training.' Contact your local outdoor store for more information regarding classes, clubs, and such.

Peakbagging is the act of climbing a mountain to 'bag' it (i.e. when you have reached the summit, you've 'bagged' that peak). Some people bag only peaks that interest them, some try to bag every peak in a region, others have attempted to bag the highest point in every state, and still others the highest peak on every continent.

The following resources can help you to identify and re-search the summits of Southern & Central California.

- *The Sierra Club* has a lot of great resources:
    1. *The Desert Peaks Section* of the Sierra Club has an extensive list of California's desert peaks, with maps and trip reports: www.angeles.sierraclub.org/peaks/dps.
    2. *The Sierra Peaks Section* of the Sierra Club has a similar listing of High Sierra Peaks: www.angeles.sierraclub.org/sps.
    3. *The Lower Peaks Committee* of the Sierra Club has a list of lower elevation peaks: www.angeles.sierraclub.org/lpc.
- *Peakware World Mountain Encyclopedia* is loaded with information on California—and the world's—mountains. Check it out online at: www.peakware.com.
- Go to www.thecaliforniahikingpage.com and click on the 'links' for tons of great trip reports.
- www.theclimber.org has lots and lots of trip reports.
- *The California Trail Connection* has trip reports, too—www.caltrails.org.
- www.outdoorsclub.org is a great website where you can find out about hikes & backpacking trips (also, ski & snowboard, kayaking, climbing, mountain biking, rock climbing, etc.) throughout California. There is a fee to join this site/club, but it is nominal and well worth it. The message board itself is worth the cost!
- The following books would be great additions to your library:
    1. *Climbing California's Fourteeners* (Stephen Porcella & Cameron M. Burns).
    2. *Desert Summits: A Climbing & Hiking Guide to California and Southern Nevada* (Andy Zdon).
    3. *California County Summits: A Guide to the Highest Point in Each of the 58 Counties* (Gary Suttle).

Mountain Biking

- Contact the *International Mountain Bicycling Association* at www.imba.com. Click on "contacts", then click on "near you", and enter 'California' to discover local clubs that offer instruction and organized rides.

Rock Art

California is home to a large amount of world-class rock art—both pictographs (rock paintings) and petroglyphs (rock engravings)—that is accessible to any adventurous spirit willing to do a bit of detective work. The following resources will help get you started:

- *"A Guide to Rock Art Sites: Southern California and Southern Nevada"* (David S. Whitley/ Mountain Press Publishing Company). This is a great book filled with lots of site locations, cultural info, and even some tips on photographing the art.
- *American Rock Art Research Association* (A.R.A.R.A.) is an organization dedicated to the study and preservation of rock art. It meets annually at various locations throughout the west, offers fantastic field trips, and publishes a monthly newsletter filled with great information. Contact them at: ARARA, Arizona State Museum, University of Arizona, Tucson, AZ 85721, or on the web at www.arara.org.
- *Piedra Pintada Books* deals exclusively in books related to rock art. For a catalog: Piedra Pintada Books, P.O. Box 1376, Claremont, CA 91711, or by phone at 909.620.6742, or online at www.rock-art.com/books.
- *The San Diego Museum of Man* sponsors a rock art symposium the first Saturday in November, and publishes the papers that are presented each year. This is a great place to meet and network with others who share your interest. Contact: The San Diego Museum of Man,

Balboa Park, 1350 El Prado, San Diego, CA 92101, or by phone at 619.239.2001.

Rock Climbing

Contact the *Southern California Mountaineers Association*—www.rockclimbing.org—for instruction, field trips, trip reports, and a great message board. Contact, too, your local outdoor stores for any rock climbing courses that they may be offering.

Whitewater Kayaking/Sea Kayaking

Contact the *American Whitewater Association*—www.americanwhitewater.org—for kayaking clubs and instruction in your area.

One Last Thing

When you have a chance, swing by <u>www.godgrowthand-greatadventure.com</u> and share how God has used this book to grow you.

While you're there you can also:

- Order additional copies of this book.
- Discover fresh outdoor tips and adventure destinations.
- Network with others who share your passions.
- Recommend outdoor locations & spiritual activities that weren't covered in the book.
- Report errors and/or update site information such as campground, or trail, conditions or closures.
- Receive help with your trip planning.
- Have your questions answered.
- Or simply say, "hey."

I look forward to hearing from you.

God bless you as you follow His trail,
Steve Sears

Printed in the United States
77170LV00003B/15